The Fundamentals of Pa
Volume I

The Method of Lu Shui-T'ien
as Taught by Park Bok Nam

by Park Bok Nam and Dan Miller

UNIQUE PUBLICATIONS
4201 W. Vanowen Place, Burbank, Calif. 91505

The Fundamentals of Pa Kua Chang:
The Method of Lu Shui-T'ien as Taught by Park Bok Nam

Copyright © 1999 Unique Publications
ISBN: 0-86568-172-4
All Rights Reserved

Published by Unique Publications
4201 Vanowen Place
Burbank, California 91505

Printed in the United States of America

The author and publisher of the book are not responsible for any injury which may result from following the instructions contained herein.

Before embarking on any of the physical activities described in this book, the reader should consult his or her physician for advice regarding their individual suitability for performing such activity.

Table of Contents

Acknowledgments

I would like to acknowledge a number of individuals who worked hard to make this book possible. Thanks to my two senior classmates, Glenn Wright and Glen Moore, for answering my many questions and providing feedback on the draft copies of this book. Thanks to my wife, Nancy Miller, for proofreading the draft text and making valuable suggestions concerning the format and layout and for putting up with the long hours I spent in preparing this book. Thanks to Greg Hatza for posing in several of the two-person photographs. Thanks to Ken Fish for providing valuable input concerning the mechanics involved in some of these exercises, for helping with the translation of Chinese terms, and for helping clear the way for me to study with Park Bok Nam. Thanks to my mother-in-law, Nobue Melton, for providing the calligraphy which is present throughout this book. Thanks to my training partner, Gene Kreyd, for putting up with the many long practice sessions which helped me think about how to put these exercises into words. Thanks to Steve Rhodes for answering all of my computer questions. Lastly, a special thanks to Park Bok Nam. Without him, none of this would have been possible.

Dedication

**Dedicated in Memory of
Pa Kua Chang Master
Lu Shui-T'ien
(1894 - 1978)**

Preface

After the first issue of the *Pa Kua Chang Newsletter* had been published in November 1990, I approached Bok Nam Park to ask if he would be interested in being interviewed for the publication. Park's response to the first newsletter was, "History does not make progress, students need to learn principles." His point was that martial arts publications print too much history, generalized information, and abstract theory when what students need is a detailed explanation of fundamental principles. Park believes that if the student does not understand the principles upon which the art is based, he or she will not progress. "Respect for parents is good, but when the baby is hungry he does not want to know who his father is and who his grandfather is - he wants food. After his belly is full, then you can tell him about his ancestors," Park added. Point well taken.

Pa Kua Chang footwork, sparring, *ch'i* circulation, *ch'i* development, meditation, breathing, palm movements, how to move the body with the steps, how to combine speed and balance with *ch'i*, how to develop power - these are some of the topics Park wanted to discuss in detail. Since arriving in the United States in 1987, Park has observed that students in this country know that Pa Kua Chang practitioners walk the circle, practice eight "mother" palms, and execute twisting and turning movements while walking and changing in circular patterns, but he does not feel that many students know why these things are practiced, how they are specifically applied in self-defense or *ch'i* development, and how they relate to the fundamental theories of the *I-Ching*, the *Wu Hsing* (Five Phases), and *Yin-Yang*. Park contends that if Pa Kua students were asked why they walk a circle or how each of the "mother palms" is used specifically, most students would not be able to give an explanation that displays any depth of understanding.

Because of the level of detail Park wished to discuss all of these topics, he asked if I would be willing to publish a series of articles which would explain Pa Kua Chang basic principles. I agreed with Park's opinion that martial arts publications should present more practical details concerning martial arts practice and application and I had received several letters from subscribers asking me to print this kind of technical information. Thus, we initiated a series of articles in the *Pa Kua Chang Newsletter* (now the *Pa Kua Chang Journal*) which discussed Park's views and instruction of the practice and application of Pa Kua Chang fundamental principles.

Our initial interview was conducted sitting in his office. He did not demonstrate any of his Pa Kua Chang, we just talked. Although I had not actually seen him do anything, I was impressed with his systematic approach to teaching and emphasis on fundamental training.

Over the next few months Park and I met several times and he showed me a number of the exercises and drills he wanted to have explained in the newsletter. Although he showed me some *ch'i kung* and some Pa Kua palm changing and palm striking exercises, his emphasis in these meetings was placed on Pa Kua Chang footwork. I still had yet to see Park demonstrate a Pa Kua Chang form or show any Pa Kua martial applications, however, I could see that he was exceptionally skilled in terms of body flexibility, body control, and speed. His smooth, precise, cat-like movements when demonstrating Pa Kua stepping exercises indicated a high level of skill. I was interested in learning more and so at this point in time I asked Park if I could change my status from reporter to reporter/student. Park agreed and I began studying with him at his school in Richmond, Virginia for five hours every Saturday afternoon.

For the first few months I was taught nothing but very basic footwork, body movement, palm work, and *ch'i kung* exercises (the contents of this book). Although it was all very straight forward, it was different than anything I had learned before and I started to see direct benefits right away. After I had learned some basic footwork drills and practiced them repeatedly until the bottom of my feet were blistered, Park said he wanted to demonstrate how the footwork could be used in fighting. He said, "You attack me, OK" I squared off with him and planned to use the jump step I had been practicing in combination with a palm strike to his head. I quickly jumped forward and threw the strike, but it hit nothing but air. Park was standing directly behind me, positioned to strike my kidneys. I could not understand how he got there, his movement had been so quick and precise I was not really aware of what was happening when it had happened. He had not even touched me as I was moving in to strike, he simply moved out of the way and stepped in behind me. I thought, well, that was pretty amazing! There must be something to this footwork after all.

I was also fortunate in that I was able to observe Park training his two senior students, Glenn Wright and Glen Moore when I was at the school on Saturdays and I was able to practice with them. There is an old saying in the martial arts that says, "If you want to know how good a teacher is, look at his senior students." Glenn Wright and Glen Moore are two of the finest Pa Kua Chang practitioners and best fighters I have ever seen. Looking at them I knew that Park could not only apply the art himself, but knew how to teach it as well.

With each successive week of practice I slowly started to get a better feel for what Park's Pa Kua Chang was about and how his training program worked. The more I learned about him and his Pa Kua Chang and the more I practiced his training methods, the more comfortable I became with my decision to train with him. His teaching method is the most systematic and most complete program I have ever encountered.

In my capacity as editor and publisher of the *Pa Kua Chang Journal*, I have had the opportunity to meet and talk with Pa Kua Chang instructors and practitioners all over the world. I have met many highly skilled Pa Kua Chang instructors in the United States, Taiwan, Hong Kong, and Mainland China, however, I have never regretted my decision of choosing Park Bok Nam as my Pa Kua Chang teacher. I say this not only because he constantly amazes me with his ability to apply Pa Kua Chang in fighting, but also because he genuinely cares about each student's development inside and outside of the kung fu studio.

Park truly believes that the relationship between a student and teacher should be the same as the relationship between a father and son and thus he looks out for each of his students as if they were his own children. Park also teaches his students that students in the same school should be as close as blood-brothers and thus the camaraderie experienced between students in Park's school is uncommon in today's world.

We present this book to the martial arts community as a perspective, not to say this is the *only* way. There are many excellent Pa Kua Chang training systems and not all of them are the same. The method presented here is the method Park Bok Nam was taught by his teacher Lu Shui-T'ien. We humbly present this book and its companion video tape so that instructor's and practitioners in the Pa Kua Chang community might gain some knowledge from this work and that it may help them in their practice. We also hope that this work will inspire others to share the Pa Kua Chang knowledge that they were taught and have worked hard to perfect so that the community will benefit from everyone's knowledge and hard work.

Dan Miller
Winter 1992
Pacific Grove, CA

Chapter 1
Introduction

Chapter 1

Introduction

It's the Chinese version of the David and Goliath story. An old white bearded man, frail in appearance, cane in hand, strolls passively down a country road accompanying his son and granddaughter to market. Just as the three happy travelers reach the outskirts of their village, a group of thugs descend upon them. The group's leader stands boldly in the center of the road and barks, "Give us your money or we take it by force and let 'Ox-breath Chiang' have his way with the girl." Ox-breath, the Chinese equivalent of a Sumo wrestler on steroids, eyes the girl and grunts, saliva dripping gingerly from the corners of his mouth. The girl's father immediately leaps forward to protect her but is caught mid-stride by a backfist from Ox-breath's bear-size hand. He lands unconscious in the ditch by the side of the road, blood ebbing from his mouth.

The ruffians break into laughter and mock the beaten man's foolish bravery. The group's leader commands a few gang members to start searching through the man's clothes for money. Ox-breath turns back towards the young girl to claim his prize, but as he reaches out for her arm, the tip of the old man's cane pierces him threw the eye and a palm strike to the chest sends blood gushing out of his nose and mouth. As the giant begins to fall to the ground, the old man hooks him under the arm and, with a tornado like spinning movement, plays "bowling for bandits" by hurling the lifeless mass into the crowd of hooligans. The group scatters like insects at a crop dusting festival, but two or three are knocked down by the flying heap of flesh. The others rush towards the old man like

hyenas on a feeding frenzy, yet he effortlessly weaves, darts, and spins in and out of the assailants' attacks; sweeping, throwing, striking and kicking until they all lie quivering in the dusty road like beached jellyfish. The young girl helps her father to his feet and the three family members continue on their journey, the "frail" old man strolling away passively.

As far fetched as this story might seem, most of us who practice Chinese martial arts, especially the so-called 'internal' styles, are fascinated with this kind of tale because its message is that highly refined skill can easily overcome brute force. This is the concept which led most of us to study these arts and this idea keeps us going through long, hard hours of training. A small guy can beat up a big strong guy without a rock and sling? A force of four ounces can deflect a thousand pounds? Where do I sign up!?!

If a student is lucky enough to find a good teacher who has a training program which is designed to develop complete martial art skill, he or she immediately realizes that developing this skill is going to take many long hours of hard work everyday. The majority of this work, especially in the beginning stages of development, is not fun. The training is basic, it is repetitive, it is exhausting, and it can easily become boring. There is no secret, there is no magic, there is no free lunch.

Many students who enter the "internal" martial arts become interested because they relate a few of the terms associated with these arts, such as "soft" and "relaxed," with "easy." However, if they find a good teacher who is teaching a complete system, they soon discover that the training is anything but "easy." At every level of practice the training is physically demanding, however, at the beginning levels the work is especially difficult.

Working hard at fundamental repetitive exercises is nothing new to anyone who has attained a high degree of skill at any discipline. The professional baseball player can knock a fastball out of the park with a swing that appears effortless. The all-pro basketball player can drive down the lane, weave around defenders, leap into the air and "hang" for what seems to be minutes, his flight ending with a reverse slam executed while his head appears to be floating above the rim. He makes it look easy. The professional football player, the baseball player, the basketball player, the concert pianist, the Olympic gymnast and the old white bearded man in our story are all individuals who have reached the highest level of excellence in their field, and they all have one thing in common; they have spent thousands of hours practicing the fundamentals of their discipline and through this practice have reached such a refined level of skill that everything they do appears to be effortless and natural.

While thousands of hours of practice is the key element to developing skill in any discipline, practice cannot be haphazard. Any good training program is systematic and progressive; there is a method. Basic skills are developed fully before more complex skills are encountered. Components of the practice are first trained separately until each component can be performed correctly in isolation before the components are integrated. The progression is step-by-step and the system is designed to develop higher and higher levels of refined skill.

In this book, Richmond, Virginia, based Pa Kua Chang teacher Park Bok Nam describes in detail the various components of Pa Kua Chang's basic training as it was taught to him by his teacher Lu Shui-T'ien (1894-1978), a native of Shantung Province, China. The book details exercises which will help any martial artist improve his or her footwork, body flexibility, *ch'i* circulation, and internal striking power. Additionally, the publisher has made available a companion video tape in which Park Bok Nam demonstrates a majority of the exercises contained in this book.

This book contains fundamental exercises and an explanation of the principles upon which they are based. There are no Pa Kua Chang forms described in this book because Park believes that Pa Kua Chang forms should not be taught to students until other fundamental skills are developed. Park is fond of saying, "I have water to give to thirsty students, but unless they have a cup for me to pour it in, they cannot hold the water." The "cup" is symbolic of fundamental skills and principles, the "water" is the complete art of Pa Kua Chang. Park firmly believes that at each level of training the student has to develop the "cup" before the teacher can pour in the "water."

While many students today are taught the Pa Kua Chang form as the sum and total of the art, Park was taught that forms practice makes up only a small sliver of the total art of Pa Kua Chang. There are many components of Chinese martial arts that cannot be developed solely through forms practice. The majority of these components fall into three broad categories. Any complete Chinese martial arts system will include elements of the following:

Ch'i Kung

1) *Ch'i Kung* - breath control, visualization, and non-specific body movement techniques for various purposes - increased circulation to the distal points of the extremities, increased vital capacity, meditation, and *ch'i* development.

Nei Kung

2) *Nei Kung* - training designed specifically for the development of muscle groups, ligaments, and tendons not usually under conscious control.

Wai Kung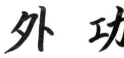

3) *Wai Kung* - external, i.e. visible, aspects of any martial art including firm balance, flexibility, good posture and stance work, proper mechanical alignment, coordination, and stability.

Ideally, these elements will be developed in a progressive, balanced curriculum designed by an experienced teacher who will guide each student's individual development. Pa Kua Chang, being a complete martial art system, contains elements of all three of these disciplines. In Park's training program, all of these elements are trained separately through basic training exercises before they are brought together in forms practice or fighting.

Beyond Pa Kua Chang Forms Training

When martial arts practitioners ask why Park Bok Nam does not teach Pa Kua Chang forms to beginners, he tells the following story.

Living at opposite ends of a remote country village by the sea, there are two families. Each family has a young son. Both of these young boys love to eat fish. In one family, every time the young son wants to eat fish, his father takes out his fishing gear and travels down to the seashore to catch fish for his son to eat. His wife cooks the fish and the family has a nice fish dinner.

In the second family, when the young boy tells his father he would like to eat fish for dinner, his father takes his son out and shows him how to find materials and construct a fishing pole, line, and hook. He then shows his son how to find and cut bait. Next he takes his son down by the sea shore and shows him the best areas for fishing, shows him how to bait a hook and teaches him how to catch fish. Once the fish are caught, he takes his son home and shows him how to clean the fish and then his wife shows the boy how to cook the fish. The second family then sits down to enjoy a nice fish dinner.

From that time forward, whenever the second family wants to have fish for dinner, father and son go together. Over the course of time the son learns how to place drop lines, how to fish with nets, how to catch crabs, how to dig for clams, when to employ specific kinds of bait, what times of the day are best for fishing, how to fashion lures, etc. The father puts forth a lot of effort teaching his son, and after a short time the son becomes a fairly skilled fisherman. In the first family the father still goes to catch fish alone anytime his family wants fish for dinner - it is easier and much less time consuming.

A year later the country is involved in a war and the men of the village are called off to fight. In the first family, the wife knows how to prepare and cook fish, but neither the mother or son knows how to catch the fish. However, in the second family, the son is now able to go catch fish easily on his own and bring it home for he and his mother to eat. Which of the fathers was smarter?

Park believes that if a student learns a form without first having a thorough experiential "body knowledge" of the principles on which the form movements are based, he is eating fish without knowing how to catch it. Someday when his teacher is not there to teach him more deeply, or when he is called on to apply his art in a fighting situation, he will be out of luck. The purpose of this book is to begin to teach the Pa Kua Chang student "how to fish."

Through form practice, a student will learn continuity, fluidity, connection, body integration and rhythm. These are all very important aspects of fighting skill and when practicing a series of Pa Kua techniques with these principles in mind, the whole will become greater than the sum of the parts. In other words, practicing a form has purpose beyond the linking together of a series of techniques. However, two elements that a fixed form sequence is missing are variation and sufficient repetition of isolated body movements.

Unless a student learns how to change, adapt, and vary his movement spontaneously, his fighting skill will always be weak. However, all variation of movement and technique will still adhere to the fundamental principles of Pa Kua Chang. The spontaneous response is efficacious, and proceeds along the path of least resistance. To this end, the body is trained and developed so that proper response is elicited out of habits which are ingrained in the body. Correct habits are formed through repetition of fundamental training methods.

Beyond building correct habits and mechanics, repetition of fundamental training methods serves another very important purpose - overall body development. The "internal" styles of Chinese martial arts are famous for the practitioner's ability to deliver a tremendous amount of power with very little visible movement or apparent effort. The Chinese refer to the highest level of this ability as *hua ching*. *Hua ching* is one of three levels of *ching*, or trained strength, which are as follows:

Ming Ching

Ming ching or "obvious power." This means that exertion of force, alignment, and the effects of the body's action are all clearly discernible to an observer.

An Ching

An ching or "hidden or covert strength." When force is exerted in this manner its origin is not visible to the untrained observer, hence the term "hidden." The practitioner at this level has begun to refine and internalize the body's movement.

Hua Ching

Hua ching or "refined force." Sometimes this term is translated a "mysterious power," however, this term really refers to strength which is highly refined. The practitioner's application of force is so subtle that the origin of this force is completely imperceptible to the opponent. When the force is exerted one's opponent may believe that he has done something to make himself miss the mark because he cannot feel the source of the strength initiating from the practitioner.

Typically when a martial artist is fighting an opponent, he or she will utilize sensory clues to "listen to" or "feel" the movement of the opponent's body in order to respond correctly to any attack the opponent is preparing to launch. The practitioner who has reached the *hua ching* level of development has completely internalized his or her movements and thus moves so efficiently that the movements are imperceptible even if the opponent is touching the practitioner's body. The movements are very small, smooth and subtle, yet extremely powerful.

In order to develop the *an ching* or *hua ching* ability, the practitioner's body needs to first be cultivated and developed. The process is progressive. Increased levels of flexibility and suppleness lead to increased *ch'i* movement; development of secondary muscle groups, ligaments and joints lead to increased body strength, coordination, and integration; and development of the mind's intention and focus leads to an increased body awareness and a connection between the mind, the body, and nervous system. If these elements have not been progressively developed and trained fully, a practitioner can perform a form movement perfectly with all of the correct body motions and alignments, yet still not have much power. The movement will be "empty." There is no *kung li*, or developed internal strength. Park believes that development of this skill requires hundreds of hours of correct practice.

A practitioner cannot jump right to the *an ching* or *hua ching* level of development without first having spent a considerable amount of time practicing on the *ming ching* level. The reason being that power has to first be developed before it can be hidden or refined. The power is developed through body conditioning on the *ming ching* level. What this means in Park's school is that when a practitioner first begins training, all of the fundamental exercises are practiced with large body articulations. The practitioner's *ch'i* pathways need to opened so that there is a full and balanced distribution of *ch'i* and the "power" resident in the body is coordinated. Large body articulations promote the movement of *ch'i* in a body which is stiff, inflexible, has *ch'i* blockages, or is uncoordinated. The body needs to be stretched, joints need to be opened and primary and secondary muscle groups need to be conditioned. Park feels that this conditioning will not occur if the practitioner starts out learning small, overly soft, subtle movements.

If a student tries to imitate the movements of an instructor who has reached the *an ching* or *hua ching* level of development, he or she will have a very difficult time developing any real skill. A form sequence is used by an advanced practitioner to refine movements that have been trained and conditioned through fundamental skills training.

Form sequences were developed in martial arts to help the practitioner's body easily remember, refine, coordinate, and link those body movements and mechanics which have already been developed in basic training.

In Park's school forms are used to refine skills that have already been developed. Park believes that a practitioner who has only worked with complex form sequences from day one of training will not progress very far in terms of internal power development or fighting skill. Their form may be pretty, however, it will usually lack internal, trained strength.

In Park Bok Nam's training program, the *ming ching* level of development is trained through a series of fundamental training exercises which are designed to increase body flexibility and joint range of motion, coordinate and integrate body movement, condition the muscles, tendons, and bones, and develop proper body mechanics. These exercises are practiced for hundreds of hours before forms are introduced to the student. These developmental exercises are the what we present in this book.

Park insists that his students learn and fully understand Pa Kua Chang footwork, body movement, and palm striking fundamentals (which includes elbow striking) before learning forms for three reasons:

1) The mechanics of movement are developed correctly.
2) The body is developed and conditioned to a certain degree in terms of flexibility, coordination, endurance, speed, power, and integration.

3) The fundamental principles on which the form movements are based will be understood experientially before the form sequence is attempted.

With a sound prerequisite "body knowledge" of Pa Kua Chang footwork, body mechanics, and palm striking application (including tactics and strategy of attack and defense) which have been developed through basic repetitive drills and two-person practice sets, the student can easily learn form movements and then extract techniques from a form and learn to vary the techniques by changing the stepping pattern or palm application in accordance with the principles he or she has developed. Park's theory is that without a strong foundation built through hours of work with simple, repetitive drills, the body will not become conditioned fully and will not be able to respond innately and spontaneously in any given situation.

Park Bok Nam is very interested in sharing the Pa Kua Chang foundation training that he learned from his teacher, Lu Shui-T'ien, with practitioners in the United States. This book and its companion instructional video are to be the first in a series of books and videos which lend instruction on Lu Shui-T'ien's Pa Kua Chang. While this book concentrates on the basics of Pa Kua Chang footwork, body movement, palm training, and *ch'i kung*, future books and videos will include more advanced instruction in all of these areas. This book and its companion video are meant to lay a strong foundation for future study for practitioners with an interest in this particular fighting system.

Pa Kua Chang Master Lu Shui-T'ien

Lu   *Shui*   *T'ien*

Lu Shui-T'ien judging Park Bok Nam's students at a promotion test at his school in Inchon, Korea, 1974

Park Bok Nam studied the art of Pa Kua Chang for 17 years with his teacher Lu Shui-T'ien. During this time period (1960-July 1978) Park did nothing but study Pa Kua Chang all day, everyday.

When he started training with Lu in 1960, Park was 18 years old. Prior to studying Pa Kua Chang, he had studied Western boxing in junior high school, however, while fighting with a classmate, he was kicked in the side. This incident made him think that he ought to study a pugilistic sport which employed kicking techniques. In high school Park switched from Western boxing to *Tang Soo Do*, a Korean martial art style. After four years of training, he earned a black belt.

Park was a somewhat wild and rebellious youth who would employ the practical side of his martial art at the drop of a hat. He was constantly in trouble for fighting and his father, concerned about his son's future, offered him an ultimatum

when he graduated from high school. Either he was to become serious about martial arts and find a good teacher to study with, or he was to forget about martial arts altogether and concentrate on his school work. As one might guess, Park chose martial arts.

It may seem surprising that a father would let his son choose martial arts practice over school or a job, but Park's father, who had been a professional soccer player in Korea, knew the value of physical training and wanted his son to enjoy himself while he was young. His father also felt that having a focus in life would help him stay out of trouble.

Park's father was hoping that he could find a martial arts teacher for his son who would provide some discipline and teach him that there was more to martial arts than learning how to win street fights. Inchon had a very large Chinese community and Park's father had seen the Chinese martial artists perform amazing skills. He felt that if his son was to excel at the martial arts, he needed to find a Chinese teacher.

The elder Park had a sister who lived and worked in Inchon's Chinatown. A few doors down from where Park's aunt lived, there lived a martial arts teacher who was famous among the Chinese. Park's aunt asked this teacher, Lu Shui-T'ien, if he would consider teaching her nephew. Lu, who had thus far only taught his art to the Chinese in Chinatown, said she could send the boy to see him.

When Park knocked on Lu's door, Lu answered and just looked at the boy. He asked if Lu would teach him martial arts. Lu closed the door. Park, knowing that Lu was a traditional teacher and was probably testing his character, went back to Lu's

Master Lu Shui-T'ien

door everyday with the same question. For four weeks he got the same response, a door closed in his face. However, one day, just as he was about to give up, Park asked the question again and was invited in to the house.

In the courtyard behind Lu's living quarters a small group of students was practicing. Park was told to sit and watch. After the students had finished, Lu turned to Park and asked him to sweep up the area and return the next day. The next day was the same, he was allowed to sit and watch, but could not practice. After everyone else had finished practicing he was told to sweep up the area. This went on for several days. Park, assuming this was another test of his patience and

dedication, adopted the pattern and each day came to Lu's home, watched practice and then swept and raked the yard after practice was complete. One day it looked like it was going to rain after practice so Park quickly grabbed his rake and broom and started working. Lu stopped him and asked him to sit back down. Lu left him sitting until it started to rain. When the rain was falling heavily, Lu turned to Park and said, "OK, now you can go and rake the yard."

Although Park thought this old man was crazy, he continued to perform his menial tasks without complaint. He was going to learn this martial art and show his father that he could stick to his decision to become serious about martial arts practice. He was determined to do whatever it took. Several weeks later, it again started to rain after practice so Park got his rake and went out to rake the yard. Lu stopped him and said, "You don't have to do that now, wait until after the rain stops." He had passed his second test. Soon after that he was allowed to join the rest of the class and start practicing, however, he was still required to sweep up the yard after everyone was finished.

Once Park started practicing with the other students, his "tests" of loyalty and dedication were far from over. For the first year of practice Lu totally ignored him. Park had to pick up what he could from the other students. During the second year of training Lu taught Park very basic, repetitive exercises and would insist that he practice each one for hours. Lu would often hit Park or have the other students beat him up. He would do whatever he could to try and upset Park and then observe his reaction. During the third year, Lu had Park spend a lot of time sparring with other students and he encouraged the other students to try and hurt him. Park was still determined to prove to everyone that he could finish what he had set out to do and so he kept practicing.

When Park began his study with Lu, his father told Lu about Park's tendency to get into trouble and run with a bad crowd and said, "If you will discipline my son, I will support him financially." As evidenced by the preceding story, Lu took this task to heart and was very strict with him. Once Park began training with Lu, his teacher insisted that he train full time. Other than one or two hours in the evening after a full day of training, Lu would only allow Park to visit with his friends one day a week, on Sunday afternoon, otherwise he was to spend all his time practicing Pa Kua Chang. If Park's friends came by to see him, Lu would run them off saying, "Go away, he is practicing now." Lu did not allow Park to date any women for the first five years they were together as he felt that women would take his mind off of his martial arts training.

Lu Shui-T'ien and his Pa Kua Chang

Lu Shui-T'ien (1894-1978) brought Pa Kua Chang to Korea when he moved his family there during the Sino-Japanese War. Lu, who was from the city of Ching Tao in Shantung Province, China, was well known in Shantung for his martial arts ability. During the Sino-Japanese War, Lu was a guerrilla fighter and killed many Japanese. He ran with a band of Chinese martial arts experts who hid in the mountains during the day and infiltrated Japanese encampments at night. Because their operation had to remain covert, the group executed Japanese soldiers without the aid of firearms. Traditional bare hand and weapons techniques were used to kill the enemy and thus the guerrillas could move in and out of the Japanese camps without being noticed.

Park states that Lu's favorite weapon was the short knife. Lu was extremely skilled at using the single knife and double knives. He preferred the single knife as this allowed one hand to remain free for grabbing and striking. Park said that Lu often demonstrated a knife throwing technique whereby a throwing knife is fasten inside the sleeve in such a manner that when the arm is whipped out properly the knife is thrown like a dart shooting out of the sleeve. Park said that his teacher was extremely accurate throwing knives in this manner. One can guess that Lu's weapon of choice when fighting against the Japanese was the short knife.

Lu Shui-T'ien became so well known for his fighting skill that the Japanese put a price on his head. When this occurred, it became too dangerous for Lu to stay in China, so he sailed from Ching Tao across the Yellow Sea to a safe haven in

Lu Shui-T'ien was still very strong and healthy in his Eighties

9

**Lu Shui-T'ien with his top student
Park Bok Nam in 1974**

Inchon, Korea. Inchon was a big trading port and ships frequently traveled to Inchon from China. When he thought the situation in China was safe for him, Lu would travel back to China and continue to fight the Japanese. During one of these trips, Lu's wife was killed while fleeing the Japanese on horseback. After this incident, Lu left for Korea once again, never to return to his native country. Lu settled in Inchon's large Chinatown with his two children, a daughter and a son. He never remarried.

Lu Shui-T'ien's Early Years in China

When Lu Shui-T'ien was young, he studied what he called "farmer style" martial arts. By "farmer style" Lu was referring to any one of the hundreds of "family style" martial arts systems that were practiced by the inhabitants of remote towns and villages.

During the Ch'ing Dynasty, police protection was only provided to those people who lived in large cities. Inhabitants of small towns and villages were left to provide their own protection against bandits and thieves. Typically, a village would hire a skilled martial artist to come live in their village for a period of time and teach the young men of the village fighting skills. Once a group was trained, the martial artist would leave town and the group he trained would train others. Over time, the system that was originally taught would change and the village would make it their own.

The martial system which was taught in Lu Shui-T'ien's hometown provided him with his introduction to combat arts.

After having practiced the "farmer style" for a number of years, Lu wanted to know more. He had heard that the best fighting art in China was Pa Kua Chang and so he sought out a Pa Kua Chang instructor. Tung Hai-Ch'uan, the originator of the Pa Kua Chang style, had taught Pa Kua Chang in the palace of Prince Su and had become well known for his tremendous martial arts skill during the mid to late 1800's (Tung taught in Beijing between 1865 and 1882). Subsequently, one of his students, Yin Fu, who also worked in the palace as a bodyguard and martial arts instructor, was chosen to escort the Empress Dowager out of Beijing during the Boxer Rebellion in 1900. The Chinese assumed that the person the Empress chose as her personal body guard was the best martial artist in China. Since she chose a Pa Kua Chang man, Pa Kua Chang gained great popularity around the turn of the century.

The Pa Kua Chang instructor Lu Shui-T'ien found was Li Ching-Wu (1864-?). When Lu met Li and began his study of Pa Kua Chang, he was still a teenager. Li did not live in Ching Tao but in a town which was about a two day ride by horse north of Ching Tao. Lu Shui-T'ien would frequently make the two day journey to his teachers town to study. When Lu left his home in Ching Tao to study with his teacher, he was typically gone for months on end. In some cases Lu was away from home and training with his teacher for as long as two years at a time. The study and practice of Pa Kua Chang was the only thing that interested him.

Not much is known about Li Ching-Wu himself. Park Bok Nam does not know who Li's teacher was, however, Lu did tell him that Li only had ten Pa Kua Chang students. Li's students kept to themselves and thus Pa Kua Chang as taught by Li Ching-Wu was not widely spread. Li Ching-Wu was very selective about who he taught.

Lu told Park that he was once traveling to see his teacher and camped over night on the side of the road. Another traveler came by and shared his camp. While conversing, Lu found out that the stranger was a practitioner of Hsing-I Ch'uan and thus the conversation naturally turned to martial arts. The two demonstrated for each other. The Hsing-I man was so impressed with Lu's Pa Kua Chang that he asked Lu if he could take him to see his teacher so he might study with him. Lu agreed and thus his new friend accompanied him to his teacher's house the next day.

When the stranger asked Li Ching-Wu if he could become a student, Li flatly refused. He told the stranger that he had as many students as he could handle. Li Ching-Wu taught each student individually and thus did not have time for many students. After the man departed, Li scolded Lu for bringing this man to see him without first asking permission.

Most of Li Ching-Wu's ten students did not live in Li's village and thus had to travel to where Li lived, train for a while, and then return home and practice what they had learned. Lu told Park that Li Ching-Wu taught each new student to specialize in a different aspect of Pa Kua Chang.

Based on the student's body type and aptitude, Li would teach a student the one aspect of the art that best suited him. After Li felt the student was somewhat proficient in that one aspect, he would send the student back home to practice that one component for at least one year before returning for more instruction.

Periodically Li would invite all ten of his disciples to his home to train together. He would have each student teach all of the other students the aspects of the art which they had specialized in. Li would oversee the practice and would suggest to each student what aspects of the art they needed to concentrate on next. Li felt that it was important for his students to research the art independently and then get together and teach each other what they had individually discovered.

Every time Lu Shui-T'ien went to visit his teacher he would be tested on his Pa Kua Chang skills when he arrived. Li would then tell Lu what

Park Bok Nam, Lu Shu-Te, and Lu Shui-T'ien evaluate students during a promotion test

11

Lu Shui-T'ien poses with two swords

The banner in the background reads:

The genuine transmission of the palm skills is complete in both loyalty and righteousness.

he needed to work on. After receiving new instruction and practicing for several months, Lu would be tested once again before he left Li to return home. After this test Li would suggest what components of Pa Kua Chang Lu should work on at home until the next time he came to see his teacher.

After Li Ching-Wu died, Lu Shui-T'ien sought out another Pa Kua Chang instructor and subsequently studied with a fourth generation practitioner in Tung Hai-Ch'uan's lineage. Lu told Park that he felt his first teacher, Li Ching-Wu, taught a more complete martial arts system than his second teacher because it combined straight line Pa Kua methods with the circle walking forms and maneuvers. Park does not know the name of Lu's second teacher. He states that Lu seldom spoke of his own background. Whenever Park would ask a question that related to Lu's background Lu's response was, "That question will not help your practice." Park also states that he was not particularly interested in his teacher's background. He knew that his teacher was good at martial arts and so he was not concerned about where it came from.

Park says that one reason his teacher did not like to tell stories about himself or other martial artists was because these stories always get blown out of proportion. Lu felt that if a student hears too many fantastic stories about martial arts ability, they will have an unrealistic sense of what can be accomplished and will aim for unrealistic goals. Focusing on unrealistic goals will take the student's mind off of the fundamental training methods which develop real skill.

Today in Beijing the name Lu Shui-T'ien is well known among the practitioners in the Yin Fu lineage. They know that he was from Ching Tao and they know that he had left the country during the Japanese war. Several of these practitioners mentioned that they thought Lu Shui-T'ien's second teacher had studied with Yin Fu's son-in-law, He Chin-Kuei. While this has not been confirmed, it would make sense that one or both of Lu's teachers were of the Yin Fu lineage because much of the Pa Kua Chang that he taught is very characteristic of the Yin Fu style.

Park's teacher did tell him that his second Pa Kua Chang instructor's Pa Kua method only

Park Bok Nam practices with Lu Shui-T'ien's son, Lu Shu-Te in Korea

contained practice which was based on circle walking. Lu felt that the straight line practice and directional footwork training he received from his first teacher was very beneficial to his development of fighting skill. He felt that his second teacher's system was lacking because this training was not included.

Park also assumes that his teacher shared Pa Kua Chang knowledge with many of his martial arts contemporaries as Lu traveled widely and enjoyed visiting other martial artists where ever he went. Park states that Lu also practiced and refined his skills everyday with the band of guerrilla fighters he ran with during the Japanese war.

Park's Pa Kua Chang Training under Lu Shui-T'ien

For the first three years of study under Lu Shui-T'ien, Park Bok Nam was only taught basic, repetitive drills. Each exercise was demonstrated only one time and there was no explanation. Lu simply said, "Go practice." If Park did not perform these exercises to his teacher's liking, no correction was given and Park was taught nothing else until the exercise was correct. Park had to work it out for himself based on the little instruction he was given by his classmates. Lu was very strict because he used this period of time to test Park's dedication to Pa Kua and loyalty to his teacher. These repetitive exercises were also mandatory for Park's future development in Pa Kua Chang.

One of the first lessons Lu imparted was the importance of the student-teacher relationship and a development of mutual trust and respect between the student and teacher, and among students of the same teacher . Lu gave Park three phrases in Chinese to memorize and live by, these phrases read as follows:

師道與父子

> • *The relationship between a student and teacher is the same as the relationship between a father and son.*

同學與兄弟

> • *The relationship between students of the same teacher is just like the relationship between blood brothers.*

敬師與敬父

> • *The respect the student shows for his father is the same he shows to his teacher.*

Lu also taught Park a motto containing four words which convey four ideals he felt all Pa Kua Chang practitioners should strive to cultivate in themselves and live by. These ideals, Wisdom, Benevolence, Sincerity, and Bravery, are continually cultivated throughout the practitioners lifetime in the martial arts and form the motto for Park's Pa Kua Chang school.

Pa Kua Motto:

Wisdom The student must have a good mind in order to grasp the depth of Pa Kua Chang theory and develop his or her skill through research. The student comes to the Pa Kua Chang school to develop wisdom, however, he or she must have initially had some wisdom to make the decision to study the art.

Benevolence The student must always be humble and never use his art in an unjust manner or for ego gratification. The student comes to the school with an "empty cup" and through benevolence also learns to approach a fighting situation with an empty mind, without preconceived ideas, and void of egotistical goals. The student must have had some degree of benevolence in order to approach a teacher and become a student. The more wisdom one gains, the more benevolent one becomes.

Sincerity The student must be willing to practice hard and be sincerely dedicated to the art and his or her teacher. Lu Shui-T'ien told Park that a teacher does not teach the student, the student teaches his or her self. The teacher simply provides knowledge and ideas. When the student practices something one thousand times, it is then theirs. Through the development of benevolence the student becomes more sincere.

Bravery The practitioner is not afraid to fight. In order to develop the art completely the student must participate in the fighting aspect and thus must initially have some bravery. By also having cultivated wisdom, benevolence and sincerity, the student's bravery does not become machismo. The student has the bravery required to do what is just and fair when it is necessary. When a fight is necessary, there is no hesitation.

Park's Early Training

During the first three years of their relationship, Park's loyalty and patience was tested again and again. Every exercise Park was taught, his teacher required him to practice for hours without stopping. All of the exercises Lu taught Park during the first three years were boring and repetitive. Anytime Park did not practice to his teacher's satisfaction, or if he asked if he could be taught more, the response from Lu would be a strike with his cane to Park's body.

In winter time, if Park showed up to practice with a jacket on, his teacher would make him take it off and practice wearing only a thin shirt. Park got wise to this and wore a thin shirt, but also wore long underwear underneath. He could not fool his teacher though, Lu would ask him to lift up his shirt prior to practice. When Park was wearing and undergarment under his practice uniform, Lu would make him take it off. Lu told Park, "If you practice hard enough, you don't need a jacket." After three years of daily abuse, Lu opened up a little and started to show Park more, however, the teaching was still very strict for the next two years.

After Park had endured Lu's strict discipline for five years he showed up to class one morning and Lu patted him on the shoulder and said, "I trust you." That was the extent of the lesson for that day. When Park returned the next day, Lu began teaching Park the Pa Kua Chang material at a faster pace. He also stopped requiring Park to perform menial chores around the school. It had

taken Park five years of daily training before his teacher felt his body and his mind were ready to really practice Pa Kua Chang. Lu also started to explain to Park why he had practiced all of the repetitive drills and how each one fit into Pa Kua Chang's training process.

While Lu's initial emphasis in training Park in Pa Kua Chang was to develop a strong foundation in the areas of flexibility, coordination, leg strength, balance, speed, mobility, suppleness, and an ability to feel natural, relaxed, and comfortable while practicing all aspects of the art, the next priority was to study the philosophy and theory upon which the art of Pa Kua Chang is based and learn how this theory is directly applied to the physical art. Lu taught Park how Pa Kua Chang's footwork, body movement, kicking techniques, and striking techniques were practiced in accordance with the theories of the *Pa Kua*, *I-Ching*, Five Phases (*Wu Hsing*), and *Yin Yang*. Once these elements were practiced separately in accordance with these theories, they were then integrated in accordance with these same principles.

Lu Shui-T'ien emphasized that if the direct physical combat technique and strategy is connected to deep principles and theories, the art can be continually researched and improved based

Lu Shui-T'ien with Park Bok Nam

15

Lu Shui-T'ien poses in Pa Kua Chang's "Sliding the Window Shutter to Look at the Moon" posture

on these theories. Once Lu felt Park had a firm grasp of Pa Kua Chang's fundamental physical principles and the theories on which they were based, Lu began to teach Park the Pa Kua Chang 64 palm combat form. However, in order to teach Park how to apply Pa Kua Chang's principles to the form's application, Lu only taught Park one section (*kua*) of the eight section form at a time and required Park to research the applications on his own.

When one form section's basic movements were taught, Park would then be required to go off and practice by himself and figure out how every move of that section could be used in combat based on the principles and mechanics of movement inherent in Pa Kua Chang. Not only would he be required to show his teacher the direct application of each movement, but he would also have to show multiple functions for each move and display how each move could be varied based on a given attack from the opponent.

In other words he was required to grasp the essence of the movement, not the technique of the movement.

Lu's theory was that Pa Kua Chang is not a technique oriented art. Each movement of a form sequence does not strictly define a unique technique applied in a given scenario. The form movements are templates which help embody principles of correct motion. These principles of motion may be applied in a large variety of situations or can be varied as a particular situation dictates. He taught that the form movements do not address specific attacks, defenses, or tactical problems as much as they convey general principles of sound tactical motion. Lu felt that the Pa Kua student should work to obtain knowledge of the principle that a given form sequence was designed to embody and then work to research how that principle of motion might be applied to any situation.

Typically Park would research the series of movements in one form section for a number of weeks and then present his discoveries to his teacher. Lu's usual response was, "That is not right." or "You missed something." This would be the only instruction he was given. Park would then have to go research the movements again and try to figure out where he had made mistakes and what he had missed. On the average, it would take Park 4 to 6 months of research before he was able to satisfy his teacher and progress to the next section of the form. Practicing in this manner it took Park three years of daily practice to learn the eight section combat form from Lu.

Lu was also fond of giving Park tactical combat puzzles to figure out for each of the form sections. Lu would present Park with a scenario based on an attack or series of attacks from one or more opponents and Park would have to explain how he would best defend himself in that scenario. Again, if Park presented a strategy he thought would work and it was not valid based on the principles of Pa Kua, Lu's response would simply be, "Not correct." Given no other instruction, hints, or critiques, Park would be required to continue his research. Some of the scenarios Park had to work on took him over two years of research before his teacher was satisfied with the answer.

This method of practice may seem harsh, however, Park states that after researching the movements and techniques of Pa Kua Chang in this manner and discovering the correct applications and variations of all the form movements on his own, he has never forgotten any of what he learned. He states that if a teacher "spoon feeds" a student and shows the student some limited applications of specific form movements without explaining the principles, theories, or strategies behind the movements, and without allowing the student to discover how the Pa Kua Chang movements are applied through his or her own hard work and research, the student will soon forget what he or she was taught and will never have a "body knowledge" of Pa Kua Chang's full expression.

Park's Fighting Lessons

While training Pa Kua Chang with Lu Shui-T'ien, Park was constantly challenged by local martial artists who were skilled at various Korean martial arts styles. The Koreans are proud of their own pugilistic arts and wanted to prove that Park was a fool for studying this Chinese style. Park's teacher had told him to ignore these challenges and concentrate on his own practice. Park did his best to ignore the taunts of others who wanted to prove that their Korean styles were better than Pa Kua Chang, however, there was one particular individual who was relentless in his challenges and finally Park could not ignore him any longer. Park met this man's challenge and flattened him within a matter of seconds. The man was knocked unconscious and taken to the hospital.

The doctors at the hospital could not find a way to help this man. He was in severe pain, however, there were no external bruises or contusions. When the doctors heard that the injury had occurred during a fight, they took the beaten man to an old Chinese martial arts teacher who was skilled at healing people who had been injured in this manner. The person the doctors took the injured man to see was Lu Shui-T'ien.

When Park showed up for his lesson the next day his teacher told him that they were going to practice spear sparring. Park was excited because he loved to fight with the spear. He squared off with his teacher to begin the lesson and within

seconds Lu had stuck his spear into Park's arm and had pinned it to the floor. When Park tried to pull away Lu followed his movement with the spear's tip and maintained constant pressure. The spear tip remained in Park's arm. Park asked why he would not take the spear out of his arm. Lu replied, "Oh, does that hurt?" When Park replied, "Yes, this hurts!" Lu said, "Then how do you think that man you hit last night feels!" Park learned the hard way that his teacher was serious

**Park Bok Nam stands with his teacher
Lu Shui-T'ien**

about Park not taking meaningless challenges from the local martial artists.

The next day Park came to practice with his arm bandaged and in a sling. He sat down to watch the other students workout. Lu said, "What are you doing?" Park replied, "I cannot practice with my arm like this." Lu said, "You still have another good arm and two legs. You change your clothes and practice." Today Park still carries the scar from the spear wound as a reminder of this lesson.

While Lu forbid Park to become involved in street fights and accept challenges outside of the school, he did give Park plenty of opportunity to practice his fighting skills. Lu's philosophy was that a student could not learn the art of Pa Kua Chang correctly without the experience of fighting. Park said that Lu used the analogy of a top when

Park at Lu Shui-T'ien's funeral in 1978

explaining why a student should be required to fight in learning the art of Pa Kua Chang. Lu said that if one were to spin a large top, the top would eventually loose momentum and fall unless someone were to continuously hit the top to keep it spinning. The same analogy could be made to spinning a basketball on one's fingertip. The ball will fall unless it is continually tapped to keep it rotating. Lu felt that the Pa Kua Chang practitioner needed to be hit in combat or else he or she would not learn the valuable lessons this experience provides and his or her practice would loose momentum and fall just like the spinning top which is not hit at opportune moments to keep its momentum going.

In addition to having Park spar with other students in his own school, Lu would periodically take him to visit other Chinese martial arts schools in Korea which were run by his friends. Lu was well known and well respected among the Chinese martial artists living in Korea and thus he had many friends. When Lu took Park to visit other schools he would talk with his friends while Park sat and watched the classes. After a while Lu would stand up and say, "OK, now it is time to fight. Who would like to spar with my student?" Park would then be required to fight anyone who wanted to have a piece of him. Lu took Park to fight at a variety of schools so that he could experience other fighting styles and research how to best handle each.

Lu Chooses His Successor

After Park had been studying with his teacher for 11 years, the lessons began to come fast and furious. Park guesses that Lu realized that he was getting old and he wanted to pass his full art on to someone. He chose Park as his successor and thus Park had his work cut out for him trying to keep up with all that Lu had left to teach.

Lu overloaded Park with information to the point where he felt that Park needed to take time to assimilate all that he had been taught. He wrote out a one year training program for Park and sent him to live in a Buddhist monastery in the mountains of Korea. The curriculum which Lu designed for Park was very difficult. It required that Park practice Pa Kua Chang almost every waking hour for an entire year. Park felt like this

The tomb site of Tung Hai-Ch'uan in Beijing, China, includes a stone depicting the Pa Kua Chang lineage as it traveled to Korea with Lu Shui-T'ien

was a final test his teacher was giving him. He states that he didn't feel like his teacher really expected him to stay hidden away in a monastery with nothing to do but practice Pa Kua Chang for a full year.

Park passed his test and stayed training in the mountains for a year. Upon returning to Inchon, he showed his teacher the progress he had made. Lu, who never once told Park that he did something good, responded by saying, "What did you do up there in the mountains, take naps everyday?" Park, determined to show his teacher that he was serious about Pa Kua Chang training, asked Lu to give him another one year training program. He wanted to go back to the mountains and train again. Lu did not give Park anything for a few days, he wanted to make sure Park was serious

about this request. Park insisted that he wanted to go back to the mountains so Lu developed another one year training program. Park went back to the mountains to practice his Pa Kua Chang for another full year.

When he returned to Inchon after the second year of secluded training Lu was happy with his progress. Park states that, although his teacher would never say it, he felt that his teacher was very happy that he volunteered to go to the mountains for a second year of training and that his teacher was pleased with the progress he had made.

Park states that his teacher was very strong and healthy up until the day he died. Lu Shui-T'ien died in 1978 at the age of 84, but not from illness or natural causes. Lu had gone to sleep one night and the gas heater which was used to heat his room had malfunctioned and the gas leaked into the room. Lu died in his sleep of gas poisoning. Since Park was Lu Shu-T'ien's top student, he was asked to wear the traditional funeral clothes which are usually reserved for close family members of the deceased.

Korean Stele at Tung Hai-Ch'uan's Tomb

Tung Hai-Ch'uan (1813-1882) is recognized by most Pa Kua Chang practitioners as the originator of the Pa Kua Chang style. Tung taught his art widely in Beijing, China from approximately 1865 until his death in 1882. While some are convinced that Tung may not have originated the style, all agree that he was the first to propagate this art widely in China. After Tung died, his students, wishing to show their respect, placed a stone stele at his burial site in 1883. Since that time, Tung's grave site and the stone monuments which mark it have had a colorful history.

Tung's original burial site, near the Red Bridge just outside Beijing's East Gate, was initially marked with one stone monument. Over the years a number of other stone markers were added by Pa Kua Chang practitioners wanting to show their respect. Tung's tomb was a great attraction and was visited by many martial artists and martial arts enthusiasts. However, this original tomb was destroyed during the Cultural Revolution and the stone markers were buried underground. In 1980-1981 the stone monuments and Tung's body were unearthed and moved to a new location. Pa Kua Chang practitioners from all over the world donated money for the restoration of Tung's tomb and new monuments were added.

Park Bok Nam with his students and his teacher in Korea

In June of 1991 a new stele was erected at Tung Hai-Ch'uan's burial site which details the Pa Kua lineage as it moved from China to Korea. The writing on this monument indicates that Pa Kua Chang was brought to Korea by Lu Shui-T'ien. Three generations of names in Lu's lineage are carved into the stone stele. The first generation, listed as the fifth in Tung's lineage, lists only Lu Shui-T'ien. The sixth generation lists six of Lu's students. Included are his son Lu Shu-Te and his number one student, Park Bok Nam. Also listed on the stele are students of Park Bok Nam in Korea and students of Park's Pa Kua "brothers."

Park Teaching Pa Kua Chang in Korea

Park Bok Nam began teaching Pa Kua Chang in Korea in 1971, however, he had not originally intended to teach or open a school. His teacher's son, Lu Shu-Te had opened a Pa Kua school and asked if Park would help teach. Park agreed to help his elder Pa Kua brother with the instruction at the school but soon found out that Lu Shu-Te did not spend much time at the school and Park ended up running the majority of the classes. When Lu Shu-Te collected the first month's tuition, he gave it all to Park. Park was puzzled, "This is your school, why do you give all of this money to me?" Park asked. Lu told Park that it was his school now. He had only opened the school because he thought Park should teach and knew that he would not take the initiative to open a school on his own.

Once Park started running his school, Lu Shui-T'ien came to the school for 4 or 5 hours everyday and began teaching Park how to be a good Pa Kua Chang teacher. When Park first started teaching, Lu would make observations about each student's body condition and suggest how Park might teach each student. Later, Park was required to set up a unique training program for each student based on what he felt were the student's needs. Lu would continually ask Park questions about the students after the classes were over. He would ask about a particular student's postures, movements, body condition, coordination, or a multitude of other aspects about each student's performance

Park Bok Nam relaxes with his teacher

or progress. Park would answer the questions based on his observations and his teacher would lend advice.

Lu continually emphasized that each student is different and thus each student must have a unique training program designed to strengthen their individual weak areas. Periodically Park would be required to present Lu with a training syllabus for each student in the school. Lu would review Park's work and make suggestions.

Each month in Park's school promotion tests were held for students who were ready to be promoted to the next level, or grade. Lu Shui-T'ien, his son Lu Shu-Te, and Park would all evaluate the students ability to perform the tasks required at each promotion level. Lu Shui-T'ien would lend advice to each student after the test. By paying close attention to his teacher's guidance to his students, Park was able to learn how to become a better instructor.

One observation which Lu had made, and passed on to Park, concerning martial arts students and their practice dealt with the personal obstacles that students will experience when training in the

Chinese martial arts. Lu said that after three days the new student's body will be sore and he or she will not want to continue practicing everyday. Body soreness is the first obstacle the student needs to overcome. Next, after three weeks of practice, the student finds that the newness of the practice has worn off and it is hard to stay interested in repeating the same exercises everyday. Any exercise which is designed to condition and develop the body will take at least three months of daily repetitive practice. The body does not change overnight. From the three week to the three month period in training Lu said that the student needs to have patience and continue diligently

Lu Shui-T'ien's son, Lu Shu-Te

practicing the exercises.

At the three month mark the student starts to become bored and begins to wonder if what he or she has been practicing is good or not. Because development in internal martial arts practice is measured in years instead of weeks or months, the student may begin to feel like no progress is being made. In order to overcome this obstacle the student has to once again be patient and remain motivated.

The next obstacle is encountered after three years of practice. Lu said that at this point in time the student will have a tendency to become lazy and loose motivation. The student may get a false sense of true accomplishment after three years of hard training and begin to become complacent. Three years is a relatively short time in terms of overall Pa Kua Chang development. The student needs to recognize that they are still "a babe in the woods" and continue to practice hard.

Park explains Lu's three day, three week, three month, and three year theory to his students so that they know that these personal obstacles to continued hard practice might be encountered, but with patience and perseverance the obstacles can be overcome and the student can continue to grow in the art.

Through his experiences as a student under Lu Shui-T'ien and being a teacher under Lu's watchful eye, Park has developed a very sound Pa Kua Chang training program. Park's students became well known throughout Asia for their fighting skills. In Korea the Pa Kua Chang of Lu Shui-T'ien was simply referred to by other martial artists as "Inchon Kung Fu" and the practitioners of this style are highly respected.

Although the Koreans are very proud of their own indigenous martial arts, Chinese Kung Fu is also very popular in Korea - much more popular than it is in the United States. In a country which is approximately the size of the state of Virginia, there are nearly 500 Chinese Kung Fu schools. Park's school was so well respected in Korea that anytime a teacher wanted to open up a martial arts school in Inchon, they would first go to Park and ask his permission.

Park Bok Nam demonstrates his flexibility in his school at an American Army base in Korea. The photograph on the left side of the back wall is of the famous second generation Pa Kua Chang Master, Yin Fu

Tournaments in Taiwan and Hong Kong

Every year or two from 1979 to 1986 Park took a team of students to fight in tournaments in Hong Kong and Taiwan. His team always performed very well in the full contact fighting events. The Chinese enjoyed watching the Korean team because of their Pa Kua Chang and the Korean team became well known for its Pa Kua Chang fighting skill in both Hong Kong and Taiwan.

Many of the Chinese were very curious about this Korean team demonstrating such good Pa Kua Chang skills and would frequently ask Park where they learned their Pa Kua. When Park stated that the Pa Kua had come from Lu Shui-T'ien, many of the older generation practitioners told Park that he was very lucky to have studied from Lu. A number of these older Chinese martial

arts practitioners who had come to Taiwan or Hong Kong from Mainland China had heard of a famous Pa Kua Chang stylist who they referred to as "Ching Tao" Lu.

On one occasion Park saw a Chinese martial artist in Taiwan practicing spear. Park commented that he also loved to practice spear. The Chinese man seemed surprised that this Korean would know anything about a spear and asked Park to spar with him. When the two crossed spears Park saw an opening, but not wishing to hurt the man, he simply brushed the spear tip against the man's arm. Park's opponent could not get in on Park at all, however, Park was able to brush this man with the spear tip many times. Finally the Chinese gentleman got frustrated and called it quits. When Park told him where he had studied, the man thought that it was very strange that a Chinese

**Park Bok Nam's senior student in the
United States, Glenn Wright (left), fights in
a full contact tournament in
Taiwan in 1979**

martial artist would have taught a Korean in such depth.

On another occasion Park was practicing his Pa Kua Chang in a park in Hong Kong. Several local martial artists stopped to watch and one man commented that Park's Pa Kua Chang was very good. One of Park's Chinese friends from Korea who was with him replied in Chinese, "He cannot understand you, he is Korean." The group that was watching was very surprised. The man that had made the comment about Park's Pa Kua wanted to see if Park knew how to apply it. Park squared off with him and the man attacked. Park avoided the attack and hit the man 3 times within one second. The man was very startled and did not want to try and attack again.

Another reason the Korean team became well known in Hong Kong and Taiwan was due to the antics of Lu Shui-T'ien's son, Lu Shu-Te. Lu Shu-Te's attitude towards the martial arts has always been "put up or shut up." He does not like to talk, but he loves to fight. On one occasion in Taiwan a large group of teachers held a meeting and the conversation turned to a discussion about which styles were better and whose students were good fighters, etc. Lu Shu-Te, becoming bored with the discussion, stood up and announced, "This talk is cheap, the only way to decide who is good and

who is not is to fight! Anyone who wants to prove they are good can come out and fight!" At this point the meeting Chairman suggested that everyone break for lunch first. After the lunch break no one came back except Lu Shu-Te.

On another occasion Lu Shu-Te felt that one of the Korean fighters had won a fight, however, the decision was given to his opponent. Lu ran up to the judges table yelling and screaming. When he reached the table he hit it with his fist and the table broke in half. Needless to say, the Taiwanese tournament officials did not soon forget the team from Korea.

The Pa Kua Chang Association in Korea

During the early 1970's Lu Shui-T'ien's son, Lu Shu-Te had formed the Pa Kua Chang Martial Arts Research Association in Korea. The membership was limited to those practitioners in Korea who had obtained a high level of skill in Pa Kua Chang. In 1978, Lu Shu-Te turned over this Association to Park Bok Nam and Park changed the name to the Pa Kua Chang Association of Korea. Park opened up the association membership to anyone who had practiced Pa Kua Chang and had an interest in its future growth. Today this association has approximately 200 active members in Korea.

Park Moves to the United States

While Park Bok Nam was teaching Pa Kua Chang in Korea, one of the classes he taught was located in a small Quanset hut on an American Army base. One of the American soldiers studying with Park in this class was Glenn Wright. He began his practice with Park in December of 1978. Glenn enjoyed practicing Park's Pa Kua Chang to the extent that he managed to get stationed in Korea five different times during his twenty year Army career so that he could continue his Pa Kua Chang study.

In 1987, Park was invited to come to the United States and perform in a Chinese Martial Arts Masters Demonstration being held in Los Angeles. Glenn Wright, who was then stationed in Ft. Lee, Virginia, flew to Los Angeles to visit his teacher. After the demonstration, Park had a few weeks to stay in the United States and site see. Glenn brought Park to Virginia with him and convinced Park to stay in the United States and open up a Pa Kua Chang school here. Since Park's Pa Kua school was very strong in Korea and he had many senior students who could take over his school there, he decided to stay.

In 1987 Park opened his school in Richmond, Virginia. For more information about Park's program in the United States, refer to the Appendix.

Park's Teaching Method

After reading about Lu Shui-T'ien's heavy-handed teaching method, readers may wonder if Park approaches Pa Kua Chang instruction in the same manner. Luckily for his students, Park is very fair and not nearly as strict as his teacher. Although Park strongly believes in the values of trustworthiness, honesty, loyalty, and respect in the student-teacher relationship, his tests of loyalty are not nearly as severe as the trials he was forced to endure in his relationship with his teacher. If a student practices very hard and shows Park common courtesy and respect, the student will be shown the same respect and thus will be taught openly. If a student is honest and opens his heart to Park, Park returns the same honesty and openness. Park does not hold back his teaching as long as a student shows dedication to the art, in fact, he usually gives students more than they can handle.

In the next section we will discuss Park's general approach to Pa Kua Chang instruction.

Lu Shui-T'ien's Grave

Park Bok Nam's Teaching Method

Park Bok Nam's approach to Pa Kua Chang training, which comes directly from his teacher, is very systematic. Park compares teaching a beginning student the art of Pa Kua Chang to transforming a family sedan into a finely tuned, high performance race car. The new student in Park's school will not learn the Pa Kua Chang form movements right away. The form is like the body of the car and Park sees no sense in building a body before the engine reaches high levels of performance. This engine is built on

fundamental principles. Forms and fighting applications are but small components of the Pa Kua Chang machine. Park firmly believes that each component and sub-component of the "engine" should be developed and balanced separately and then brought together to form a complete equation which will equal perfect health and self-defense.

In designing an engine, an engineer will start with the theories and principles of mathematics, physics, electronics, thermodynamics, and mechanics. Similarly, when training the Pa Kua practitioner, Park starts with the principles and theories of Pa Kua Chang. Park believes that unless the practice is based on sound principles and theories, the student will be practicing blindly. He is quick to point out that the principles of Pa Kua Chang are not strictly physical, but include in-depth research into tactical and strategic methods of improving physical combat.

Some very small advances can be made practicing a form without knowledge and development of the principles behind the movements, but in practicing only forms, one will quickly reach a peak, past which there will be little progress. The essence of applying Pa Kua Chang in a fighting situation is spontaneous correct response, adaptability, variation, and change. Park asks, "How are any of these elements going to be applied if all the practitioner has is knowledge of a structured form?" Park was taught that in order to change, create, and respond to any situation a "body knowledge" of fundamental Pa Kua Chang physical and tactical principles is required.

Park's approach to teaching Pa Kua is through a very systematic, progressive development of these fundamental principles. Like the engineer designing his engine, Park builds his theories of Pa Kua practice utilizing sets of equations. The equations he uses break down the separate components and sub-components of Pa Kua practice and describe how these components fit together to produce a final result. The students are trained first to develop skills on the most basic sub-component level. Then, as these skills develop, sub-components are added together to build higher level sub-components, and then these are added together to create other higher level components.

The engineer must learn how to add, subtract, multiply, and divide before he can learn algebra, and his knowledge of algebra must be sound before he can utilize differential and integral calculus. Pa Kua Chang training in Park's school evolves in similarly progressive stages.

At each stage of training Park's students must demonstrate a degree of proficiency in each exercise before Park will begin to teach the follow-on exercise. To Park, proficiency not only entails proper execution of the movements themselves and knowledge of how the movements are employed, but also a high degree of reflex body response. When he attacks a student, he wants to see that the student executes the proper mechanics of Pa Kua Chang movement without having to think about it - the body should respond correctly and spontaneously. If there is any hesitation in the student's response to an attack, the student is not ready to move on.

When Park was training with his teacher, he was required to spend many hours everyday for months at a time repeating the same exercise. Eventually Park would become bored with the exercise and ask his teacher if he could move on to something else. Lu Shui-T'ien would say, "So you are ready for something else?" and launch an attack at Park. If Park did not respond correctly, Lu would say, "I think you need more practice." Although Park is not as harsh as his teacher (who would usually attack Park with his cane), Park came to realize that although the repetitive training drills were boring, in order to develop a reflex body response, they were necessary.

Reflex Body Response

Success in internal boxing requires an experiential understanding of the principle the Chinese call *wu wei*. *Wu wei* is one of the most important principles applied to any internal martial art in a self-defense situation. *Wu* literally means "non", "negative", "not", or "none" and *wei* means "action", "doing", "striving" or "straining." The common English translation of *wu wei* is "non-action," however, many incorrectly interpret this translation to mean laziness or passivity.

Wu   Wei

Wu wei is action through non-action. It is spontaneous action which does not arise from a motive or seek a result. In modern phraseology *wu wei* can be interpreted as "going with the flow" or "rolling with the punches", but requires that the practitioner do so spontaneously, skillfully, efficaciously, and along the line of least resistance. When the practitioner has embodied the principle of *wu wei* in martial arts, he or she has developed an innate body response which is spontaneous, correct, without thought and requiring what appears to be little effort in the execution of a difficult task. This response is based on a knowledge of principles, structures, alignments, rhythm, timing, optimum angles of attack and defense and economy of motion which is resident in the body, not just the mind. *Wu wei* does not stem from intellectual intelligence, but an "unconscious" or innate intelligence in the physical body that can only be developed through hours of correct repetitive training.

Park emphasizes the importance of this "body knowledge" in his teaching. He believes that when something is "known" in the body, it becomes a reflex action which will not soon be forgotten. His approach to Pa Kua Chang instruction is to start the student with very simple movements and exercises. These exercises, which are based on fundamental principles, are repeated hundreds, if not thousands of times under Park's watchful eye until the student has embodied the principle and it becomes a natural reflex. Park states that the exercise should be repeated so many times that when the student stops, the body still feels as though it is going through the motions of the exercise - like when getting back on land after a long boat ride and the body still feels like it is rocking back and forth.

Once Park feels the student has "body knowledge" of the principle as it is applied in the simple exercise, he will teach the student a slightly more difficult exercise with which to work in the same manner. Park feels that if the student is initially given exercises that are too complex, or is given too many different exercises to practice, then he or she will never develop skillful innate body response. He is fond of saying that "If I give you too much food, you cannot digest it all and some of it gets thrown away. It is the same with Pa Kua. If you are taught too much at one time, you will never digest it all."

The development of skill in internal martial arts not only requires that the student work to gain this "body knowledge" of the principles, but the body also has to change and develop physically. Flexibility, balance, and overall coordination are important components of training the body for martial arts. However, since Pa Kua Chang is an "internal" style, additional training which works to properly develop the tendons, bones, joints, ligaments, and secondary muscle groups must be executed in a progressive manner. Development of the physical body requires many hours of repetitive practice with fundamental drills designed to initiate such development. The student needs to develop what Park refers to as the "kung fu body."

Developing the "Kung Fu Body"

The Pa Kua Chang practitioner's body movement has typically been compared to that of a snake or dragon. References to snake or dragon like movement in Pa Kua Chang literature are numerous and many of the popular Pa Kua forms are called "snake" or "dragon" form Pa Kua (*she hsing* and *lung hsing* respectively). The turning, twisting, coiling, circling and whipping movements of the skilled practitioner will indeed remarkably resemble the movements of a snake and have inspired further descriptive analogies of Pa Kua movement such as *yu shen* (swimming body) or *lien huan* (continuous circling).

The snake-like movements of the Pa Kua

practitioner are never restricted to the arms, but involve a connected full body movement. There are no breaks or "dead spots" along the chain of movement from the foot to the hand. Movement in every part of the body is supple, smooth, fluid, and continuous. In order to accomplish this technique, the practitioner must be extremely flexible in the joints, especially the hips (*yao k'ua*), waist, spine, and shoulders. Full body integration and connection in conjunction with the flexible, relaxed, and unified movement are prerequisite to correct Pa Kua Chang technique application.

Development of a body capable of this great degree of flexibility and connection (what Park refers to as a "kung fu body") requires training exercises designed to develop muscle, ligament and joint flexibility and training the body to move in a unified manner. In addition to overall body flexibility, integration, and coordination, development of internal martial arts power, or the ability to apply great force through very small body articulations, also requires repetitive training drills designed to isolate and train secondary muscles groups, tendons, and joints. To be trained properly and completely, these components are trained in isolation before being applied in Pa Kua Chang form techniques.

Another important component in development of the "kung fu body" is a balanced, unified, smooth movement of *ch'i* throughout the body. The classics of Pa Kua Chang speak frequently of the "*I ch'i*," or "one *ch'i*." This is referring to the ability of the practitioner to unify the movement and function of the body in such a way that the entire body, mind, and spirit are working to achieve a common goal in a given instant, creating a "whole body power." If the body's *ch'i* is not full and balanced, the body will not work in complete harmony and the power will not be full. There will be "weak links in the chain."

Park believes that learning to apply the complex Pa Kua Chang forms before the body is well on its way to being developed properly in terms of flexibility, strength, balance, integration, alignment and coordination is analogous to entering high school without first learning how to read. Park is fond of saying, "You cannot give a baby steak; a baby needs milk."

The exercises presented in this book are

designed to help the practitioner begin to develop the "kung fu body" and gain an experiential understanding of the principle of *wu wei*.

Research

Once the Pa Kua Chang practitioner's body has been developed through a series of repetitive exercises designed to train component parts, Park introduces the student to new exercises which are designed to bring all of the parts together. Park says that no matter how good the engine parts are, if you don't know how to put them together to build the engine, you don't have anything but a pile of expensive parts.

Usually when the parts first come together the student will experience some awkwardness. Park's approach is to add small bits and pieces together a little at a time to allow the student to transition from simple repetitive drills to more complex repetitive drills (forms and fighting applications for example) so that eventually correct, spontaneous free form movement which adheres to the principles of Pa Kua Chang can be attained.

Park, who likes to teach through the use of analogy, explains that when the Wright Brothers built their plane, it flew successfully, but it didn't fly very far. This first attempt was defined as "flying" but it is trivial compared to what aviation has become today. To evolve from the Wright Brothers to the Space Shuttle, engineers had to research and develop each component of the plane and bring all the components together into a fine working balance.

The physical components which Park corresponds to the engineer's numbers are the body's joints. The numbers zero through nine are the basic building blocks of mathematics. By combining these numbers, any other number can be constructed. Similarly, by utilizing the body's joints, any attack or defense can be created. The major attack weapons are the fist (knuckle joints), palm and wrist (wrist joint), elbow, shoulder, hips, knees, heels (ankle joints), and feet (toe joints).

Skill in utilizing numbers depends on the level of sophistication of the mathematics employed in utilization of those numbers. The skill in fighting arts depends on how efficiently and effectively the body's attacking and defense weapons are employed. If the practitioner can punch and kick well, he or she has grasped " basic math." If they can use footwork to evade and set up an attack, the math is a little higher. If they can utilize the elbows and knees in combination with the punches and kicks, the math is still higher. If they can utilize all of their available weapons from all angles in continuous, fluid combinations of attack and defense, the math is becoming very sophisticated. If they have refined their skill so that all of the above can be accomplished with subtle movements executed efficiently and effectively without waste, then the "mathematics" is extremely high. Park views Pa Kua Chang practice as equating to very high level math, however, he feels that before high level math can be absorbed, basic math should be studied thoroughly.

While the student in Park's school is developing the "kung fu" body, they will also train exercises which develop power and speed in utilizing each of the body's attack weapons. In other words, they start out with basic math. These exercises include various footwork drills, palm striking exercises, elbow striking exercises, and kicking exercises designed to develop power and speed in the utilization of all the body's weapons. After the student has worked to develop power and speed in utilizing all of the basic attack weapons, he or she will then learn how to combine these attacks with Pa Kua Chang footwork. The key to Park's system of developing Pa Kua Chang skill with a systematic, complete method is the theory and strategy which forms the "math" of Pa Kua Chang.

As stated previously, all of Park's training methods are based upon the principles and theories of Pa Kua Chang. Throughout this book, component parts of Pa Kua Chang footwork, body movement, palm striking, and *ch'i kung* will be defined through the use of equations which describe how sub-components of each of Pa Kua Chang's major component come together in a systematic fashion. Once the student has an experiential understanding of the major components of Pa Kua Chang (and body knowledge of these components) Park encourages the student to research the art and improve his or her knowledge through the use of the primary theoretical equation associated with this art. This equation is based on the theories of *Yin/Yang*, Five Phases (*wu hsing*), and Pa Kua (Eight Diagrams).

Once the student learns how these philosophical concepts relate directly to the art of fighting in the context of the body movements of Pa Kua Chang, he or she can then use this philosophy as a tool in order to efficiently and effectively research and develop their understanding of the art.

Once an elementary school student learns the rules of addition and subtraction, they can easily add and subtract any numbers. The rules of addition and subtraction are the tools the student will use in adding or subtracting those numbers. Park's approach to teaching Pa Kua Chang fighting is not to "spoon feed" his students by showing application after application, his method is to give the student the tools and let the student figure it out themselves.

If the student has learned the basic fundamental movements of Pa Kua Chang and how to use the theories of *yin* and *yang*, five phases and *I Ching*, he or she can figure out the best defense or attack for any given situation. Park was required to learn in this manner and he requires this of his students. His philosophy is that if a student can figure out on their own the most efficient and effective way to handle a situation using Pa Kua Chang, then they will never forget how to handle that situation and they will be able to figure out how to handle any other situation.

When a student in Park's school is given a new movement, Park does not show the application, the student has to show Park the applications, or variations of that movement. If the student has not figured out the most effective way to use the movement Park will lend advice and tell the student to do some more research. Through this type of learning process the student eventually learns how to handle any situation.

Without the theoretical principles of *yin* and *yang*, five phases and *I Ching*, Park believes that the student will be blindly conducting research by trail and error. Trial and error will get you there, but it is not the smart way nor the efficient way. In every application a student employs, Park will look to see if the student is employing the theories

of *yin* and *yang*, five phases and *I Ching*. If one of these elements is missing, Park will say that the technique is not "balanced" and thus it is not the best, or most effective way.

These theoretical concepts and Park's applications of them to Pa Kua Chang practice will be discussed briefly in the next chapter. Specific examples of how these theories are applied to separate components of Pa Kua Chang practice will be discussed throughout the book.

Conclusion

When a student enters Park Bok Nam's Pa Kua Chang school, the priority for Park is to design a program which will develop the student's "kung fu body," enable the student to gain a "body knowledge" of the mechanics of movement and body alignments inherent in Pa Kua Chang by training those mechanics and alignments repeatedly, and enable the student to understand the theory and principles behind Pa Kua Chang employment in combat. Once the student has gained an experiential understanding of these three components, he or she is well on their way to becoming a skilled Pa Kua Chang practitioner.

Lu Shui T'ien and Park Bok Nam

武 明 武 武
義 門 藝 聖
双 弟 眞 先
全 子 傳 師

The late sagacious teacher of martial arts,

Passed on true martial skills.

His most insightful students,

Are both righteous and skilled in martial arts.

Chapter 2
The Philosophical Roots of Pa Kua Chang

Chapter 2

The Philosophical Roots of Pa Kua Chang

hy did Tung Hai-Ch'uan call his art *Pa Kua Chang*, or "Eight Diagram" Palm? Was this an arbitrary name that he chose or is there a connection to the theory of the *Pa Kua*, or Eight Diagrams, or the *I-Ching*? Although the origin of Pa Kua Chang is a popular topic of debate among Pa Kua Chang stylists and martial arts historians, many martial arts scholars believe that this art was created by Tung Hai-Ch'uan in the mid-1800's. Research indicates that after studying indigenous Northern martial arts for the first thirty or forty years of his life, Tung was taught a circle walking meditation practiced by Taoists of the *Chuan Chen Chiao* (Complete Truth) sect. Tung took this circle walking practice, which the Taoists called *Chuan T'ien Tsun* (Rotating in Worship of Heaven) and combined it with the martial arts he had studied and devised what we know today as Pa Kua Chang. However, Pa Kua Chang was not the first name that Tung chose for this art. Research reveals that he originally called his art *Chuan Chang*, or "rotating palm" and there was no apparent connection to the Pa Kua theory.

Tung changed the name of his art to *Pa Kua Chang* and connected the theory of his fighting art to the theory of the Pa Kua, or Eight Trigrams of the *I Ching*, late in his life. Perhaps his intent in doing this was to give his students a theoretical basis by which they could continue to research and develop the art after Tung was gone.

Regardless of where Pa Kua Chang originated and how it was handed down by Tung Hai-Ch'uan, Lu Shui-T'ien's intent in teaching Park Bok Nam

this art based on the theories and principles of Chinese philosophy was for the exact reason stated above. Lu was already 66 years old when Park started studying with him in 1960. Lu knew that Park, who was only 18 at the time they met, would spend the majority of his life studying Pa Kua Chang without him. Therefore, during the 17 years they spent together, Lu emphasized the theoretical foundations of the art so that Park would have tools to utilize in order to continually develop his skill for the remainder of his life. Lu Shui-T'ien was taught in this same fashion by his teacher Li Ching-Wu.

If our ancestors who invented simple electronic instruments such as the electric light bulb or the telegraph had handed their descendants the instrument without the mathematical and electrical theories to explain how it was developed and how it worked, it would have been much more difficult for those who followed to invent the electronic instruments of today. What Lu provided to Park was the "mathematics" of Pa Kua Chang so that Park could continue to improve his skill after Lu was gone. Park's feeling is that just as the engineer cannot get very far in his design work without mathematics, the Pa Kua Chang practitioner cannot get very far with his or her art without the theoretical components of that art.

Lu's approach to drawing connections between Chinese philosophy and Pa Kua Chang practice is far from anything metaphysical, astrological, or otherwise mystic, esoteric, or secretive. Lu's only real interest in Chinese philosophy was how it could be directly and practically applied to the principles of health building and physical combat. Unless theory and philosophy can be applied simply and directly in the physical world of martial arts, it does not do the practitioner much good in practice or when "push comes to shove" in a fighting situation.

The three philosophical principles which Park relies on to help him research and improve his fighting art are outlined in the following equation.

Pa Kua Chang Philosophy = Yin Yang Theory + I-Ching Theory + Wu Hsing (Five Phase) Theory

In this chapter we will briefly discuss the background and history of these philosophical theories and explain how they are applied to the fighting art of Pa Kua Chang in Park Bok Nam's school.

無　極
Wu　*Chi*

太　極
T'ai　*Chi*

陰　陽
Yin　*Yang*

Yin and Yang Theory

The ancient Chinese people were very practical and straight-forward in their philosophy. In many instances, the foundation of their belief system was based on what was occurring naturally around them. They noted that nature was in constant change and that there were noticeable patterns, rhythms and cycles inherent in this change. They observed daily cycles, monthly cycles, and yearly cycles and they sought to symbolize them to better understand patterns of nature and conditions of human life.

The two extreme ends of the observed cyclic continuum they called *yin* and *yang*. The idea of *yin* and *yang* became a kernel that sprouted more complex patterns, models, and ideas. The Chinese saw the dynamic interaction of *yin* and *yang* springing forth from stillness. This stillness they called *wu chi*, an emptiness or "void." Because nature is continually changing and thus nothing remains indefinitely still, the Chinese theorized that from any form of stillness, motion will naturally manifest. The movement which springs forth from the *wu chi*, they defined as *t'ai chi* (supreme ultimate) - a dynamic interaction of *yin* and *yang*. Everything under the sun was said to have originated from *wu chi* through the *t'ai chi*

interaction of *yin* and *yang*.

The diagram which symbolizes the *t'ai chi* is shown below. The white areas of this diagram represent *yang* and the black areas represent *yin*. The movement of the diagram is described as demonstrating a never ending, cyclical changing from *yin* to *yang* and back again. When *yin* has reached its apex, there is a return to *yang* and subsequently, when *yang* has reached its apex there is a return to *yin*. *Yang* in extreme becomes *yin* and *yin* taken to extreme becomes *yang*. The black and white dots in the diagram are

The *T'ai Chi* Diagram

representative of *yang* always containing aspects of *yin* and *yin* always containing aspects of *yang*. One is never present without the other. Additionally, the white (*yang*) dot present in the largest area of black (*yin*) is representative of the "seed" of *yang* being present in the belly of *yin*. The same is said of the black dot in the white area.

In the West, many individuals tend to incorrectly think of *yin* and *yang* as strictly defined "opposites" - typical examples being darkness and light, male and female, night and day, etc. While these simple correspondences are representative of *yin* and *yang* qualities, one should keep in mind that all relationships based on *yin* and *yang* are relative and the mutual interaction of both aspects should be considered, therefore, nothing can be defined as strictly *yin* or strictly *yang*. Additionally, *yin* and *yang* are never to be considered in a permanent state. There is always interplay, change, and dynamic movement.

Yin and Yang Relativity

When Park Bok Nam describes the relative nature of *yin* and *yang* and how it applies to Pa Kua Chang training and fighting application, he uses the number line (as shown below) as a simple example. If we look at a number line, we can identify the negative numbers as being generally *yin* and the positive numbers as being generally *yang*. However, each number can only be strictly identified as *yin* or *yang* in relation to another number. For example, the number 3 is *yang* compared to the number -4, however, the number 3 would be considered *yin* in comparison with the number 6.

Park views the zero mark on the number line as the balance point and states that in all training, whether for health or self-defense, the balance point should be sought. In practice, the *yang* (expressive, external) training is always balanced with the *yin* (meditative, internal) training. Additionally, the practitioner of Pa Kua Chang seeks a balance of *yin* and *yang* in every movement. The Pa Kua Chang practitioner is never too soft, or too hard; when he moves forward, he is aware of

what is behind and is ready to move back, when he engages the opponent high, he is conscious of what is happening low, etc.

In interaction with an opponent, the *yin* and *yang* balance is also sought. If an opponent is expressive or hard in his technique, the technique is met with a soft, absorbing force and redirected. If the opponent is very soft, the practitioner applies expressive force. While this general rule is common knowledge to most "internal" style martial artists, Park's variations and quick changes on this theme are numerous.

Pa Kua Chang stylists are famous for their ability to change rapidly from firm to gentle, fast to slow, right to left, inside to outside, high to low, etc. While the aim is to always reach the point of balance, the Pa Kua Chang practitioner will typically offset and confuse the opponent with his or her quick variations. The Pa Kua Chang practitioner is able to maintain his own balance through the myriad of changes because his footwork and body movements are rotating around balanced central points. An opponent who is not accustomed to the centripetal and centrifugal forces expressed through the Pa Kua Chang stylist's movements will be easily offset. Study and application of the constant and continuous interchange between *yin* and *yang* elements of the fighting art aids the Pa Kua Chang practitioner's application.

Yin and Yang in Cycles

Because *yin* and *yang* are viewed as the extreme ends of a natural cyclic continuum, there is a constant cyclic changing from *yin* to *yang* and from *yang* back to *yin*. The time of change between *yin* and *yang* in these cycles is viewed as containing the strongest force, inertia, or energy. In all cycles of nature, the Chinese view the time of change from *yin* to *yang* or *yang* to *yin* to hold the greatest energy, or the greatest strength. For example, night time is generally considered to be *yin* in nature while day time is *yang* in nature. When day changes to night or night changes to day at sunrise or sunset, the energy of the day is strongest, clearest, freshest and well balanced. Most everyone has experienced the strong, fresh sensation of the morning air. Because the energy is strongest, freshest and well balanced at these times of the

Yin   Yang

-8 -7 -6 -5 -4 -3 -2 -1 0 1 2 3 4 5 6 7 8

Yin Palms   **_Yang_ Palms**

day, these times are the ideal times for practicing *ch'i kung* exercises and meditation.

While practice at anytime of the day, or season of the year, can be beneficial, Park believes that practicing specific exercises, such as breathing and *ch'i* cultivation exercises, while the *ch'i* in the air is the freshest, strongest, and most balanced will greatly enhance the practice and thus the progress will be faster. He believes that the most efficient way to practice is in accordance with the rules of nature as symbolized by the cycles of *yin* and *yang* in the day (and during the year) and thus he applies this theory to all of his practice and teaching.

The cyclic change between *yin* and *yang* also applies to Pa Kua Chang's palm articulations. In the Pa Kua Chang parlance, a palm that is facing up is called a *yang* palm and a palm that is facing down is called a *yin* palm. In accordance with the *yin yang* theory, the palm movements are most powerful when the *yin* palm is changing to the *yang* palm or when the *yang* palm is changing to a the *yin* palm. In other words, the power, or strength is the strongest when there is change, not when maintaining a static position.

As an example of this idea of a changing force being stronger than a static force, imagine someone driving along in a car with a baseball bat stuck out the window. If this person holds the baseball bat static, as if bunting, and the bat hits a mailbox, the force striking the mail box will be equal to the force generated by the speed of the car. However, if the person holding the bat were to swing the bat

and strike the mailbox, the force hitting the mailbox would be equal to the speed of the car plus the force of acceleration from the person swinging the bat. In Pa Kua Chang, many strikes are applied as the palm is changing from *yin* to *yang* or from *yang* to *yin* in order to add the extra force produced by the crisp rotation of the palm. Additionally, the palm rotation also helps increase the flow of *ch'i* and blood to the palm.

Typically the *yin* palm changing to *yang* palm will be used in conjunction with a defensive maneuver, such as a parry or when freeing one's self from an opponent's grab, and the *yang* changing to *yin* will be used in conjunction with an offensive strike. The *yin yang* palm relationship is one small example of how the theory of *yin yang* is applied directly to the physical movements in Pa Kua Chang.

Another direct representation of *yin* and *yang* to the physical aspects of Pa Kua Chang is symbolized by the interplay of *yin* and *yang* in the *t'ai chi* diagram. The diagram displays a constant movement from *yin* to *yang* and back again. The diagram representation symbolizes this movement as flowing smoothly and continuously. This idea can be interpreted as representing a smooth interchange and continuously flowing motion in physical practice. When one changes from slow movement to fast movement, from hard movement to soft movement, from high to low, low to high, inside to outside, outside to inside, forward to backward, etc., the movement should be continuous and flow smoothly.

Yin and *Yang* Combinations

In order to represent, and therefore further understand, the patterns of nature beyond the dynamic interplay of *yin* and *yang*, the Chinese created *yin* and *yang* combinations. The first of these combinations represents the maximum number of sets that can be formed by combining two differing elements in sets of two. In other words, if one was given *yin* and *yang* as two unique items and asked to combine them in sets of two, the maximum number of unique sets obtainable is four. This simplest representation of *yin* and *yang* in combination is called *Szu Hsiang* (four figures).

Yin and *yang* are symbolically represented by

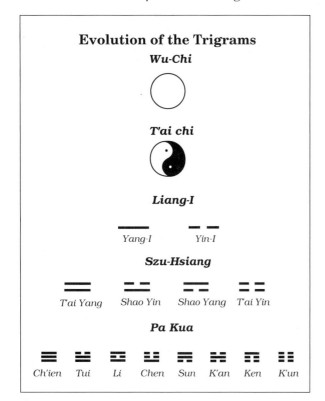

Evolution of the Trigrams

Wu-Chi

T'ai chi

Liang-I

Yang-I   Yin-I

Szu-Hsiang

T'ai Yang   Shao Yin   Shao Yang   T'ai Yin

Pa Kua

Ch'ien   Tui   Li   Chen   Sun   K'an   Ken   K'un

combinatorial analysis, which are modeled by these *yin* and *yang* combinations, in his approach to Pa Kua Chang training and Pa Kua Chang fighting. However, we will first further explore the theory of the Eight Trigrams.

Pa Kua Theory

Most Westerners who are somewhat familiar with Chinese philosophy will recognize the eight trigrams as the building blocks that form the 64 hexagrams of the *I-Ching* or *Book of Changes*. However, the majority of *I-Ching* texts available today in English dive directly into commentary on the hexagrams without fully explaining the meaning and usage of the trigrams.

An understanding of the eight trigrams and the two primary trigram arrangements can provide great insight into a study of the *I-Ching* and facilitate a deeper understanding of the patterns of change inherent in nature and in human life. The ability to understand the combinatorial theory upon which the trigrams and hexagrams are built, and an understanding of the nature of change inherent in the changing lines of the *I-Ching*, are important components in understanding the art of Pa Kua Chang as taught by Park Bok Nam. This section will briefly look at the history, meaning, and usage of the eight trigrams as representations of combinatorial analysis, and as arranged in the *Fu Hsi* (also called *Hsien T'ien* or Early Heaven) and *King Wen* (also called *Hou T'ien* or Later Heaven) diagrams.

The trigrams are essentially codifications of naturally occurring processes. By combining symbols that reflect dynamic elements in nature and the human process, the Chinese have sought to understand and predict patterns, cycles, and polarities which are present in nature and human development. Two such trigram combinations, the *Hsien T'ien* (Early Heaven) and the *Hou T'ien* (Later Heaven), represent the balance of polar elements and the nature of cyclical change, respectively. By studying the relationships of the trigrams in these configurations, one can learn to apply these symbols directly to the practice of Pa

the *Liang I* (two symbols). The *Yang I* is represented by a continuous straight line and the *Yin I* is represented by a broken line. The *Szu Hsiang* are formed by combining the *Yin I* and the *Yang I* as shown in the illustration above. The *Szu Hsaing* are given names of *T'ai Yang* (Greater Yang), *Shao Yin* (Lesser Yin), *Shao Yang* (Lesser Yang), and *T'ai Yin* (Greater Yin).

If one were to add one more element to the *yin yang* set, and thus create all of the possible combinations of *yin* and *yang* in sets of three, the result is the *Pa Kua* (Eight Trigrams or "Three Line Markings"). Starting from nothing (*Wu Chi*) the one (*T'ai Chi*) was created; from the one, two were created (*Yin and Yang*); from two, four were created (*Szu Hsiang*); and from four, eight were created (*Pa Kua*). Similarly, from the eight, sixty-four are created and form the hexagrams of the *I Ching* (*Book of Changes*). Looking at this progression from the standpoint of mathematics it is easy to see that the pattern fits that of simple combinatorial theory.

Throughout this book we will describe how Park Bok Nam was taught to use the theories of

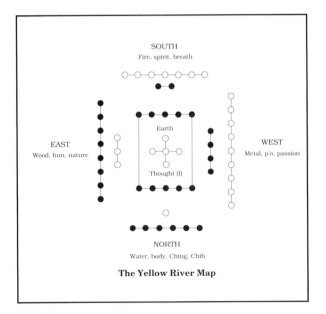

SOUTH
Fire, spirit, breath

EAST
Wood, hun, nature

Earth

Thought (I)

WEST
Metal, p'o, passion

NORTH
Water, body, Ching, Chih

The Yellow River Map

Kua Chang. We will describe how this is done in Park's Pa Kua Chang method throughout this book.

Through identification with the trigram arrangements and the natural development process, one can adapt to fit smoothly into patterns of change and balance within cycles of change. While these theories can be applied to most any human condition or life process, in this book we will only be concerned with how they apply directly to Pa Kua Chang training and fighting.

The ability to smoothly change from one technique to another when it is least expected by the opponent and to do so in an efficacious manner is characteristic of Pa Kua Chang and thus understanding combinatorial analysis and the theory of change when researching and practicing Pa Kua Chang techniques is to the practitioner's advantage.

The History of the Eight Trigrams

In pre-dynastic times, China was ruled by the mythical Five Emperors *(Wu Ti)*. The Five Emperors ruled in succession during the "golden age of antiquity" (prior to 2357 B.C.) and have traditionally been considered sages and cultural heroes, if not semi-divine beings, by the Chinese. Therefore we find that these Five Emperors; Fu Hsi (Subduer of Animals), Shen Nung (the Divine

Farmer), Huang-Ti (the Yellow Emperor), Shao Hao, and Chuan Hsu, have each been credited with many inventions. Fu Hsi was credited with the discovery of the *I-Ching* (as well as inventing hunting, fishing, and trapping) nearly 5,000 years ago.

There are any number of stories that have been written pertaining to Fu Hsi's discovery of the trigrams. One story says that he derived the eight trigrams from the Yellow River Map *(Ho T'u)*. This map was revealed to him on the back of a supernatural animal called a "Dragon Horse" that rose from the waters of the Yellow River. Another story describes Fu Hsi as finding the trigrams hidden in the patterns on a tortoise shell. Still another tale states that he created the trigrams after careful observation and contemplation of the natural objects around him.

While accrediting the discovery of the trigrams to a mythical Emperor has a nice mystical flavor to it, there is no evidence that the trigrams existed prior to the Shang Dynasty (1766-1123 B.C.). Of course, actual archaeological existence of anything prior to the Shang Dynasty is scarce (within the last 15 years there have been Hsia Dynasty findings). However, analysis of inscriptions found in tortoise shell and bone from the Shang period leads some scholars to believe that the Shang people practiced divination using the tortoise shell, not the trigrams or hexagrams.

It is speculated that the Shang people heated the tortoise shell with fire until cracks appeared. The Diviner would read the cracks and be able to intuitively answer questions about one's future. It is thought that the patterns that typically reappeared when the shell was heated were given meaning, and this practice eventually led to the formation of the trigrams and hexagrams.

While tortoise shell divination could very well have led to the formation of the trigrams and explain one of the Fu Hsi myths, I tend to believe that the formation of the trigrams and hexagrams came about through an evolutionary numerological process which started with the concept of *yin* and *yang*. This evolution could have occurred prior to the Shang period and the trigrams adopted by the Diviners at a later time.

The Eight Trigrams Theory

The *Pa Kua* (eight trigrams) were said to have been instituted by the sages through their observation of the *Szu Hsiang*. They represent the maximum number of combinations of the *Yin I* and the *Yang I* in sets of three. Their names are *Ch'ien, Tui, Li, Chen, Sun, K'an, Ken,* and *K'un*. The trigrams are frequently associated with natural objects (Heaven, Lake, Fire, Thunder, Wind, Water, Mountain, and Earth respectively), as well as animals, members of the family, numbers, colors, shapes, sounds, hours of the day, weather patterns, astrological animals, parts of the body, directions on the compass, seasons of the year, etc.

Although the trigrams have many names and attributes associated with them, one should not attach too much importance to the name or any other unique association. Though the components of transformation may share some characteristics with the natural object for which it is named, the trigrams represent transformations that cannot be tied adequately to a given name in the literal sense. The concepts represented by the trigrams are dynamic and associating them too closely with physical objects or concrete ideas will usually tend to undermine and limit the symbology.

Just as the trigrams should not be limited in use by associating them too closely with specific ideas or objects, they should also not generally be thought of as mystical symbols having powers of their own. Although some *Feng Shui* (practitioners of the "Wind and Water" art or geomancy) will hang the trigrams on walls to "ward off evil spirits" or balance the "energy" of a room and there are religious factions in China which believe these symbols can hold mystical powers, one should keep in mind that the trigrams are fundamentally codifications or models of naturally occurring processes. It is the movement and change that they

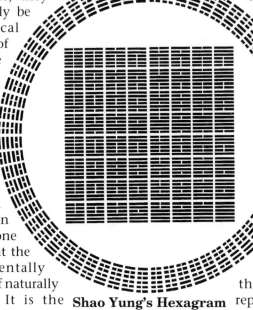

Shao Yung's Hexagram Circle and Square

represent that we seek to understand through the use of the trigrams. While some people believe that archetypal images can hold certain powers, this esoteria often turns into misinterpretation, illusion, and fantasy. Unless one has been fully initiated into a religious or spiritual discipline that believes in and understands these "powers," it is probably best to avoid the attachments.

Also, it should be said that the trigrams and hexagram symbols provide far more than a basis for an oracle used for fortune telling, prophecy, or divination. Although it is frequently used as such, many books that have been published on the *I Ching* over-emphasize this aspect and thus students loose sight of the underlying system and structure which profoundly expresses patterns of movement and change. The trigrams and hexagrams have been used widely in the fields of philosophy, astrology, medicine, geomancy, numerology, emblemology, martial arts and mathematics.

Of great significance is the fact that the Chinese took symbols such as the *Yin I* and the *Yang I*, which are representations of dynamic concepts, and used them as building blocks to represent and allude to other ideas (*Szu Hsiang, Pa Kua,* etc.). In this sense, the combinations of the *Yin I* and *Yang I*, especially as they are used in the areas of numerology and emblemology, are algorithmic.

An algorithm is a recursive mathematical rule or procedure. Modern day computers perform almost all of their functions based on algorithms and the only language computers understand is the binary language. Everything the computer does—mathematical calculations, word processing, graphics, you name it—is performed using binary arithmetic and binary representation.

If we let the *Yang I* represent the number one and the *Yin I* represent a zero, it is easy to see that the combinations that form the *Szu*

40

Hsiang and the *Pa Kua* follow the rules of binary arithmetic. In fact, in the well known hexagram circle of the Sung dynasty philosopher Shao Yung (1011-1077), the hexagrams are arranged in an exact representation of binary arithmetic (each hexagram in succession is a binary representation of the numbers from 0 to 63).

In the West, binary arithmetic was discovered by the German mathematician Gottfried Willhelm Leibnitz (1646-1716), who published his findings in 1679. In the field of mathematics, Leibnitz excelled in the areas of combinatorial analysis and symbolic reasoning. While he is noted as a pioneer in these fields, Shao Yung is the true trailblazer—he worked out his arrangement of the hexagrams in 1060.

Shao Yung combined "emblemology" and numerology derived from the teachings he received from Li Chih-Ts'ai (died 1045) to form his diagram. These teaching included explanation of the diagrams and emblems of the *Ho T'u* (River Chart), the *Lo Shu* (Lo Writing), the hexagrams of the *I Ching*, and the *Hsien T'ien T'u* (trigram arrangement of Fu Hsi). According to Ch'eng Hao (1032-1085) in his "Epitaph to Shao Yung," Li had received these ideas through a line of Taoists which can be traced back to Ch'en T'uan (906-989). Shao Yung's biography is recorded in the *Sung Shih* (History of the Sung Dynasty).

Combinations - From Theory to Practical Application

Lu Shui-T'ien's method of applying the theory of the *I Ching* to Pa Kua Chang had little to do with divination or the exact meaning or attribute of the hexagrams. However, he did impart to Park Bok Nam the importance of combinatorial analysis and the *I Ching*'s message of continuous change. The first lesson which Lu taught Park was that in Pa Kua Chang there are eight upper body weapons and eight lower body weapons which the Pa Kua Chang practitioner will use most often to strike or block an opponent. All of these weapons are associated with the body's joints.

The upper body joints which can be described as weapons include the knuckle joints in both hands (weapons associated with these joints would include the fists and fingers), the two wrists (weapons here would include the palms and the wrist joints), the two elbows, and the two shoulders. The lower body joints are the two hips, the two knees, the two ankles (heel kicks), and the two feet. All of these weapons can be used in attack or defense. The practitioner can either strike or block with any of these weapons and they are also key points of attack on the opponent's body when striking, grabbing, controlling, or otherwise attacking.

Given these weapons of attack and defense, the next lesson Park was to learn was the mechanics of applying each of these weapons efficiently and effectively on the left side and right side, high and low, inside and outside, and at long and short range. Each component was trained individually through a series of kicking exercises, palm striking exercises, elbow striking exercises and straight line combative technique forms. After learning the body mechanics involved in applying each of these weapons effectively, Park was then taught a series of "speed combination" exercises which develop the ability to use combinations of these weapons with the greatest speed and power.

The "speed combination" principles are designed so that the practitioner can develop an intuitive feel for how to apply combinations of his weapons quickly and accurately while taking away the opponent's ability to use his or her weapons. The intricacy and complexity of Lu's Pa Kua theory as it is applied to speed combinations is beyond the scope of this book. However, we will provide some very simple examples of how this theory is applied on the most basic level so that the reader can grasp the fundamental concept involved.

Just as *yin* and *yang* can be combined to form more complex sets such as the *szu hsiang* and the *pa kua*, elements of the fighting art can be similarly combined. Instead of *yin/yang* pairs, in boxing one can pair sets such as attack/defense, long range/short range, left/right, inside/outside and high/low. Applying the most basic level of combinations to a set such as attack and defense (letting A = attack and D = defense) we can arrange them in sets of two in four possible ways as follows:

$$A + D, \ D + A, \ A + A, \ D + D$$

The other paired sets can be similarly combined. Taking the combinatorial sequence one step farther, one can combine the same two element pair in eight possible ways as follows:

$$A + D + A$$
$$D + A + D$$
$$A + A + D$$
$$D + D + A$$
$$A + D + D$$
$$D + A + A$$
$$D + D + D$$
$$A + A + A$$

When studying combinations of attack/defense, left/right, long range/short range, high/low, or inside/outside, the student in Park's school will use the combinatorial analysis tool as a model so that research will be thorough. After simple combinations are practiced, more complex combinations are explored by combining the different paired elements.

Lu taught Park that if he was given an attack/ defense combination with the right hand followed by an attack/defense combination with the left hand in a given form or exercise, based on combinatorial analysis of this combination, there are many possible combinations that the practitioner can use which stem from this one combination. If we let A = attack, D = defense, R = right, and L = left, we can see that some of the possible combinations are as follows:

1) AR DR AL DL
2) AR DR DL AL
3) DR AR AL DL
4) DR AR DL AL
5) AL DL AR DR
6) AL DL DR AR
7) DL AL AR DR
8) DL AL DR AR, etc.

By combining the paired sets in constructing exercise sets, there can be many possible combinations. In this simple example, one can see that for one attack, say a strike with the palm, and one defense, say a subsequent block with the elbow, there are 16 different combinations one can practice stemming from these two simple techniques. For each of the simple combinations Park was given, his teacher required him to practice all of the combinations of those techniques which were possible and demonstrate how each of the combinations might be best employed. Simple combinations were followed by more complex combinations.

All combinations Park was taught involved a series of tactically sound movements using the body's sixteen joints for attack and defense in rapid succession and were later combined with Pa Kua Chang footwork. All combinations were efficient and effective. While some of the combinations which result from applying the combinatorial analysis to one given combination might not work as well as others, the practitioner will have at least been complete in his study of the technique if all possible combinations are researched. The practitioner can later discard the ones that do not work well.

When the practitioner has been trained to employ all 16 of the body's joints as weapons in an efficient and effective manner and can apply these weapons on the left and right side, high and low, and at short and long range, the number of combinations the practitioner can devise to handle any given situation is enormous. When these weapons and combinations are combined with an intricate usage of footwork, the fighting system is very thorough.

Lu Shui-T'ien always stressed to Park that theory was useless if it was only known in the head. In order to gain a "body knowledge" of the theory of combinations Park was required to practice each combination sequence of a particular combination of techniques hundreds of times so that all of the combinations would become reflex body reactions.

The series of "speed combination" drills which Park learned from his teacher are all based on the theory of combinatorial analysis utilizing the body's 16 weapons to strike the opponent while simultaneously robbing him of his weapons. Park's teacher taught him two rules of thumb to use when fighting. The first is that "if you take it away from them, they can't use it." In other words, if the opponent kicks, damage his leg and then follow up. If he puts out an arm to block or strike, damage it or break it and then use it as a bridge to get inside and continue the attack.

The other rule used when fighting is applied in controlling the opponent. Park states that "if you want to stop a four blade fan, you only have to hold one of the blades." Applying this principle, Park was taught how to control the opponent's body in any given situation simply by controlling one of the opponent's sixteen joints. Which joint the practitioner attacks or controls depends on the spacial relationship between the practitioner and the opponent. Park utilizes Lu's theory of studying the use of the body's joints through combinatorial analysis in all of his combat instruction.

Once a student practices the speed combination drills for a sufficient amount of time, his or her ability to inflict an incredible amount of damage on an opponent in a very short period of time is greatly increased. Swiftness in overcoming an opponent is not only gained through the development of fast, powerful, continuous attacks, but also in the practitioner's ability to know exactly where to strike the opponent to inflict the most amount of damage in the shortest period of time. Therefore, Park's method of combination study is very thorough. Additionally, because the student has practiced every possible combination of a series of techniques in training, his or her ability to respond to any of the opponent's movements in combat and vary the techniques based on the situation is easily accomplished.

Practicing repetitive sets of the "speed combinations" allows the practitioner to train the body to respond quickly, accurately, and continuously without having to think. In combat, there is no time to think, the body should respond to any of the opponent's movements spontaneously. If the practitioner has to stop and think, the response will be far to slow. When Lu Shui-T'ien took Park to other Chinese martial arts schools to fight other students and test his skills, he would not allow Park to use the speed combinations because they are too brutal. When these speed combinations are trained and applied correctly, the fight is over in a matter of seconds. Park states that he can train any student to be able to strike eight times in one second. Park has been clocked striking as many as 13 times in a second.

Typically when Lu had Park fight against opponents from other schools there was something specific he wanted Park to work on and the best lessons could be learned through testing the particular skill in a fight against an unknown opponent. These fights were learning experiences, not contests to see which school was better. However, on one occasion a group had said something derogatory about Pa Kua Chang to Lu and upset him. When Park went to fight, Lu told Park to take the guy out quick. Park utilized his speed combinations and won the fight in a matter of seconds. This is typical of Pa Kua Chang fighting, the practitioner's application is very fast, brutal, and continuous.

On another occasion, Park was taken to a Chinese martial arts school to fight with some of the students. Park had engaged in several sparring matches in order to work out whatever techniques or principles his teacher had wanted him to train during these matches. During the last fight Park engaged in, Lu felt it was time to leave. He stood up while Park was fighting and announced, "Finish it." Park applied the speed combinations and quickly knocked out his opponent. The techniques were applied so fast that the opponent and members of the other school could not figure out what had happened.

By applying combinatorial analysis to basic Pa Kua Chang fighting principles utilizing paired sets such as defense/attack, long range/short range, high/low, left/right, or various combinations of these paired sets, the practitioner can develop an extensive arsenal of applications to use in a fighting situation. By utilizing this theory, a practitioner can take any given movement from a form and create dozens of variations of any one movement or combination of movements based on the theory of the *I Ching* (discussed at the end of this chapter). However, Park always stresses that even if a practitioner discovers the best combination or technique in the world, if he or she only knows it in the head and not in the body, it will not be of much use. Every element of Pa Kua Chang must be practiced until it is "known in the body" before it can be effectively applied in a self-defense situation.

Pa Kua Geometry - The Eight Trigram Diagrams

Combinatorial analysis is not the only way one might employ the wisdom of the Pa Kua theory to the art of Pa Kua Chang. Another very important research device which the Pa Kua Chang practitioner can utilize is the principle of movement associated with the geometry of the two Pa Kua diagrams. In this section we will introduce the reader to the two primary Pa Kua diagrams, the Early Heaven arrangement (*Fu Hsi*) and the Later Heaven arrangement (*King Wen*), and then explain how these diagrams are used by Park in his training methods and his implementation of this art in combat.

Early Heaven and Later Heaven

Before we go any further with the discussion of the eight trigrams, a discussion of the terms "Early Heaven" and "Later Heaven" is appropriate. These concepts have deep meaning in Chinese thought and we would be remiss if we did not address the subject before turning to a discussion of the *Fu Hsi* (Early Heaven) and *King Wen* (Later Heaven) trigram arrangements.

The Chinese terms *Hsien T'ien* (Early Heaven or Pre-Heaven) and *Hou T'ien* (Later Heaven or Post-Heaven), which describe the two trigram arrangements, also have been translated conveniently to English as "prenatal" and "postnatal," respectively. In general terms, Early Heaven represents the innate and Later Heaven represents the acquired. Innate, or prenatal *ch'i* in the body is genetic and hereditary in nature - it is life energy that represents life potentiality, or the possibility of life manifestation. The acquired, or postnatal *ch'i* is created from the prenatal energies after the manifestation of life. In the human, postnatal energies are formed upon conception.

Early Heaven energies are not strictly related to the human, but represent all environmental elements that are involved in conception of new life. Once life manifests, these elements remain active in guiding the growth and maturation of that life. When the Early Heaven energy has been exhausted, life in its material form will typically end. Movement launched by the Early Heaven energy is developed and nourished by Later Heaven

energy. Later Heaven energy is manifest the moment life is conceived and is sustained by the Early Heaven force and nourished by the environment through the intake of food and air. The Early Heaven energies form a foundation for the Later Heaven energies to build upon.

In accordance with these concepts, the Later Heaven arrangement of the trigrams shows a self-generating cyclic movement while the Early Heaven arrangement indicates the interaction of the polar forces which actually bring about creation. It is said that knowing how to relate and work with the symbology depicted by these two trigram arrangements when practicing Chinese *Ch'i Kung* or Internal Martial Arts will lead to internal restoration and completion of one's *ch'i*. Knowing how to preserve Early Heaven energy (the body's innate energy) and cultivate pure Later Heaven energy (energy derived from food and air) in the body are key aspects in maintenance of health through Chinese *Ch'i Kung* or Internal Martial Arts practice.

The *Fu Hsi* Arrangement

The *Fu Hsi* or "Early Heaven" arrangement of the trigrams is said to have existed prior to the *Book of Changes*. As discussed previously, the trigrams themselves are formed by combining the *Yang I* and *Yin I* as shown in the illustration on the next page. Study of this progressive combinatorial sequence will reveal that the *Szu Hsiang* are formed by duplicating two sets of the *Liang I* and adding

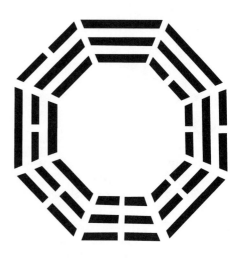

The Fu Hsi Trigram Arrangement

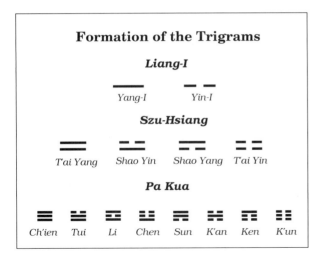

Formation of the Trigrams

Liang-I

Yang-I   Yin-I

Szu-Hsiang

T'ai Yang   Shao Yin   Shao Yang   T'ai Yin

Pa Kua

Ch'ien   Tui   Li   Chen   Sun   K'an   Ken   K'un

the *Yang I* under the first set, and the *Yin I* under the second set (the first set being the set on the left).

Similarly, the Pa Kua are formed by duplicating two sets of the *Szu Hsiang* and adding the *Yang I* to the bottom of the first set and the *Yin I* to the bottom of the second set. In the Early Heaven arrangement of the trigrams, the first set of four trigrams occupy the left side of the circle, running from top to bottom, and the second set occupy the right side of the circle, also running from top to bottom. The four trigrams on the left pertain to Heaven, are creative and move upward. The four on the right pertain to Earth, are receptive and move downward. The Fu Hsi trigram arrangement is shown on the previous page.

The Early Heaven arrangement is based on a balance of opposing forces representing a primordial order rooted in stillness and reaching beyond space and time parameters. The eight universal forces represented by these trigrams are balanced axially and the diagram of *Fu Hsi* is read along these four axes. If one studies the relationship of the symbols in this arrangement, it is easy to see that trigrams occupying a position directly across from each other are indeed symbolic opposites. Wherever there is a *yang* line in any one trigram, the trigram across from it will have a *yin* line in that same position and vice-versa.

At the ends of the vertical axis of this arrangement are the trigrams representative of Heaven and Earth (*Ch'ien* and *K'un* respectively) and thus extreme *yin* and extreme *yang* balance

the polar (positive and negative) positions of this diagram. At the ends of the horizontal axis are the trigrams representative of fire and water (*Li* and *K'an* respectively). Fire is positioned in the East (South is at the top) and moves upward, thus representing the rising of the sun. Water is positioned in the West and moves downward, representing the setting of the sun and darkness of night. These four trigrams make up the *Szu Cheng* (four sides) of the Fu Hsi arrangement.

The *Szu Yu* (four corners) of the Fu Hsi diagram are composed of the trigrams *Sun, Chen, Tui,* and *Ken*. To the right of the Heaven trigram (Southwest) we find the trigram *Sun. Sun* is one of the Earthly trigrams and represents the Wind (the Gentle). This trigram is balanced with the *Chen* (Thunder) trigram positioned in the Northeast. Thunder is seen as a dynamic force, a sudden spark of energy, with the ability to arouse and stimulate. Wind (also related to the Wood element) balances this force with a gentle, receptive nature. In the Southeast we find the *Tui* (Lake) trigram symbolizing joyfulness, transparency, and lightness. This trigram is balance in the Northwest by the trigram *Ken* (Mountain) which represents steadfastness, resistance, and solidity.

In accordance with the concept of "Early Heaven," the *Fu Hsi* arrangement, with its polar opposites placed in axial positions around the circle, represents the innate, primal, time-independent forces. This symbol can thus be interpreted as representing the perfect balance we imagine existing prior to the conception of life, the complete stillness prior to initiation of movement, and the void which exists beyond space/time parameters.

The image this trigram arrangement gives to the Pa Kua Chang practitioner is one of stillness, centeredness, and balance. The movement of this trigram arrangement is from the center outward. The practitioner utilizing this movement principle will visualize his or her self in a stable, still, balanced, central position focusing outward with a balanced awareness of all sides. The *Pa Feng Ken Pu* (Eight Direction Rooted Stepping) footwork introduced in the next chapter, which trains the practitioner to move linearly in one of an infinite number of directions from a stable central location, is theoretically based on the *Fu Hsi* diagram.

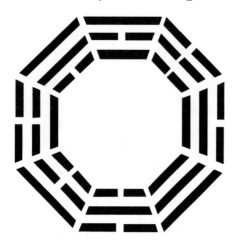

**The King Wen Trigram
Arrangement**

The King Wen Arrangement

While Fu Hsi is said to be the inventor of the hexagrams of the *I Ching*, Wen Wang, who was given the title of King posthumously, is credited as being one of the authors of the *I Ching* commentary, along with the Duke of Chou and Confucius. It is said that King Wen constructed his interpretation of the hexagrams of the *I Ching* through contemplation of the trigrams while he was in jail (around 1143 B.C.). Additionally, Wen is credited with devising the "Later Heaven" arrangement of the eight trigrams. King Wen's arrangement is shown above at left.

We can guess that this trigram arrangement was probably devised from the *Lo Shu* (Lo Writings or Lo Scroll), which is said to have been derived from the markings on the shell of a "spiritual turtle" that crawled out of the Lo river when the Emperor Yu was draining off the floods (shown above). From this scroll the *Chiu Kung* (Nine Halls or Nine Palaces), which have an important place in Chinese numerology, were also derived.

The Nine Palace numerological arrangement is depicted in the "magic square" shown below. In the magic square the numbers 1-9 are assigned to each "palace" in accordance with the Lo scroll. Pa Kua Chang literature is full of references to the Nine Palaces. The nine post, or nine circle practice in Pa Kua Chang is derived from the arrangement of the Nine Palaces.

Investigating the "magic square" one will discover several numerological correspondences. The most obvious pattern one will encounter is that the sum of any row, column or diagonal equals 15. The numbers in the four primary directions (sides) are odd, while the numbers on the corners are even. Summing the numbers on the corners equals 20, the sum of the sides also equals 20. The numbers associated with each of the trigrams in the King Wen arrangement are identical to the numerology of the "magic square." The number five does not relate to any trigram and thus it is the unifying number which is placed in the center.

It is possible that the Later Heaven arrangement

4	**9**	**2**
3	**5**	**7**
8	**1**	**6**

The "Magic Square"

SOUTH

EAST

WEST

NORTH

The Lo Scroll

South

Mid Summer
12 noon

Clinging

Li
(Fire)

South East

Starting of Summer
9 a.m.

South West

Starting of Fall
3 p.m.

Gentle

Sun
(Wind)

Receptive

K'un
(Earth)

Dividing of Spring
6 a.m.

East

Arousing

Ch'en
(Thunder)

Tui
(Lake)

Joyful

Dividing of Fall
6 p.m.

West

Keeping Still

Ken
(Mountain)

Ch'ien
(Heaven)

Creative

Starting of Spring
3 a.m.

North East

K'an
(Water)

Beginning of Winter
9 p.m.

North West

Abysmal

Absolute Winter
12 midnight

North

Later Heaven

of the trigrams was derived from either the Lo Scroll or the Nine Palaces since the numerological arrangements of the three diagrams coincide.

When looking at the Later Heaven (King Wen) arrangement, we read the progressive pattern along the periphery in a clockwise rotation. Reading the trigrams in a circular arrangement symbolizes the elements of infinity and continuity. The movement in this arrangement flows from the superficial qualities to deep qualities, from new life to maturation of life, and from the physical existence to the spiritual existence. Whereas the Early Heaven (*Fu Hsi*) arrangement is based on a balance of opposing forces representing a primordial order based in stillness, the Later Heaven arrangement depicts the development of life in the time-space conditioned world.

We read the Later Heaven sequence starting with *Chen* trigram (Thunder - the arousing). The *Chen* trigram is representative of Spring, the 6th hour, and the East, and thus expresses the dynamic appearance of life force. It is all that stirs up latent energies and stimulates them into movement and growth. It is the beginning, the seed, the inspiration that leads to development. The *Chen* trigram stimulates a firm base for all growing things, it is the striving of new growth towards the light. The arousing energy is carried in the direction

47

of growth, development and maturation by the energy of the *Sun* trigram (Wind - the gentle). It is in the *Sun* trigram that the latent energies stimulated by the arousing *Chen* are shaped. The gentle wind nurtures and guides.

The new consciousness that received the spark of Thunder and is directed by the Wind reaches maturation in the *Li* trigram (Fire - the clinging). The *Li* trigram is representative of Summer, the 12th hour, and the South and thus expresses the attainment of full maturity. The clinging nature of this trigram is representative of the attachment one has to the new energy that took form under the *Sun* trigram. Under the *Li* trigram, one is exploring the possibilities of new creation and thus have an intense inquisitive kind of interest. One is, in a sense, like a child clinging to a new toy.

The seed that was planted in the Spring reaches maturity under the Summer sun. Once nourished in the creative faculties of light and heat under the *Li* trigram, movement into the receptive and productive *K'un* trigram (Earth - the receptive) occurs. In the *K'un* trigram that which matured an outward sense under the trigram *Li*, is assimilated, digested, and integrated. The *K'un* trigram represents openness to new knowledge and the ever changing condition of the world. It is the extreme *yin* and thus totally receptive. That which is explored under the *Li* is absorbed into the being under the *K'un* trigram. This is the beginning of the transition from superficial to deep; from a physical consciousness to a spiritual consciousness; from a mental idea to intuitive knowledge.

The knowledge assimilated under the *K'un* trigram moves inward under the *Tui* trigram (Lake - the joyous). The Lake trigram is representative of Autumn, the 18th hour, and the West. It is a time of harvest and celebration and moves towards quiet and contemplation. That which is received under the *K'un* trigram is accepted internally under the energy of *Tui*. It is an internal harvesting of new knowledge.

Once movement turns inward under the *Tui* trigram, it is touched by the spirit under the *Ch'ien* trigram (Heaven - the creative). This trigram represents the *yang* aspects of heaven, health, and strength. Deep contemplation and movement towards a greater connection manifests under this trigram. Creative inner forces begin to stir. The

Using the Two Trigram Arrangements to Construct the Hexagrams

seed that sprouted in the Spring, was nourished and reached maturation in the Summer, and harvested in the fall has been consumed and is digesting under the *Ch'ien* trigram. The creative nature of this trigram comes forth when the outer idea moves inward and inner growth begins.

The creative inner forces dive deep into the essence of the being under the *K'an* trigram (Water - the abysmal). The *K'an* trigram is representative of Winter, the midnight hour, and the North. There is deep contemplation, meditation, and inward movement. The abysmal represents spiritual depth and inner stillness. From the depths of the water arises the steadfastness of inward assurance represented under the *Ken* trigram (Mountain - the resting). In the mountain there is completeness in the sign of keeping still. Development has come full circle. The stillness and meditative poise of the mountain is a preparation for new life. For as the mountain sits in stillness, clouds begin to form above and stimulating energies are released once again under the Thunder (the arousing) trigram.

In general terms, what this says to Pa Kua Chang practitioners is that the Later Heaven arrangement of the trigrams are arranged in accordance with the eight directions of the compass and represent a cyclical pattern as is evident in the continuous daily and yearly cycles inherent in nature. This cyclical pattern forms a basis for Pa Kua Chang's characteristic circular body movement and the circle walk practice. Additionally, one will note that the development of any skill will follow the maturation process symbolized by this trigram arrangement.

Combining the Two Pa Kua Diagrams

One method used in forming the sixty-four hexagrams of the *I Ching* involves combining the Fu Hsi and the King Wen Pa Kua diagrams as shown in the illustration on the previous page. In this arrangement, the Fu Hsi diagram is placed in the center of the King Wen arrangement. The Fu Hsi diagram remains stable and the King Wen diagram rotates around it. Each time the King Wen diagram is rotated one-eighth of a turn, eight new hexagrams are created by combining each pair of two trigrams sets which line up with each other. In this manner, once the King Wen arrangement has made one full revolution, all of the sixty-four hexagrams will have been identified.

In Park Bok Nam's advanced fighting instruction, the student will use this eight diagram construction in studying the possible combinations and changing variations in Pa Kua Chang tactical movements. Further discussion regarding this advanced theory is beyond the scope of this book.

Using the Pa Kua Diagrams in Pa Kua Chang Practice

While the names and representations of the Pa Kua in the *Fu Hsi* and *King Wen* arrangements may be interesting to study, the utility Park Bok Nam takes from these diagrams when teaching beginning and intermediate students is revealed in their geometry. From these two diagrams Park interprets three geometrical principles of movement. The *Fu Hsi* diagram reveals movement

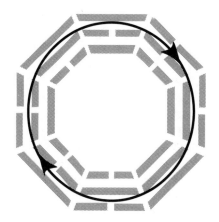

1 - Circular Rotation

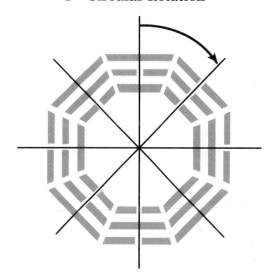

2 - Angular Rotation

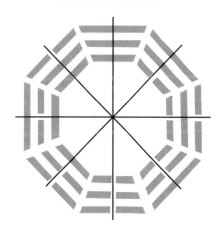

3 - Eight Directions

49

from a balanced central position extending out to one of eight directions. Since the eight trigrams in this arrangement are balanced in each direction with their respective polar opposites, one can carry the symbology further to say that whenever one moves the body along one of these eight directions, he or she maintains balance and awareness in all directions.

The *King Wen* diagram reveals circular movement around a central axis. This movement would include cyclical, or continuous, circular movement as well as movement in a spiralling pattern. Pa Kua Chang practitioners are well known for their circular movements. While the circular walking patterns of the style are the most obvious representation of Pa Kua's circle principle, circular and rotational articulations of the body and limbs are also included in this theory of movement.

The third principal of movement which Park derives from these diagrams is formed by combining circular movement around a central axis with movement in eight directions. This combination forms a pattern of movement in an angular rotation around a central point. Again, this theory will apply to footwork as well as hand, leg, and body motion.

While these three principles of movement are born out of the Pa Kua diagrams, Park does not make any connection with trigram meaning. At this point the student only needs to study the straight-forward geometry of the Pa Kua diagrams. Looking at the trigram circle, it is not difficult to see the geometric elements mentioned above. Figure 1 (at left) illustrates circular movement around a central axis. Figure 2 illustrates angular rotation around a central axis. Figure 3 illustrates linear movement along eight directions.

The theoretical principles of motion relating to circular movement around a central axis, angular rotation around an axis, and linear movement in eight directions apply to Pa Kua Chang footwork, body movement, and arm/hand movements and a study of these theories in any one of these areas can be very deep. Examples of how Park applies and combines these theories of movement in each of these areas, as well as how they are applied in Pa Kua Chang tactical fighting, are discussed throughout this book.

Change and the *Book of Changes*

Nothing in nature stands still. Observing the natural process, the ancient Chinese sought to model patterns of change so that they might better understand what was occurring naturally around them and predict what the future might bring. As addressed previously in this chapter, change, or movement, at its most basic level is represented symbolically through the interplay of *yin* and *yang*. From the idea of *yin* and *yang*, combinations were formed to represent more specific assignment of meaning to events in nature and in the human condition. Simple combinations (*liang-I* and *szu-hsiang*) led to more complex combinations (trigrams and hexagrams).

The Chinese sought to represent all aspects of nature and the human condition by constructing sixty-four six-line *Yin-I* and *Yang-I* combinations and studying their changing patterns through the *I-Ching*, or *Book of Changes*. This may seem like an impossible task until one considers that modern day computers can perform a seemingly infinite number of operations through the combination of two elements (one and zero, or on and off), the compact disk player can play a binary representation of any piece of music, and a digital camera can represent any scene through combinations of two simple elements.

Previously in this chapter we have discussed the combinatorial process by which the trigrams and hexagrams are formed and we have briefly explained how the combinatorial process can be applied to studying combinations of simple Pa Kua Chang techniques. After the student of Pa Kua Chang studies techniques and combinations

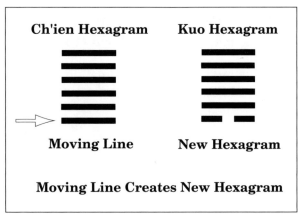

Moving Line Creates New Hexagram

of techniques and works to obtain a "body knowledge" of these techniques, the next step in the training process is learning how to vary and change those techniques in any given situation.

Although Park Bok Nam utilizes the *I-Ching* theory in teaching a student about change, a study of the hexagrams and their specific meaning is not the exercise a student will engage in to learn this concept. What Park borrows from the *I-Ching* is the general idea of changing combinatorial elements, not the specific meaning of each hexagram as written in the *I-Ching*.

In the *I-Ching*, symbolic meaning is derived from each individual hexagram, however, the hexagram representations are not static. In all aspects of Chinese philosophy, the idea of dynamic movement and unceasing change is apparent. It is the changing lines of the hexagrams which provide this dynamic aspect of the *I-Ching*. When any of the *Yin-I* or *Yang-I* lines of a hexagram change, an entirely new hexagram is created (see illustration on the previous page).

In the illustration we see that by changing one line of the hexagram *Ch'ien*, and new hexagram, *Kuo*, is formed. Since *Ch'ien* is the extreme *yang* hexagram (all lines are solid), there is no doubt that when *Ch'ien* changes, the change will produce a hexagram which is less *yang* (contains one or more *yin* lines). This is a very simple example of how one might predict change.

The simple example above can be easily examined in the realm of martial arts. If an opponent assumes an extremely extended stance (what Park would refer to as a *yang* posture), the next change of stance or posture will become more *yin*. Either he extends farther and looses his balance, or he withdraws. A practitioner recognizing the overly *yang* stance or posture of the opponent can predict what the opponent will do next and respond accordingly. He or she may add to the force of the opponent's extension and help cause the opponent to loose his balance, or the practitioner may "stick" and follow the opponent's withdraw and use it as a bridge to close the gap and attack. Again, these responses are studied and cultivated in training so that they become natural. There is no time to think about the theory of change in the *I Ching* while one is fighting.

Predictable Change

Just as there are predictable patterns of change inherent in nature, there are also predictable patterns of change when two opponents clash in physical combat. It is these patterns that the Pa Kua Chang practitioner seeks to understand to help research the fighting art. Understanding patterns of change inherent in boxing will allow a practitioner to gain knowledge of how an opponent might respond to any given offensive or defensive gesture.

If a Pa Kua Chang practitioner initiates an attack, a palm strike to the opponent's face for instance, one can predict with relative certainty what the opponent's reactions might be. There are a certain number of ways that the opponent might block that strike or there are a given number of ways that he might choose to move out of the way of that strike. The opponent might block with the left hand or the right hand, he might block to one side or the other, he might block up or down, he may move his body right or left, he may move straight back or straight in, he may duck, etc.

The changes an opponent might make in order to avoid or block an attack are reflective of the changes made when one hexagram changes to another hexagram in one of sixty-three possible ways. When researching patterns in boxing, the Pa Kua Chang practitioner first tries to obtain an intuitive feel for the opponent's predictable movements regarding the hands, body, and feet. In Park's school this study is conducted during two person partner practice. To help facilitate this study of the opponent's movements, the opponent's body movement can be easily broken down into upper body movement (handwork), middle body movement (bodywork), and lower body movement (footwork).

Once the practitioner begins to get a basic feel for predictable patterns regarding the hands, body, and feet, he or she can then examine patterns of movement further by studying the possible movements of all of the opponent's joints. In other words, the practitioner studies higher level math. With each successive weapon the opponent has available, the "mathematics" of his movement becomes more complicated. A Western boxer will have two skilled weapons, a Western "sport" kickboxer will have four skilled weapons; with the addition of weapons, the combinations become more complex. One reason Pa Kua Chang is referred to as a "graduate" level martial art is because the skilled practitioner knows how to continuously, rapidly and effectively employ 16 or 17 weapons from all angles and in a seemingly infinite number of combinations.

A detailed study of how the practitioner might damage the opponent's attacking weapons, continuously control the opponent's body, and always remain in an optimum position to attack begins with a study of predictable patterns of change associated with basic attack or defense. The Pa Kua Chang practitioner will study which of the opponent's possible reactions might be most likely to occur in any given situation and then he will devise combination attacks or counter-attacks which will overcome those predictable reactions. He will then practice these combinations on his own and against partners in practice. He will keep the combinations and counter-attacks which work well in partner practice and train those to become natural body reactions. The ones that don't work so well, he will discard. This is the way a student in Park's school will research the fighting method. Park is fond of saying, "If the student thoroughly researches one Pa Kua Chang technique he will learn one hundred techniques." In this manner, one technique becomes "no technique."

Consistent with the study of predictable patterns is the study of body types and fighting styles. The student will research how to best fight an opponent who is tall, or thin, or big, or fat, or small, or slow, or quick, etc. Additionally, the student will consider the best methods to use in fighting a boxer, a wrestler, a good kicker, someone skilled and *chin na*, etc. The ability to quickly recognize an opponent's strong points based on his body type, character, and fighting style is an important part of studying predictable change.

As in all research, if there is sound philosophy, the research method is not haphazard. We described earlier how Park was taught to research and build combinations based on combinatorial analysis. After the combinations were practiced, Lu taught Park how to change and vary combinations based on opponent responses. The exact method for this research is beyond the scope

of this book, however, the theory is similar to that used in the moving line prediction of the *I Ching*.

Consistent with the theory of "patterns of change" symbolized by the hexagram and trigram models, there are patterns, or principles, of movement associated with the Pa Kua Chang form maneuvers and sequences. Just as the trigrams and hexagrams symbolize dynamic concepts and thus cannot be too strictly tied to any particular association or correspondence, a particular Pa Kua Chang movement in a form sequence should not be strictly associated with a given "technique." Pa Kua Chang is not a technique oriented art. The beginning student may start by training technique application, however, as the student progresses he or she should look beyond technique and try to capture the underlying principle of the movement.

The movements and sequences in any Pa Kua Chang form relate to patterns and principles of the fighting system, not "techniques." The student's job is to strive to understand the movement beyond a handful of attack and defense techniques and capture the principle which any given movement in a form is conveying. Once the essence of the movement is understood, there are a limitless number of variations that one can derive from the principle. Making attachments to specific attack and defense techniques will severely limit one's understanding of the principles of movement inherent in Pa Kua Chang.

Unpredictable Change

Another reason a Pa Kua Chang practitioner will research predictable patterns is so that he or she can make his or her own attack combinations and counterattacks unpredictable. As soon as an opponent is committed a certain way, the practitioner will change unpredictably. When sparring with Park the student will get hit with palm strikes that seem to come out of nowhere. This is because Park is a master of making the opponent think he is going one way when he is really going another. This ability is characteristic of any skilled Pa Kua Chang practitioner.

Pa Kua Chang practitioners are famous for their ability to change rapidly in response to any of the opponent's movements. Their rapid changing movements also serve to confuse the opponent. As soon as the opponent commits in one direction, the Pa Kua Chang practitioner has changed and is attacking from another direction.

Any good fighter is going to be able to "listen" or feel what an opponent is doing, or detect what an opponent is about to do, and respond accordingly. So what is different about Pa Kua Chang? The difference is that in Pa Kua Chang the change is continuous, it is unpredictable, and it is powerful. Like flowing water constantly changing direction in accordance with the path of least resistance, the Pa Kua Chang practitioner continually changes and flows smoothly into his or her opponent's weak areas of defense. Once a fight begins, the Pa Kua Chang practitioner never quits moving, changing, and attacking until a positive outcome is obtained.

While T'ai Chi Ch'uan practitioners are also fond of relating the flowing water analogy to their art, the Pa Kua Chang practitioner is very crafty in his application of the ability to "flow" while changing suddenly and unpredictably to inflict the greatest amount of damage on an opponent in the shortest amount of time. For instance, if a Pa Kua Chang practitioner initiates a throwing technique, he or she might choose not to continue the full execution of that throwing technique as a judo practitioner might. The judo practitioner will initiate the throw and then follow through with that throw until the opponent is on the ground. The Pa Kua Chang practitioner might initiate the throw and then as soon as the opponent is off balance and moving towards the ground, the Pa Kua Chang practitioner will change quickly so that a palm strike can be delivered to the opponent's face while he is falling toward the ground. Quick and complete destruction is the rule.

In many Pa Kua Chang applications, the practitioner will initiate a technique to get the opponent moving one way, then suddenly change to strike directly into the direction the opponent is moving. Using the opponent's momentum, or inertia, against him is a favorite technique of the Pa Kua Chang practitioner.

Knowing how to change and when to change is a skill that will only come through many hours of research and partner practice. Once a practitioner in Park Bok Nam's school has studied the fundamentals of Pa Kua Chang as described in this book, Park will teach eight basic Pa Kua Chang fighting techniques which are practiced on a straight line repeatedly. When the student has obtained a certain level of skill with these eight basic movements, Park will encourage the students to pair up and use these attacks against a partner. Each partner will study what defensive techniques and counter-attacks work well against these basic attacks.

Only by spending hours with a training partner acting out "what if" scenarios will a practitioner gain an innate ability to learn how to apply Pa Kua Chang. The theory as outlined in this chapter simply provides the student with a road map.

Five Phase Theory

Everyone who has been associated with any element of Chinese religion, philosophy, medicine, or martial arts is probably familiar with the Five Phase (*Wu Hsing*) model and its associated creative and destructive cycles (shown in the illustration below).

In the creative cycle we see that Water creates Wood, Wood creates Fire, Fire creates Earth, Earth creates Metal, and Metal creates Water. Like the cycle represented by the Later Heaven trigrams,

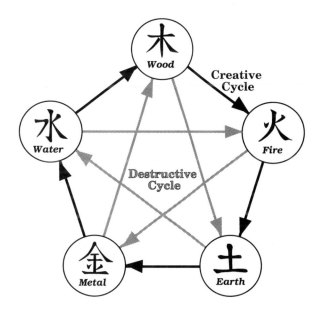

The Five Phases

the creative cycle of the five phase model depicts a never ending generative process. The destructive cycle depicts Earth destroying Water, Water destroying Fire, Fire destroying Metal, Metal destroying Wood, and Wood destroying Earth.

Wu   **Hsing**

This model is deeply ingrained in Chinese society and an integral part of Chinese philosophy, medical theory, martial arts, astronomy, and many aspects of daily life. While many refer this model as the "five element" model, the term "phase" may be more appropriate because it implies that the model is dynamic. The word "element" implies a static or concrete representation. Just like there is a dynamic interplay between *yin* and *yang*, there is also a dynamic interplay between the five phases and continuous movement among them. Additionally, there is a continuous ebb and flow of *yin* and *yang* aspects of each of the unique phases and thus they cannot be considered as representing static concepts.

Each specific discipline employing the five phase model will have their unique five phase correspondences. The relationships of the five phases as depicted in the creative and destructive cycles represent a dynamic interplay which is seeking balance or harmony. The interaction of the five phases form a system of checks and balances. If something is in excess it can be put in check through the destructive cycle, if something is depleted it can be revived through the creative cycle. The constant movement of the five phases in the never ending search for the elusive "perfect" balance can form a complex web of checks and balances.

The study of these relationships and correspondences associated with this model can become very deep and is well beyond the scope of this book. However, Park's application of this model in his fighting art is very straight forward and thus a detailed study of this model as it is applied in a field such as medicine is not necessary.

Park Bok Nam was taught to employ this model

in two ways. The first method Park was taught is similar to the way this model is used in some Hsing-I Ch'uan schools. In Hsing-I Ch'uan, each of the five elements is associated with one of five basic striking techniques, or five fists. For example, on the most basic level, Hsing-I practitioners relate force applied in a vertical plane (*p'i ch'uan*) to the Metal phase. Force applied in a horizontal plane (*peng ch'uan*) corresponds to Wood and force applied on a inclined plane (*ts'uan ch'uan*) corresponds to Water, etc.

In application of this model, the Hsing-I Ch'uan practitioner might use the Metal technique to create an opportunity to use the Water technique, followed by the Wood technique, etc., as depicted in the creative cycle. Similarly, if an opponent attacked with a Wood technique, the practitioner might counter that technique with a Metal technique as depicted in the destructive cycle. In this manner the Hsing-I Ch'uan practitioner uses the destructive and creative cycles as research tools to built attack and defense combinations.

Although the technique correspondences are not exactly the same as used in Hsing-I, Park was taught to use this model in a similar manner. Attack combinations can be built by utilizing the creative cycle and defense strategies can be studied utilizing the destructive cycle. For instance, if an opponent attacks with a quick, fast, expressive technique (Fire) such as a palm strike to the chest, the practitioner would counter that with a receptive, Water, technique such as a *yin* to *yang* changing palm to parry combined with a pivot step to evade.

The other method Park uses in applying this model is not so dependent upon exact five phase correspondences as it is on the general idea of the creative and destructive cycles. The creative cycle corresponds to the principles of "joining", "following", "adhering", "sticking", and/or "guiding." These principles all describe the practitioner's ability to follow, guide, stick to, adhere to, or join with the opponent's force. In contrast, the destructive cycle corresponds with the practitioner's ability to damage, destroy or lock the opponent and/or cut off the opponent's power.

Many Pa Kua Chang applications, rely on the ability to adhere or "stick" to an opponent's force, follow, lead, or deflect that force, and then strike effectively when the opponent is off balance, or "open." The trick to attaining this skill is in the development of an innate feel for the "adhere" component, knowing how to easily and effectively apply the "deflect" component based on a knowledge of angles and controlling points, and then finally apply the "damage" component powerfully, swiftly and effectively.

In Park's Pa Kua Chang system he trains his students how to get from the "adhere" to the "damage" phase of the encounter as rapidly as possible. As depicted in the five phases model, the "adhere" and "deflect" components are usually applied through circular movements while the "damage" component is applied in a direct, linear fashion. This concept applies to the footwork, bodywork, and handwork of Park's Pa Kua Chang. Park states that if both opponents continue to move in circles, they will potentially continue following each other forever. The key is in knowing how and when to change from the circular to the linear and vice-versa. The adhering and deflecting is used to create an opening or an opportunity for attack. A skilled practitioner can create that opportunity within seconds of the initial encounter.

In Park's method, the study of knowing how to adhere and deflect and when and where to attack is facilitated through practice of two man drills which utilize the five phase model correspondence as a research device.

Conclusion

Given numbers without mathematics, use of those numbers would be terribly cumbersome. One could count objects, but counting groups of objects one by one would prove to be a very laborsome task. With the tool of addition, groups of numbers can be counted more efficiently and thus the job becomes easier. But then again, with the tools of multiplication and division, performance of the job becomes even more efficient. The higher the math becomes, the more efficiently one can work and the sophistication of the tasks one can undertake and complete increases exponentially.

Park Bok Nam states that everyone who has two arms and two legs starts out with the same set of "numbers." The skillful, efficient, and effective application of those numbers dictates the outcome of a physical encounter. Like in mathematics, the more highly evolved the principles and theories of the system, the more efficiently the task can be accomplished. In the realm of mathematics there is theoretical mathematics and then there are applied mathematics. The ones who apply the mathematics are the ones who get things done. They design things and they build things.

The Pa Kua Chang theorists were the scholarly ancestors who took the Chinese theoretical models and applied them to the art of Pa Kua Chang. The fighters do not spend much time thinking about the theory, they simply learn the theory and apply it. No matter how sound the theory, it does not do the practitioner much good unless it can be applied. Although Park relies heavily on the theory to teach his students, he is also found of saying, "This martial art should be in your body, not in your head, and not in your mouth."

In applying the philosophical principles of the art, Park emphasizes that all three of the principles which form the equation below should be evident in every movement of the practice:

Pa Kua Chang Philosophy = Yin Yang Theory + I-Ching Theory + Wu Hsing (Five Phase) Theory

Park teaches that if one of these elements is missing from any movement or application, then that movement or application is not balanced. His students strive to seek this balance in their own movements and also learn how to recognize a lack of this balance in their opponent. Park states that developing the physical manifestation of the principles in oneself is only half of the work. The other half is learning to recognize what principles the opponent lacks so that he can be quickly defeated.

The "research" component of Park's Pa Kua Chang training and the principles and theories which form this component provide the student with the tools necessary to continually strive to perform the art with more speed, more power, more efficiently, and more efficaciously. With these tools at his or her disposal, the student is always thinking, researching and growing.

If an opponent attacks me, I can simply move out of the way, and at the beginning levels of training that is all I might train to do. However, once I can do that effectively, then I have to think about a better way. When during the opponent's attack is the best time to move out of the way? In which direction should I move? How close or far away should I be to set up an optimum counter-attack? At what angle should I orient myself in order to set up for an optimum counter-attack? What hand technique should I use to parry? Should I simply parry, or should I also use the parry as a strike? Remembering that my counter-attack should be aimed at an area that will cause the opponent the most damage and executed so that I can follow the counter-attack with a rapid

follow-on attack, what counter-attack would be best for me to employ?

All of these questions are answered while researching the art in two-man partner practice. The road map which is used to help answer the questions concerning distance, timing, syncopation, evasion, opening, closing, set-ups, rhythm, angles, combinations, targeting, and all other attack and defense strategies is drawn from the Pa Kua Chang theories. The method Park uses to teach these theories so that they are resident in the student's body as reflex reactions is to teach every level of development based on these principles. Throughout the remainder of this book, we will discuss how all of Park's fundamental exercises are built within the framework of these theories.

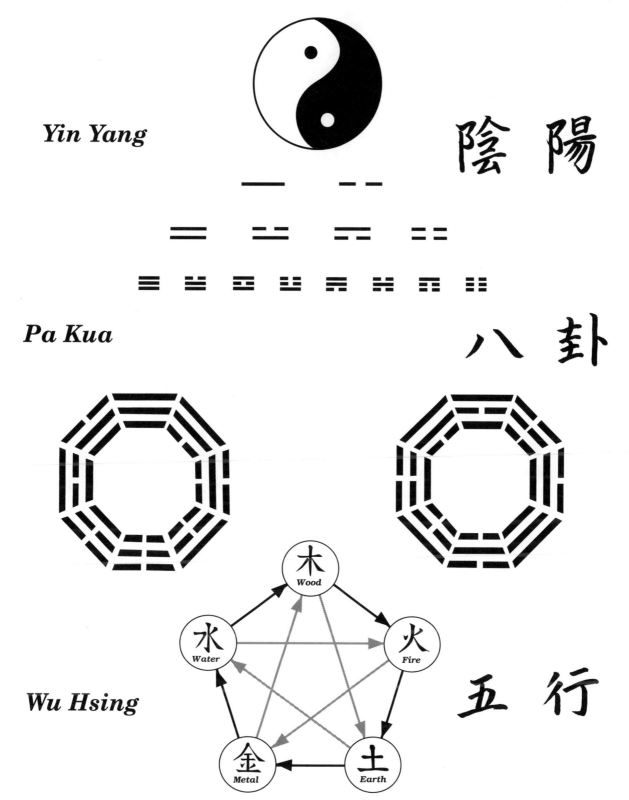

Yin Yang 陰陽

Pa Kua 八卦

Wu Hsing 五行

Chapter 3
Pa Kua Chang Footwork

Chapter 3

Pa Kua Chang Footwork

Introduction

If you have ever tried to catch a fish with your bare hands, then you know the frustration of a martial artist trying to combat a Pa Kua Chang stylist. Rapidly executed evasive footwork and swift elusive twisting and turning body movements are distinctive of Pa Kua Chang. Like the T'ai Chi Ch'uan practitioner, the Pa Kua Chang stylist's movements are relaxed, supple, smooth and continuous. However, while the T'ai Chi Ch'uan practitioner will usually practice at a slow steady pace, the Pa Kua Chang practitioner will vary his rhythm and change directions quickly. His movements are continuous, but they are sometimes fast and sometimes slow, and his flexible body is always twisting, turning, coiling, and circling. Highly evasive footwork and snake-like body movements are characteristic of the style.

One of the most difficult, and perhaps the most misunderstood, aspects of the art of Pa Kua Chang is its employment of footwork. The fluid, swift, continuous movements and applications of the Pa Kua style are motivated by rapid change of direction and constant interchange of weight while the practitioner executes quick, accurate stepping maneuvers. The practitioner relies on his footwork to optimally position his body to avoid an opponent's attack or to set up his own attack.

The skilled Pa Kua Chang practitioner can strike an opponent repeatedly with incredible speed and power while continuously moving and remaining highly mobile. All Pa Kua technique is initiated by combining footwork and handwork with hip (*yao k'ua*) and integrated body movement. Integration and connection between step, body, and hand are essential elements to successful technique application.

Rooting

In stepping, the Pa Kua Chang practitioner is fluid, quick and light. His aim is to remain highly mobile while maintaining body connection and stability in motion. This stability in motion, or rootedness, is primarily a product of alignment, connection, and full body integration. Maintaining rootedness while remaining light, agile, and highly mobile is characteristic of Pa Kua Chang. To some, being light and rooted at the same time may seem like a contradiction. However, rootedness results from alignment, not "heaviness."

When asked to "root," some practitioners will make their body heavy and imagine that they are like trees with roots extending from their legs into the Earth. While this method may help to form a connection to the Earth, and thus may be a valid technique in some forms of standing meditation and *ch'i kung*, this method is not ideal when executing the swift foot movement required in a combat situation. In making the body "heavy," foot and body movement become sluggish. If root is to be maintained while moving rapidly, this method must be transcended. Park Bok Nam likes to compare the movement of a Pa Kua Chang stylist to that of a cat. He states that a lion or tiger has a very heavy body, however, all of their movements appear to be light, supple, and nimble.

While in Beijing, China, in October 1992, I asked several elder Pa Kua Chang practitioners what made Pa Kua Chang different from other martial arts. They stated that the genius of Tung Hai-Ch'uan's art was that the practitioner could issue powerful strikes while the feet were in constant motion. In most martial art styles the practitioner is mobile, however, prior to striking he will stabilize himself in order to issue power from a firmly rooted, or grounded, posture. The mechanics and training of Pa Kua Chang are such that the practitioner can issue his power while the feet are continually moving. Through the correct practice of Pa Kua Chang footwork and body movement, the practitioner can develop a "moving root."

In Pa Kua Chang the practitioner's body remains light and ready to move even when he is assuming a static posture. He does not bounce up and down like the Kickboxer, nor does he anchor himself into the ground like a practitioner of T'ai Chi Ch'uan's fixed-step push hands. He is like a cat ready to pounce. His exterior is still, while his intention is focused on moving quickly. In most instances, moving the feet is his first reaction to an opponent's attack. The practitioner's root is a function of body alignments and structural integration. Structural dynamics utilized to develop *ken* or "root" in the static "guard stance" or "dragon posture" of Pa Kua Chang are described later in this chapter.

Although Park Bok Nam teaches a number of static postures to his students in the course of their training program, in execution of Pa Kua Chang, the static postures are very transitional. The Pa Kua Chang practitioner will rarely hold a static stance in combat for more than a second or two. Pa Kua Chang's strength is in its ability to apply footwork and thus fighting while continuously moving the feet is stressed in Park's school.

The *Sung* Principle

In addition to correct alignments, the practitioner of Pa Kua Chang will also incorporate the *sung* principle. *Sung* is a Chinese term which cannot be correctly translated into English using

a one word definition. *Sung* is often incompletely translated as "relax." This convenient one word translation can lead to misunderstanding as *sung* has meaning in the martial arts beyond "relax" in the dictionary's sense of "to make lax or loose."

Sung

The Pa Kua Chang practitioner does not let his muscles relax in such a manner that the body is like that of a rag doll. In applying the *sung* principle, the body is loose, but it is a rubbery, springy, "ready for action" kind of looseness. The muscles do not hang on the structure like heavy, dead flesh and the eyes to not glaze over like a zombie or droop as if one is ready to fall asleep. The whole body should be relaxed, but at the same time it is alive, alert and ready to move. The body is like that of a cat ready to pounce on its prey. The muscles are relaxed, but the intention puts life into them. If alignment and posture are correct and the body is *sung*, the practitioner will be relaxed and rooted, but the body will be light and ready to move, the mind will be alert and the spirit radiant.

Footwork Training

The only way to train stability in motion is to move. However, the way many martial arts train alignment, in the developmental stages, is in standing still. Most martial art training systems are progressive, starting with static postures designed to develop connection, alignment, flexibility, and leg strength. However, in Pa Kua Chang, since the focus of the art is on moving the feet, the basic training does not usually include standing in one place very long. For instance, in Park Bok Nam's school the student will practice stepping exercises which require the student to stop briefly and examine alignments and structural integration in-between stepping maneuvers. The student will step, check the posture, step, check the posture, step, check the posture, etc.

By practicing basic stepping maneuvers such

as the "Eight Direction Rooted Steps," and the "pivot steps" while focusing on maintaining structural alignments and checking these alignments in-between steps, the student develops structural integrity and coordinated movement while also training mobility. As body alignments become second nature, the student can increase the speed of consecutive stepping maneuvers and increase his or her mobility. The goal is to be able to move swiftly, continuously, smoothly, and lightly while maintaining structural alignments and proper full body integration. Executing consecutive steps in rapid succession also trains leg strength, stamina, endurance, and concentration.

In Park's school of Pa Kua Chang the basic training also involves learning the continuous movement of Pa Kua Chang circle walking and the associated *k'ou pu* and *pai pu* footwork. Because the Pa Kua circle walking requires constant movement and transition of weight, maintaining root at all times is difficult and so the beginner spends *a lot* of time "walking the circle."

Most practitioners are familiar with Pa Kua's signature circle walking and the various walking steps (lion step, dragon step, chicken step, etc.) as well as the *k'ou pu* and *pai pu* stepping maneuvers. However, Pa Kua Chang also employs a great number of other stepping techniques that are not commonly associated with the art's popular forms. Many martial arts practitioners only think of Pa Kua stepping as being circular because the majority of popular Pa Kua forms consist mainly of the circle walking techniques. However, looking closely at the lineage of Pa Kua Chang as it descended from Tung Hai-Ch'uan, one will note that in most lines of transmission the circle walking was not the only stepping technique which was taught. In conjunction with the circle walk the practitioner was also required to become skilled at a number of other stepping techniques.

For most of Tung's students the foundation work for other various stepping maneuvers was done while the practitioner studied another martial art style. Tung did not accept many students that did not have a solid background in another art. Circle walking maybe considered an "advanced" technique because it requires that one maintain rootedness while in constant motion. Tung taught his students to employ the circle walk and the Pa Kua Chang techniques based on what they already knew from studying other systems.

Not all Pa Kua teachers required their students to have a solid foundation in another art before studying Pa Kua, but would have the student become proficient in basic stepping methods along with the circle walk. When the student was taught fighting skills, the basic stepping methods would be combined with the circle walking techniques in order to provide a complete arsenal of Pa Kua Chang stepping maneuvers. This is the approach that Park takes in training his students and this is the approach that is outlined here in this book.

In terms of functionality, all of these stepping techniques are very useful fighting maneuvers and are combined with circle walking and *k'ou pu pai pu* in order to provide the Pa Kua practitioner with a full range of stepping techniques to use in combat. Thus, although they come from exercises supplementary to the popular Pa Kua Chang circle walking forms, these stepping techniques should not be thought of as being separate from the art Pa Kua Chang.

Why Concentrate on Footwork First

Park's reason for insisting that the student concentrate on Pa Kua Chang footwork first is two-fold. First, he feels that practicing many hours of *Pa Fang Ken Pu* (Eight Direction Rooted Stepping), pivot stepping, *k'ou pu pai pu* stepping and circle walking will give the student a strong foundation in terms of leg strength, physical endurance, proper stepping mechanics, and correct Pa Kua Chang body movement. Pa Kua Chang is an art famous for its footwork and all its fighting tactics rely on the high degree of mobility and precise body positioning that correct footwork provides. While students like to ask about practicing palm striking methods, fancy form movements, and offensive fighting tactics, Park will always tell a story about a strong man trying to catch a fly, "If a strong man cannot catch a fly, who is actually stronger?"

Park got his first taste of the effectiveness of Pa Kua Chang's foot work shortly after he began practicing at Lu Shui-T'ien's school. Park had been very proud of the "spinning back kick" that he had developed when he was in high school studying *Tang Soo Do*. He had become so fast with this technique that he could use it with ease against his *Tang Su Do* sparring partners. Naturally when Park first started sparring with Lu's students he tried to use this technique. Lu saw Park's kick and said, "You better not do that, you are going to get hurt." Park didn't believe Lu and so he tried it again. Lu then whispered something to Park's sparring partner. The next time Park tried that kick he found himself flat on the ground. He could not figure out what had happened. He tried it again and the same thing happened.

Park was intent on finding out how his opponent was dumping him on the ground so easily and so he continued to try his kick. The result was the same each time and he still could not figure out what was happening. He tried to vary his approach, his delivery, his set up, and his timing, but every time he kicked he ended up on the ground. Finally he became frustrated and gave up. Lu said, "I told you, if you try that kick you will get hurt."

Later, Park became famous in Korea for his ability to employ fast and effective footwork. While training with his teacher, he was allowed to enter several national martial arts tournaments in Seoul, the nation's capitol. In every fighting event Park entered, each of his opponents was knocked on the ground in a matter of seconds. Park would step, move in and throw. He positioned his body so quickly and accurately that his opponent did not have a chance to react before Park had obtained the optimum throwing angle and executed his technique. Park moved so swiftly that spectators wishing to observe how he was throwing his opponents so fast could not detect what he was doing.

The second reason Park feels that footwork is the number one priority in Pa Kua Chang training, is that by executing these stepping patterns the practitioner is physically ingraining three of the fundamental movement principles of Pa Kua Chang - namely, circular movement around a central axis, angular rotation around a central axis, and movement to one of eight directions. With a knowledge of these three movement theories, the Pa Kua Chang student can take any Pa Kua Chang technique executed in a form and

research an unlimited number of combinations and variations based on these principles of movement.

The theories of circular movement around a central axis, angular rotation around an axis, and movement to one of eight directions are derived from the Eight Trigram circle and are used as research tools (along with *yin/yang* theory and five phase theory) to examine how fighting techniques might vary or how they can be improved.

Every Pa Kua Chang technique has an optimum angle from which it is applied. The difference between a technique performed adequately and one performed masterfully is dependent upon the practitioner gaining the optimum positioning before the technique is applied, applying the technique at the opportune instant in time, and maintaining optimum angles during the technique's execution. Pa Kua Chang is an art of angles. In all technique execution the Pa Kua Chang practitioner seeks the path of least resistance by attacking where the opponent is weakest. The skilled Pa Kua Chang practitioner has an innate knowledge of how to seek and maintain the path of least resistance in applying any technique. The ability to "be in the right place at the right time" will first manifest through the footwork skill.

About This Chapter

In this chapter of the book, we will focus on the four basic components of Pa Kua Chang footwork: *Pa Fang Ken Pu* (Eight Direction Rooted Stepping), Pivot Stepping, Circle Walking, and *K'ou Pu/Pai Pu* Stepping. We will detail their execution and explain how they are derived from the theory of the Pa Kua diagrams. We will also examine how these techniques are trained on the intermediate level and how a practitioner can improve his or her Pa Kua Chang footwork by researching these techniques in accordance with the Pa Kua principles.

Before detailing any of the stepping techniques in this section it is important that the reader understand how Bok Nam Park recommends his students train any Pa Kua Chang exercise or form. There are six basic training levels to any exercise in this system. We will outline these levels here in the footwork chapter, but the reader should keep this training sequence in mind when practicing any of the exercises explained in this book.

Training Stages

1) Slow and Exact   First, each exercise is executed very slowly with concentration on the proper body alignments and movements. The student works the exercise slowly until it can be executed with exactness and fluidity. In stepping the student will execute the step, stop to check the posture and adjust accordingly, then step again.

2) Power   The second stage in training is to execute the exercise with power. The power in the stepping techniques is demonstrated when the steps are executed quickly, fluidly and with exactness while maintaining a light and agile body. When this stage is executed, the upper body, shoulders, and arms are very relaxed and the footwork is executed quickly without any wobbling or wavering. Each step is crisp and explosive.

3) Power and Speed   The third stage of execution of any exercise in Park's system is to execute the exercise with power and speed. In the stepping exercises this is trained through the execution of repeated steps or a combination of different steps performed in rapid succession. There should be no bouncing up and down, shifting of weight from one leg to the other, or swaying back and forth. The body moves quickly and smoothly.

Although combinations of techniques and combinations of body, foot, and hand movements are an integral part of Park's training program, he stresses that the student should first work so that he or she can execute each individual component with power and speed before combinations are practiced.

4) Hand + Body + Step   Once the practitioner has developed the ability to execute hand techniques and footwork with speed and power in isolation, the fourth stage of execution is to combine the footwork with body, arm and hand movements. In Park's system, no movement is executed without a full hand/body/footwork integration.

The fundamental methods of how to combine the footwork with the various palm maneuvers are contained in a later section of this book.

5) Refinement As a fifth stage of training any exercise, the student will work to refine the movements of the exercise so that the large movements which were executed in the beginning stages of training become very small. In footwork training this would consist of the execution of footwork combinations in a combat situation such that there is no wasted movement. In Pa Kua Chang, all movement is quick and efficient.

6) Continuity The sixth and last major stage of focus in training is to learn how to continuously connect all movements, applications, and techniques. The student works to integrate component parts and develop tactically sound combinations of hand, arm, body, and stepping motions. The "linking" of component parts occurs in a smooth, natural, fluid, and continuous manner. The student researches how components are best connected and then practices combinations in order to ingrain a reflex body knowledge of the patterns.

Eight Direction Rooted Stepping

The Standard Circle Walk Posture

八方根步

Pa　　**Fang**　　**Ken**　　**Pu**

There are a complete set of "Eight Direction Rooted Stepping" exercises designed to develop quick, accurate, rooted, and coordinated stepping for use in fighting. We will describe the basic set of exercises in this book. In the basic set of exercises the practitioner will learn to step straight forward or backward, side to side, and forward or backward at 45 degree angles utilizing the "follow step" or "jump step" foot movement. Basic exercises also include full stepping (back foot becomes front foot as in walking) in all directions. All directional stepping patterns used in these exercises are based on the geometry of the Pa Kua diagram as described in the previous chapter.

The basics of some of the "Eight Direction Rooted Stepping" exercises will be described in this chapter. However, before we can discuss stepping, the first requirement is to become familiar with the "guard" posture Park uses in fighting.

The Stance for Combat

Most practitioners are familiar with Pa Kua Chang's signature "guard" or "eight" stance which is used in forms practice and "walking the circle" exercises. The spine is straight, the lower back is flat, the head is held erect, the shoulders are relaxed and dropped down, the elbows are pointed down, the arms are curved, and the knees are bent.

Park states that practicing forms is good exercise for developing the body and the *ch'i*. He also states that the forms contain fighting applications, however, in order to develop the muscles, joints, tendons, bones and *ch'i*, the forms are usually practiced with the body extended or "open."

The first component of Park's Pa Kua Chang footwork training, referred to as "Eight Direction Rooted Stepping" or *Pa Fang Ken Pu*, conditions the practitioner to be able to coordinate the body and hand with footwork in order to move quickly out of harm's way and position the body for optimum angles of counter-attack. The *Pa Fang Ken Pu* exercises taught to Park by his teacher Lu Shui-T'ien teach the student highly functional stepping patterns utilizing basic stepping techniques executed in eight directions. These techniques facilitate the student's development of root while remaining light and mobile.

Park Bok Nam Demonstrates His Combat Stance

When training specifically for fighting, one will "close the door" by modifying the body position slightly so that the opponent's access to the body's center line above and below the waist is shut off. "Closing the door" protects the body's *chung men* (center gate) and covers avenues of attack. Park states that in his teacher's Pa Kua Chang system the rule was; "When practicing for health the body is open, when practicing for fighting, the body is closed."

The "guard" stance, or "dragon posture," which Park teaches to use in fighting is similar to the stance used by many schools in forms practice, but there are some minor differences. In the fighting stance, the weight shifts slightly forward so that approximately 60% of the weight is on the back leg and 40% is on the front leg and the forward foot tucks in slightly. The toes of the front foot are roughly in line with the toes of the rear foot as shown in the illustration at right. As the weight shifts forward, the body is bent slightly at the hips, but the spine remains straight. In Chinese martial arts parlance this bending slightly forward at the hips is called the "tiger's crouch" and is employed by most systems of boxing.

When assuming this posture, two things occur, first, and most obvious, is that the knees and thighs naturally come closer together and thus the groin area is protected. Secondly, when the posture is correct, the hip joints will open up and therefore facilitate flexibility and ease of motion in the hips. Additionally, when the hips open, the *tan t'ien* will expand.

The *tan t'ien* is located a few inches below the navel and in towards the center of the body. This place, which roughly coincides with the body's center of gravity, is believed to be the body's central storage and distribution area for *ch'i*. When the body posture is correct, the pelvic region will relax and expand and thus allow the *tan t'ien* to store and distribute *ch'i* more efficiently and effectively. Park will sometimes encourage students to place their hands over the *tan t'ien*

Foot Alignment for the Dragon Posture

region while standing straight up and then feel the area expand as the body sinks down into the proper stance.

Tan **T'ien**

The bending of the knees will lower the body's center of gravity and thus increase stability. In this position the body is "ready" to move and thus movement in any direction can be executed quickly. Park teaches that the knees should be bent so that the body is comfortable and relaxed. If the body is too upright, balance, stability and quickness of motion will not be optimal. If the knees are bent too much, movement will be sluggish. When training to develop strength in the legs Park feels that it is all right to assume a low posture, however, when training for speed, the body should be in at a mid-level, comfortable position.

In the combat stance, there should also be a "spring loading" of the legs. The front leg pushes towards the back and the back leg pushes forward. However, this "pushing" is subtle. The practitioner should not push so hard that he or she becomes less mobile. The body remains light and ready to move and thus this "pushing" should simply stem from an intention to move forward or backward rapidly.

The forward hand is held at nose height and the eyes look straight ahead using the space between the thumb and index finger as a "gun sight" (see photographs at the top of the previous page). The lower hand is held three to five inches below the elbow of the upper arm. Bringing the lower hand under the elbow of the upper arm facilitates a rounding of the back and allows the chest to relax, providing further protection to the center line. Also, this posture will allow the shoulders to drop down in a relaxed position and as the lungs move back, breathing becomes easier.

The shoulders are relaxed, the elbows point down and the arms maintain a roundness. The hips are positioned naturally, the navel facing roughly the same direction as the toes. In this posture, the hands, forearms, knees, and thighs are in position to easily guard the center line of the body with little or no wasted movement.

By "spring loading" the legs, the practitioner can move forward, backward, or side-to-side very quickly. In fighting, the only time the practitioner executes a walking step (where the back foot steps out to become the front foot as in walking) is to travel a relatively long distance to close the gap between himself and the opponent, or to maneuver around the opponent as in circle walking.

In many fighting circumstances the opponent will be within close range and thus the follow-step could be better employed. (Keep in mind that when we speak of combat, we are not talking about the choreographed dance routines that are displayed in martial arts movies or contemporary "wushu" fighting sets. Most real fights are executed at close range and will be over in a matter of seconds.) The follow step, which is a familiar move to Hsing-I Ch'uan practitioners, is the best way to travel a short distance rapidly with root and control. The 60/40 weighted stance facilitates maximum mobility in all directions with the greatest speed.

If the practitioner is completely back weighted as in the "guard" stance employed by many styles in forms practice, it is difficult to move backwards a short distance with speed. Maintaining high levels of mobility and speed while traveling relatively short distances are essential elements in combat. The Pa Kua Chang practitioner relies on his footwork to quickly avoid attack and rapidly seek the optimum angle for counter-attack. Speed and agility are paramount.

This "combat posture" will feel a bit awkward to practitioners who have not sufficiently opened the hip joints. Flexibility and strength in hip movement is an important component in internal martial arts practice. When the posture is correct and the hips open, the student will notice that the *tan t'ien* will naturally expand. Most beginning practitioners are extremely tight in the hips. Working to achieve the correct body alignment and distribution of weight in the "combat posture" and practicing the "Eight Direction Rooted Stepping" exercise will greatly increase hip flexibility and strength in hip movement as well as improve speed, agility, body control, and root.

When Lu Shui-T'ien was training with his teacher in China, his teacher would have him stand in the back of a horse cart and assume the dragon stance posture. His teacher, Li Ching-Wu, would then drive the horse cart at high speeds down bumpy country roads while Lu was in the back trying to maintain his balance. Lu Shui-T'ien did not have a horse cart in Korea, but he would require Park to engage in a similar practice by having him ride the bus out into the country side and back while standing in the isle in the dragon posture stance.

Some might argue that having a "combat" ready stance is not realistic because in a real self-defense situation one will not likely have the time to assume a "guard" posture. Most real self-defense situations will occur quickly and in close quarters. While this is true, training the guard posture, with a "closed" body, will ingrain good habits in terms of structure, alignment, balance, coordination, and body covering that will serve the practitioner well if there is the time and space available.

Every fighting situation is different. In some cases there may only be enough physical space and time to throw a quick series of elbow strikes to defend oneself and thus the dragon posture will not be utilized. However, in many other situations having a good natural guard posture will be of great value. Park believes that the more familiar the practitioner becomes with this posture and the execution of his or her techniques from this posture, the faster and more accurate all of the techniques will become.

Basic *Pa Fang Ken Pu* Practice

In the previous section we introduced *Pa Fang Ken Pu* by explaining the "ready" or "guard" posture utilized in this exercise set. Familiarity with this posture (which Park refers to as the "Dragon Posture") is essential to success in the *Pa Fang Ken Pu* exercise because this posture is assumed at the conclusion of every stepping movement. In this section we will describe two of the fundamental rooted stepping techniques - the "jump" step and the "full" step. After explaining the fundamental mechanics of these steps and their variations, we

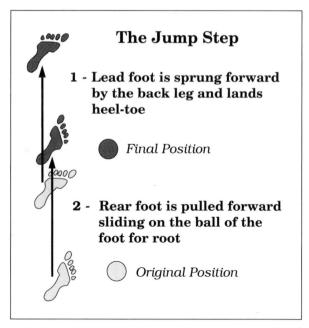

The Jump Step

1 - Lead foot is sprung forward by the back leg and lands heel-toe

● *Final Position*

2 - Rear foot is pulled forward sliding on the ball of the foot for root

○ *Original Position*

will then describe basic stepping patterns utilized in practicing these steps.

In this section of the book we will talk about the foot movements alone. We will not discuss the arm movements which accompany the steps until a later section which will explain the *fan chang* or "overturning palm" mechanics. Park is adamant when imparting to his students the importance of ingraining a physical reflex habit with the footwork movements before attempting to combine the footwork with hand and arm techniques. If the footwork is weak, there will be no foundation.

The Jump Step

The "jump step," also referred to as the "follow step" or "forward step" (*shang pu*), is utilized to rapidly travel a relatively short distance with root, balance, and body control. This stepping maneuver is one of the first stepping exercises Park teaches. Ideally the practitioner will want to be able to execute this step quickly in any direction and, upon conclusion of the first step, be immediately ready to step once again in any direction. This requirement makes continuous root, body control and balance mandatory.

If the practitioner were to step forward and

allow the forward momentum of the first step to throw the body slightly out of alignment with the principles of the "guard" stance (outlined in the previous section), the next move could not be executed immediately. When initially practicing any stepping movements, it is imperative that the student work to fall directly into the proper "guard" stance upon conclusion of the movement. The conclusion of each step is the guard stance, there should be no extra adjustment necessary.

Grossly defined, the jump step movement requires the front foot to step out, landing heel-toe as in walking, and then the rear foot to follow (traveling the same distance) by dragging on the ball of the foot to maintain root. Upon conclusion of the movement, the practitioner assumes the "guard" stance without having switched the forward foot. When the front foot steps out and lands, it remains "tucked in" at a 45 degree angle from the direction of travel (see illustration on the previous page and photo sequence below).

This step sounds relatively simple, however, in order to put "spring" and "power" into the step, the front foot does not "step" out forward as in walking, but is sprung forward by the back leg. Remember that in the "guard" stance the legs are spring loaded. The front leg is pushing towards the back and the back leg is pushing forward. In order to jump step forward the practitioner will release the front leg and allow the spring loaded back leg to push the body forward while stepping. The step is executed explosively. It may help the student to imagine that all of the joints are like springs.

As soon as the front heel hits the ground, the rear foot is brought forward with the ball of the foot dragging the ground for stability and root. Again, in order to maintain power in the step, the rear leg is not haphazardly brought forward. The rear leg is quickly pulled forward by contracting the adductor muscles in the back leg (inner thigh) and pulling with the hamstrings in the front leg. When the rear foot reaches its final destination, the heel is quickly placed on the ground.

When stepping, the body must move as an integrated piece. A common mistake when jump stepping forward or backward is to let the hips lead the shoulders causing the body to move in two separate pieces. The entire body must move together. The movement should be smooth and exact. When Park performs this footwork, his movement is very smooth and natural - cat like. There is no bobbing, hesitating, weaving, wobbling, or swaying. All of his moves are very fluid, swift and exact. Although one is rooted, the body remains light and very agile. Beginning students will usually be too heavy and therefore their movements are slow and cumbersome.

Perhaps the hardest aspect of practicing the jump step is ending the movement in the picture perfect "guard" stance. When the step is complete, the foot spacing should be the same as it was before the step was executed - the front toe is angled in, the weight distribution is 60% on the back leg and 40% on the front leg, the front leg is pushing back, the back leg is pushing forward, and the spine is straight, but slightly inclined forward (we will not worry about the arms right

| 5 | 4 | 3 | 2 | 1 |

The Jump Step

now - they can hang down by the body's sides or the hands can rest on the hips). When the student begins practicing this step, it is best to check the body's posture at the end of each step and make corrections accordingly. Eventually, no corrections should be required.

As in all stepping exercises, the jump step is first practiced at a slow, deliberate pace. Concentration is placed on executing the step correctly while maintaining proper body integration and alignments. After the student has become comfortable with the mechanics of the step, he or she will then practice executing the step quickly and powerfully one step at a time. The step is executed, the student checks alignments, then the next step is executed, etc. After the student is comfortable with stepping quickly one step at a time and has trained the body to move fluidly without bouncing or wobbling, then he or she will practice repeated steps performed in rapid succession to develop speed, strength and stamina.

A common mistake in jump step practice is allowing the front foot and/or rear foot to vary from the 45 degree "toe-in" position. Typically, when jump stepping many times in succession, the beginner will end up with the front foot pointing straight ahead and/or the back foot pointing out 90 degrees (to the side). Proper jump step execution requires flexible ankles, loose hips, and strong thighs. Until these components are developed and the proper jump step can be executed naturally, the student should pay special attention to maintaining correct alignments after each successive jump step.

The back jump step (jump stepping backwards) contains the same mechanics as the front step, however, the back foot moves first (being sprung back by the forward leg) and lands toe-heel instead of heel-toe. After the rear foot steps, the front foot slides back on the ball of the foot maintaining the 45 degree "toe in."

A common mistake beginners make when jump stepping backwards is to simply step back and then drag the forward foot back, this is incorrect. The back leg steps back, but only after the body is propelled backwards by the front leg pushing back. The movements are crisp and explosive. The entire body springs backward with the push of the front leg. As soon as the rear leg hits the ground, the front leg is pulled back swiftly.

The Full Step

The full step movement is executed as in walking - the rear foot steps forward to become the front foot. This sounds easy, however, there are a few details to consider:

1) Because the front foot is angled in at about a 45 degree angle in the "guard" stance, the practitioner needs to pivot the front foot as the back foot steps forward. The front foot will rotate through a 90 degree angle so that it ends up angled about 45 degrees to the other side (the direction of forward movement being the zero degree reference line). The front foot pivots on the heel for best speed and stability.

| 5 | 4 | 3 | 2 | 1 |

The Full Step

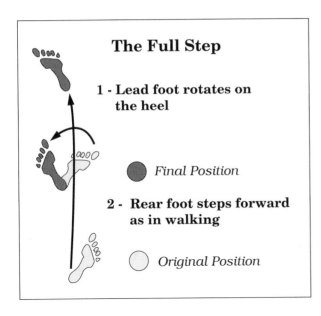

The Full Step

1 - Lead foot rotates on the heel

● *Final Position*

2 - Rear foot steps forward as in walking

○ *Original Position*

2) As the back foot steps forward, it does not step too high or too wide - remember the groin area must remain protected. The stepping foot should not drag the ground - it is brought up off the ground a few inches.

3) The student should not allow the body to bob up and down when stepping - the head stays at the same level. The movement should be smooth and fluid. When executing any Pa Kua Chang stepping maneuver the upper body should remain very steady and move as an integrated unit with the lower body movements.

4) As in the jump step, move the entire body as one integrated piece. At the conclusion of the step the body should be in the correct guard stance position.

The full step is illustrated at left and demonstrated in the photo sequence on the previous page.

The student should practice this stepping technique repeatedly until the movement can be

4　　　　　　3　　　　　　2　　　　　　1

7　　　　　　6　　　　　　5

The Full Step with a Jump

71

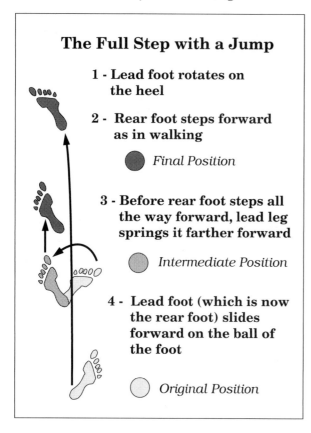

The Full Step with a Jump

1 - **Lead foot rotates on the heel**

2 - **Rear foot steps forward as in walking**

⬤ *Final Position*

3 - **Before rear foot steps all the way forward, lead leg springs it farther forward**

⬤ *Intermediate Position*

4 - **Lead foot (which is now the rear foot) slides forward on the ball of the foot**

◯ *Original Position*

executed quickly and continuously in a smooth, fluid manner. In fighting an opponent will be keen to any visual or sensory clues which will "telegraph" a practitioner's movement. When practicing the stepping exercises, the student should work to keep the upper body movement very smooth and subtle so that there is no "telegraphing" of the footwork by the upper body movement. If there is any unnecessary movement of the upper body before, during, or after the stepping is being executed, the opponent will key on these movements and use them to his or her advantage.

The full step movement becomes extremely important when the practitioner begins to learn how to employ Pa Kua Chang's various weapons. If this step has not become a reflex body action when the practitioner starts to practice basic weapons skills, maneuverability when working with a weapon will suffer.

Full Step with a Jump

If the practitioner needs to travel a longer distance in one step than that covered by a comfortable full step, he or she can combine the full step with a "jump" in order to rapidly travel a longer distance. Before the stepping foot of a full step hits the ground, the back leg springs the step forward, and the stepping foot lands a bit farther than a normal stride length. As the front heel hits the ground, the back foot is brought up by dragging the ball of the foot along the ground (as in the jump step) so that the feet are spaced the same distance apart after the step is executed as they were before stepping. See illustration at left and photo sequence on the previous page.

The "full step with a jump" (as it will be called in the remainder of the book) should add approximately a foot or two to the stepping distance. One should not try to extend the stepping distance too far, however, or root, body control, and stability will be jeopardized.

There are a number of techniques in Pa Kua Chang which are employed while "stepping through" the opponent. Once the practitioner has gained an opening along an angle conducive to offsetting the opponent's balance, stepping through the opponent while applying a strike, throw, or other technique will render the opponent incapable of swift counter-attack. The full step with a jump is ideally used in conjunction with this variety of technique as the full step helps to close the gap and the added jump provides the necessary force to step through the opponent's center.

The back full step with a jump contains the same mechanics as the front step, however, the front foot moves to become the back foot and lands toe-heel instead of heel-toe.

To effectively utilize these stepping movements in a self-defense situation they must become second nature. This requires hours of practice with basic stepping patterns in order to develop the muscles properly and attain a "body knowledge" or "muscle memory" of the proper stepping movements. In combat the practitioner cannot think about which step to utilize. Correct footwork must spring forth spontaneously without conscious thought.

Before teaching the student the first basic *Pa Fang Ken Pu* combination pattern, Park requires the student to practice straight line stepping exercises in order to become familiar with the jump step, the full step, and the full step with a jump by themselves. First the student will jump step forward (with the right leg as the lead leg) the length of the workout space. Next he or she will jump step backwards back down the length of the workout space. After going up and back numerous times with the right leg forward, the student will perform the same exercise with the left leg forward. The next drill is to utilize the full step going in a straight line forward the length of the workout space, and then full stepping backwards back to the starting position. After a number of repetitions, the student will then be required to perform the full step with a jump in the same "straight line" manner.

The Basic *Pa Fang Ken Pu* Stepping Patterns

Once the student in Park's school learns the basic *Pa Fang Ken Pu* stepping techniques and has executed them repeatedly in "straight-line" sets, the next stage of training involves combining the stepping techniques in a number of different stepping patterns. In this section we will describe some of the basic *Pa Fang Ken Pu* stepping patterns.

Turn Around and Jump Pattern

After practicing the basic *Pa Fang Ken Pu* straight line exercises, the student will then practice an exercise which combines the forward jump step and the backward jump step with a full 180 degree pivot between jump step combinations.

The 180 pivot is a simple "in place" turn-around executed from the guard stance posture. Standing in a 60/40 posture the student will simply pivot on the heels of both feet simultaneously and turn 180 degrees to face the other direction (see illustration at right). This maneuver will be referred to as a "turn-around."

The first *Pa Fang Ken Pu* stepping pattern requires the practitioner to jump step forward, jump step back, turn-around, jump step forward in the other direction, jump step back, turn-around, etc. This exercise is executed for many repetitions in order to train the ability to jump forward and immediately jump back. The turn-

around maneuver is also very useful when one is training to fight against multiple opponents.

This exercise is depicted in photographs on the following page. Photos 1 through 4 show the first forward jump step. Photos 5 through 7 show the jump step back. Photos 8 and 9 show the turn-around. Photos 10 and 11 show the jump step forward in the other direction. Photos 12 and 13 show the jump step back and photos 14 and 15 show the next turnaround.

When Park Bok Nam was first taught this exercise, his teacher left him alone to practice it stating, "You practice this until I come back." His teacher did not return for several hours. In his teacher's absence Park had become bored with the exercise and had practiced other things. When his teacher returned he was asked, "How was your practice?" Park responded that he had worked hard on what he was taught. This response was met with a solid whack to the shoulder from Lu Shui-T'ien's cane. Lu Said, "You did not practice

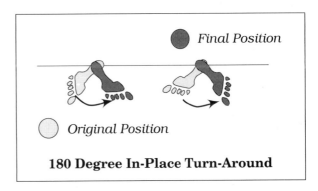

Final Position

Original Position

180 Degree In-Place Turn-Around

5   4   3   2   1

10   9   8   7   6

15   14   13   12   11

Turn Around and Jump Pattern

hard enough. Start over and practice again until I come back!"

Lu knew that Park had not practiced this one exercise continuously the entire time he had been gone because the dirt where Park had been practicing was not worn down sufficiently to display several hours of practice with this single exercise.

After becoming comfortable with the turn around and jump pattern, the student can practice a slight variation of this pattern. The variation simply adds another jump step forward to each repetition. The pattern will now be: Jump step forward, jump step forward again, jump step back, turn-around, jump step forward, jump step forward again, jump step back, turn-around, etc.

The ability to jump step forward twice in rapid succession will be a valuable skill in any self-defense situation. Once the practitioner has "opened" his or her opponent and gained an

The 90 Degree Turn Step

1 - Rear foot steps up and then out at a 90 degree angle

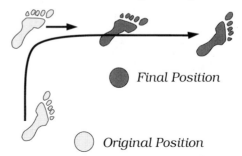

Final Position

Original Position

2 - Before rear foot steps all the way forward, lead leg springs it farther forward

3 - Rear foot (original lead foot) slides forward on the ball

optimum angle of attack, the technique applied with the first jump step forward will damage or otherwise offset the opponent while the technique applied with the second jump step forward will finish the job. When Pa Kua Chang is applied as a fighting art, the practitioner will continuously attack once he or she gains advantage on the opponent. These continuous attacks are executed in rapid succession until the opponent is rendered incapable of continuing the fight.

In Park Bok Nam's school, once the student has learned how to combine the upper body movement with the stepping, the repeated jump step stepping technique is combined with palm, elbow and shoulder striking combinations so that the student learns to attack swiftly, continuously and accurately using combinations of long and short range attacks. Practicing the two successive jump step maneuvers in the "turn around and jump" exercise will serve to build a strong foundation for future study.

The 45 Degree Turn Step

1 - Rear foot steps up and then out at a 45 degree angle

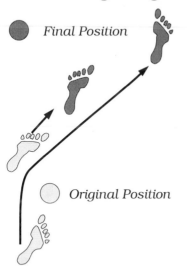

Final Position

Original Position

2 - Before rear foot steps all the way forward, lead leg springs it farther forward

3 - Rear foot (original lead foot) slides forward on the ball

The Full Step with a 90 Degree Turn and the Full Step with a 45 Degree Turn

Before the next two *Pa Fang Ken Pu* stepping patterns are taught, there are two other stepping maneuvers, which are variations of the full step, that need to be practiced. These are the "full step with a 90 degree turn" and the "full step with a 45 degree turn." In the 90 degree step, the rear foot is brought up to the position of the forward foot and then, instead of stepping straight forward as in the full step described above, it steps out straight to the side (90 degrees). See the illustration on the previous page and photo sequence below.

The full step with a jump is usually utilized in conjunction with the 90 degree turning step. If the left leg is forward, the 90 degree turn will be to the right. It is important to bring the stepping foot up close to the stationery foot before turning to step out 90 degrees so that the groin will be protected when stepping out. The turning of the upper body is coordinated with the stepping. This stepping movement is practiced in isolation by first stepping to turn 90 degrees to the right, then to the left, then to the right, etc. moving the length of the workout space in a zig-zag pattern.

The second step, the full step with a 45 degree turn is executed exactly like the full step with a 90 degree turn, however, the practitioner will angle 45 degrees from the forward direction of travel instead of 90 degrees (see illustration on the previous page). Actually, any angle of turn between a full step straight forward (0 degrees) and 90 degrees is acceptable to practice. Before practicing the next pattern drill the student should become familiar with these two turning steps.

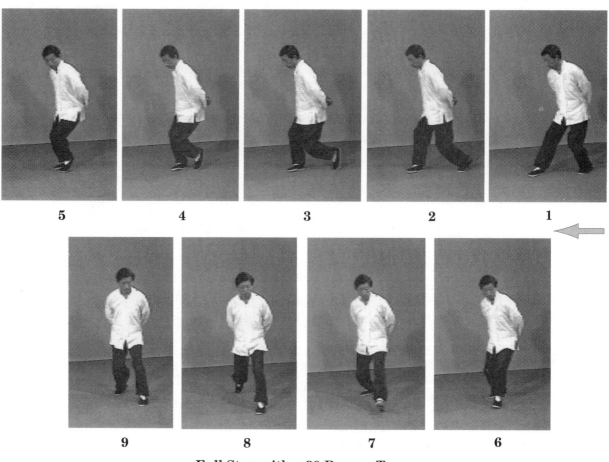

| 5 | 4 | 3 | 2 | 1 |

| 9 | 8 | 7 | 6 |

Full Step with a 90 Degree Turn

Stepping to Four Directions

Once the student has spent a sufficient amount of time with the stepping exercises described above, he or she learns another of the many *Pa Fang Ken Pu* stepping patterns. This next pattern is arranged in four directions. The student starts in the center of an imaginary "+" sign or cross. The stepping movements are as follows:

1) The first movement is to jump step forward along one of the four directions. For ease of explanation we will assume the right leg is forward and the practitioner is facing North when the exercise begins (see illustration 1 below).

2) The second movement is a full step with a jump back along the same line of travel (now the left leg is forward and the practitioner is back in the center of the cross, still facing North - see illustration 2 on the next page.

3) The third move will be a 90 degree full step with a jump turning to the right (East). The practitioner is now at the far end of the eastern leg of the cross with the right foot forward (see illustration 3).

4) The fourth move is a full step back with a jump (now the left leg is forward) The practitioner is back in the center of the cross and is still facing East (see illustration 4).

5) As one can probably guess, the next move is a 90 degree full step with a jump, again turning to the right. The practitioner is now facing South and the right leg is forward (see illustration 5).

6) Another full step back with a jump will place the practitioner back in the center, left leg forward, facing South (see illustration 6).

7) Another 90 degree full step with a jump, turning to the right will place the practitioner out on the Western leg of the cross, right leg forward (see illustration 7).

8) A full step back with a jump and the practitioner is back in the center of the cross, left leg forward, and facing West (see illustration 8).

9) The ninth move will be a 90 degree full step with a jump to the North and will end up being the same step as the original step of the exercise. The practitioner will end up with the right leg forward, facing North (see illustration 9).

This pattern is repeated over and over transitioning the four legs of the cross as many times as desired. To balance the exercise, the practitioner will start with the left leg forward and perform the same exercise rotating in the other (counter-clockwise) direction the same number of times that he or she performed in the clockwise pattern.

This pattern is excellent for building experience in learning how to maintain balance and stability while moving rapidly. To execute this pattern rapidly the student should work to assume the perfect guard stance at the end of each stepping maneuver. The reader also may notice that many of the combination stepping patterns are trained so that one may engage multiple opponents. Pa Kua Chang practitioners are famous for their ability to fight with several opponents at the same time and all Pa Kua Chang schools include training which addresses the multiple opponent scenario.

While practicing any of the *Pa Fang Ken Pu* stepping patterns, Park encourages the student to take the basic pattern and create variations. For example, examining possible variations of the stepping to four directions pattern, the student might add a jump step forward followed by a jump step backward after executing each of the 90 degree full step maneuvers. In this manner the "cross" pattern is maintained, however, a few extra steps are added to the end of each leg.

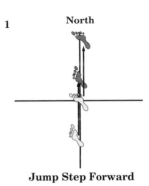

1   **North**

Jump Step Forward

2

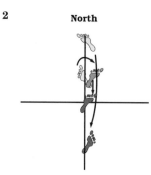

Full Step with a Jump Backwards

3

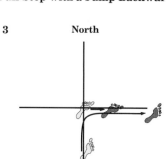

90 degree Full Step with a Jump

4

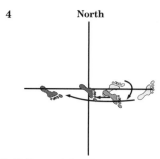

Full Step with a Jump Backwards

5

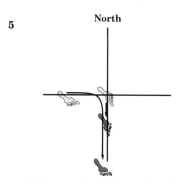

90 degree Full Step with a Jump

6

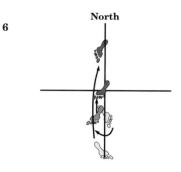

Full Step with a Jump Backwards

7

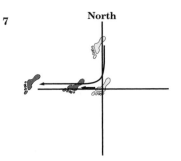

90 degree Full Step with a Jump

8

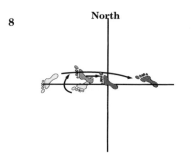

Full Step with a Jump Backwards

9

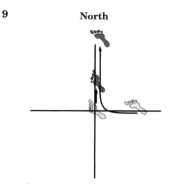

90 degree Full Step with a Jump

Stepping to Four Directions

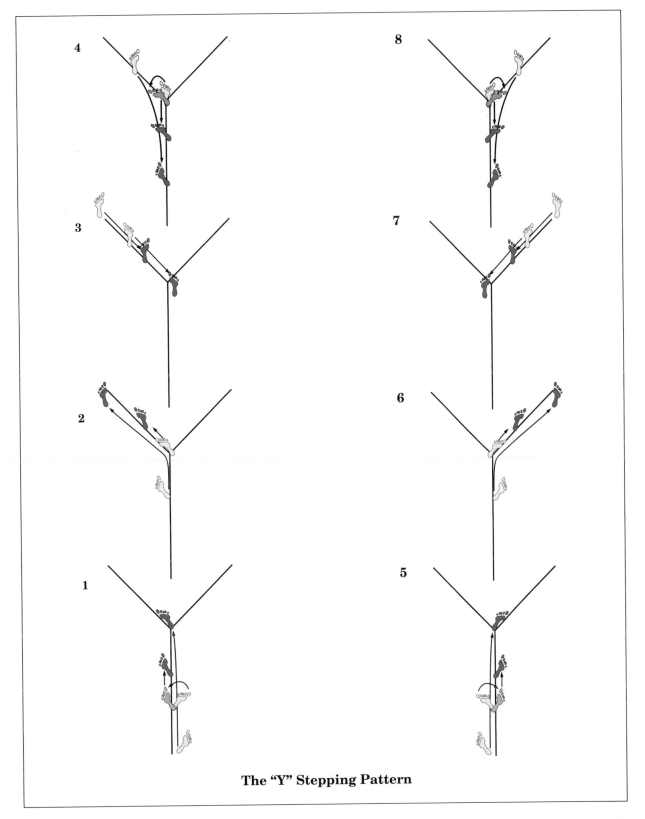

The "Y" Stepping Pattern

The "Y" Stepping Pattern

The next stepping pattern which is practiced in conjunction with the *Pa Fang Ken Pu* steps is the "Y" pattern (see illustrations on the previous page). With the left leg forward in the dragon posture, the practitioner will first execute a full step with a jump (figure #1). This step is followed by a full step with a 45 degree turn (figure #2). This 45 degree step is executed exactly like the full step with a 90 degree turn, however, the practitioner only angles 45 degrees. The practitioner has now traced one half of a "Y" pattern on the ground.

The next step is a jump step straight back (figure #3) and this is then followed by a full step back, however, the full step back is executed so that the body turns as it is stepping back so that the feet trace the base of the "Y" as shown in the illustration (figure #4). The practitioner is now back at the starting position, however, the right leg is now forward.

The steps are now repeated. Since the right foot is now forward, the full step with a 45 degree turn is executed to the right (as shown in illustrations 5-9 on the next page) and thus the other side of the "Y" is traced by the movement of the feet. This pattern, as shown in the two illustrations, is practiced repeatedly.

Once the student has a good feel for the "Y" stepping pattern, he or she can vary this pattern by adding the "Y" step to the Four Corners Stepping Pattern. In this variation, once the student has traced the first "Y," the next step executed is a 90 degree turning step along the second direction of the four corners. By replacing the first full step of each repeating "Y" pattern with a 90 degree turning step, the practitioner will be tracing the pattern shown in the illustration at right.

In execution of both the Four Corners Stepping pattern and the "Y" stepping pattern the practitioner works to transition smoothly and fluidly from one step to the next. The student will first execute the steps slowly in order to concentrate on the exact stepping movements. Later, the student will practice stepping quickly.

When stepping quickly, using any combination of *Pa Fang Ken Pu* preset patterns, there is a tendency to anticipate the next step in the

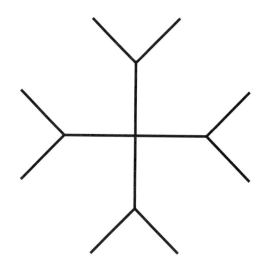

Four Direction "Y" Stepping

sequence. If the next step is anticipated, the student becomes sloppy in that the guard stance posture is not executed fully at the conclusion of each step. The importance of landing exactly in the guard stance posture at the conclusion of each stepping movement cannot be overemphasized. The practitioner should never sacrifice accuracy in order to increase speed. Ideally, one will practice such that accuracy can be maintained while moving quickly.

The "V" Step

There is one last *Pa Fang Ken Pu* step which we would like to cover in this chapter. Park refers to this step as the "V" step. The "V" step combines the jump step and the full step with a jump, however, the angles at which these steps are executed are slightly different from the standard steps. Additionally, the steps are combined in such a manner that the jump step has not quite been completed before the full step with a jump is executed. This step is used to move out of the path of an opponent's attack and rapidly counter-attack in the same stepping motion.

To execute this step from the guard stance posture, the practitioner will first jump step,

Pa Fang Ken Pu Stepping and the Pa Kua Diagram

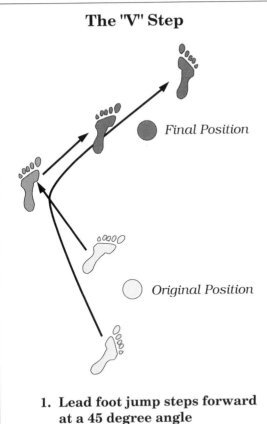

The "V" Step

Final Position

Original Position

1. **Lead foot jump steps forward at a 45 degree angle**

2 - **Rear foot steps up and then out at a 90 degree angle**

3 - **Before rear foot steps all the way forward, lead leg springs it farther forward**

4 - **Rear foot (original lead foot) slides forward on the ball**

Previously we discussed three different movement principles which were based on the geometrical configuration of the Pa Kua diagrams. These were: circular movement around a central axis, angular rotation around an axis, and linear movement in eight directions. It is not difficult to see that all of the *Pa Fang Ken Pu* maneuvers and patterns are derived from the Pa Kua diagrams principle of linear movement in eight directions. The basis of this theory of movement, simply stated, is that if the practitioner is standing in one location focusing outward (the center of the practitioner's body being viewed as the point from which movement is initiated), there are an infinite number of linear directions the practitioner could move. A workable model which is used in theory to represent the infinite number of directions which move outward from a central point is given by the eight major directions of the Pa Kua (or the compass) as shown in the illustration below.

Utilizing this model (with the understanding that the eight directions are really representative of an infinite number of possible directions), we can expand the concept by recognizing that once the practitioner moves along one of these eight directions and stops, he or she again has the ability to move along one of the eight different directions. We can represent this expanded view

however, the jump step is executed at a 45 degree angle instead of straight forward. Additionally, the rear foot is not brought forward as in the standard jump step. As soon as the front foot lands, the rear foot steps out as in the full step with a 90 degree turn. Just before the rear foot reaches it's final destination, the original lead foot springs the step forward as in the full step with a jump. This step is depicted in the illustration above.

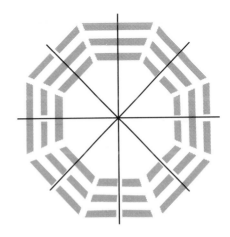

Illustration 1 - The Eight Directions

by placing another Pa Kua diagram at the tip of each of the lines of the original diagram as shown in illustration 2 below. This view could again be expanded by placing another Pa Kua diagram at the tip of each of these diagrams. This model indicates that each time a practitioner moves the center line of the body, there is once again an infinite number of directions he or she could move.

Looking at these two illustrations, we can see how all of the basic *Pa Fang Ken Pu* exercises were developed. If the practitioner is located at the center of the Pa Kua diagram (illustration 1), he or she could jump step or full step forward or backward along the three forward moving lines, or the three backward moving lines. In most cases, movement along the forward moving lines would be on the offensive, while movement along the backward moving lines would be defensive. Movement along the lines which go to either side is accomplished by executing the full step with a 90 degree turn. Therefore, all eight directions of the Pa Kua diagram are covered by utilizing the basic *Pa Fang Ken Pu* steps. Similarly, looking at illustration 2 below, we can see that all of the basic stepping patterns conform with the patterns

depicted in this diagram. For instance, the "Y" pattern begins on the center diagram, moves to the top diagram to transverse the upper portions of the "Y" and then proceeds back to the central diagram.

With the knowledge of the directions and patterns of the Pa Kua diagrams as depicted in illustration 2, the practitioner can develop a large number of stepping combinations to practice when utilizing the *Pa Fang Ken Pu* steps. Intermediate and advance *Pa Fang Ken Pu* stepping methods are all based on this formation of multiple Pa Kua diagrams. Employment of this theory assumes that the central axis of the practitioner's body is the center of the diagram. The relationship of the practitioner's center to the opponent's center is of concern to the Pa Kua Chang practitioner in combat.

By practicing the *Pa Fang Ken Pu* stepping exercises, and the follow-on *Pa Fang Ken Pu* two-person drills, the practitioner will gain an experiential knowledge of how to move his or her center body in relation to an opponent's center body movement. The Pa Kua practitioner will constantly seek to open up the opponent's center door, or *chung men*, while guarding his own from being opened by the opponent. The *Pa Fang Ken Pu* stepping exercises teach the practitioner how to avoid an opponent's attack and how to attack, or counter-attack the opponent's body utilizing optimum attacking angles. In order to fully appreciate how this theory further applies to Pa Kua Chang combat tactics, we must first examine the other two theories of movement associated with the Pa Kua diagram's geometry by discussing the other Pa Kua Chang basic footwork components.

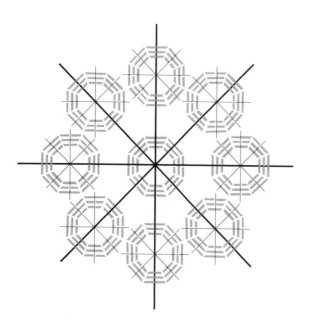

Illustration 2 - Multiple Eight Direction Patterns

The Pivot Step

In the last section, the basics of the jump step, full step, and full step with a 90 degree turn were explained and a few stepping exercises were outlined. In this section the pivot step will be described and exercises which combine the pivot step with the full step and jump step will be presented.

The pivot step is primarily employed as a defense maneuver to avoid an attack and position one's body optimally for counter-attack without loosing any ground. As the attacker advances, the practitioner will pivot to the right or left on the front foot. The front foot is planted and the back foot moves through an arc which is consistent with the degree or angle of the pivot. The exact angle of the arc that the back foot travels will depend on the body's position in relation to the opponent and his direction of attack and thus is situational. Although there are a infinite number of pivoting angles, the primary angles are consistent with the eight directions of the Pa Kua diagram, i.e. 45, 90, 135, and 180 degrees. When pivoting, the practitioner will seek to place his or her body at an angle conducive to optimal counter-attack. The beauty of this move is that the practitioner can avoid the opponent's attack with minimal engagement and no loss of ground.

Although pivoting angles are numerous, the mechanics of the 90 degree pivot will be described here to facilitate easy explanation. The 90 degree pivot should be practiced first and the mechanics of the 90 degree pivot applied identically to all pivoting angles. As in the last section on *Pa Fang Ken Pu*, we will only concern ourselves with the movement of the legs for now. Adding arm movements to the stepping techniques will be described in a later section of the book.

Assuming the guard position ("dragon posture") with the left foot forward, the 90 degree pivot to the right is executed by simultaneously shifting the weight forward slightly while pushing off the back foot and "swinging" the body 90 degrees to the right as a door swings on its hinges. The pivot occurs on the ball of the front foot. The movement should be swift and fluid and the body should move as one integrated unit. The body does not bob up and down or wobble side to side. The foot, leg, and body pivot together, as one piece, around the fixed front foot - it is a one-count movement.

The back foot movement and the torquing of the body around the ball of the front foot occurs simultaneously and all parts of the body stop moving at the same instant. The final position should be exactly the same as the starting position (the guard stance). During the transition the weight is shifted from 40/60 to approximately 50/50, however, when the movement is finished the practitioner is once again in a 40/60 stance.

If the left foot is forward and the practitioner is

| 5 | 4 | 3 | 2 | 1 |

The 90 Degree Forward Pivot Step

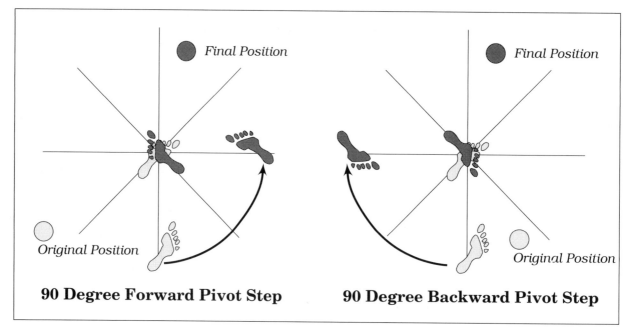

90 Degree Forward Pivot Step

90 Degree Backward Pivot Step

pivoting forward (to the right), the back foot will only come off of the ground slightly while it is in motion. When pivoting back (to the left) the back foot will not come off the ground at all. The ball of the foot will drag the ground as the body pivots into position. The forward and backward pivot steps are illustrated above and demonstrated in the photo sequences below and on the previous page.

There are a number of ways to practice the pivot step by itself. One can pivot 90 degrees to the left and then pivot 90 degrees back to the right, or pivot 90 degrees to the right, then another 90 degree to the right, then back 180 degrees, etc.

Any combinations of pivoting angles and directions is suitable to practice.

The 90 degree pivot step will typically be utilized to move to the side of an opponent when the opponent is striking or kicking forcefully. If the pivot is timed correctly in this situation, the momentum of the opponent's force will carry him forward and the practitioner will end up at an optimum angle for counter-attack. The 135 degree step is an excellent maneuver to use in combination with the *k'ou pu* step in order to quickly position oneself behind the opponent. The pivoting angles which are less than 90 degrees are typically utilized to make small adjustments when preparing to

5   4   3   2   1

The 90 Degree Backward Pivot Step

jump step forward for an attack.

After having gained some familiarity with the pivot step, it is advantageous for the student to practice this maneuver in conjunction with the jump step or full step techniques that were presented in the previous section. There are two main combination patterns that Park Bok Nam has his students practice. The first pattern Park refers to as an attack-defense-attack sequence.

In this exercise the practitioner jump steps forward to simulate an attack, then pivot steps to the left or right to simulate avoiding an opponent's counter-attack, and then the practitioner jump steps forward once again to initiate another attack. This sequence is performed rapidly, however, stability, accuracy, and control must be maintained. The full step can be substituted for either of the jump step portions of this sequence.

The next exercise is similar to the first, but it is practiced in a defense-attack-defense order. The practitioner will first pivot step to the left or right, then jump step forward and lastly pivot step again to the right or left. By practicing these two exercises, the practitioner will become accustomed to combining the pivot step with the other stepping maneuvers and the combination of defense and immediate counter-attack or attack and immediate counter-defense will become habit.

Practicing the pivot step as a defensive maneuver and the jump step or full step with a jump as an offensive maneuver in combination forms the basis of Park's stepping combination drills. Consistent with combinatorial analysis, given two unique items (attack and defense) in sets of three (as in attack-defense-attack) one will find that there are eight possible combinations of stepping patterns. Letting A = attack (jump step) and D = defense (pivot step), the eight possible three step combinations are as follows:

$$A + D + A$$
$$D + A + D$$
$$A + A + D$$
$$D + D + A$$
$$A + D + D$$
$$D + A + A$$
$$A + A + A$$
$$D + D + D$$

Students in Park's school will practice all of these combinations, however, the first four are practiced the most frequently. Although it is an option, Park is not particularly fond of the D + D + D combination as he feels that if the practitioner utilizes three defensive maneuvers without an attack, he or she is simply running away.

Once the practitioner has become familiar with these combinations, the combinatorial patterns become slightly more complex. The attack component of the previous equations is divided into long attack (full step with a jump) and short attack (jump step). With this added into the number of possible combinations, letting LA = long attack and SA = sort attack, the first combination of A + D + A now expands to become:

$$SA + D + SA$$
$$SA + D + LA$$
$$LA + D + SA$$
$$LA + D + LA$$

The student will now practice the basic combinations with this added variation to obtain skill in combining pivot steps with both long and short range attacks.

Pivoting Around the Rear Foot

After the student has become comfortable with the ability to pivot around the front foot to the right and to the left, there are some more advanced pivoting techniques to practice which involve pivoting on the rear foot. A pivot on the rear foot which is less than or equal to 90 degrees is very similar to Pa Kua's characteristic *pai pu* step which is covered later in this section of the book. Additionally, if you think about it, a 180 degree pivot around the rear foot is exactly like the full step backwards which was discussed earlier in this chapter. The rear foot pivot step which Park teaches that is different than other steps, is a 270 degree pivot of the front foot around the rear foot.

In executing this 270 degree pivot, the practitioner will bring the front foot back as if to step straight back, however, the foot will continue moving back passed the 180 degree position until it reaches the 270 degree position as shown in the

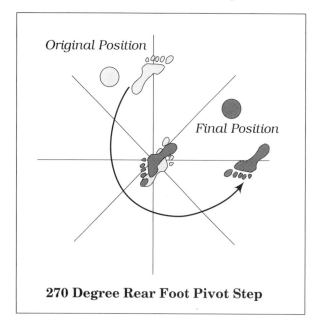

270 Degree Rear Foot Pivot Step

illustration on the next page. This step is executed when the opponent is moving towards the practitioner's center line at a high speed and with excess momentum. This step allows the practitioner to step back out of the way of the aggressive forward attack and pivot the body to set up for counter attack. As the front foot is arching back into the 270 degree position, the ball of the foot will drag the ground for stability.

Of course, most of the time the correct counter attack angle in this situation will be closer to a 225 degree angle than 270 degree, however, in practicing the more difficult 270 degree pivot the practitioner will easily be able to execute pivoting angles less than 270 degrees.

Pivot Stepping and the Pa Kua Diagram

In the section on *Pa Fang Ken Pu* stepping we described how the *Pa Fang Ken Pu* steps were associated with the Pa Kua diagram's eight directions. As one might guess, the pivot steps are also associated with the eight directions of the Pa Kua diagram, but in a slightly different manner. The pivot steps adhere to the theory of angular rotation around a central axis. In this case the central axis is the ball of the foot which the

practitioner is pivoting on and the body's central axis is rotating around that point.

In the *Pa Fang Ken Pu* steps, the center of the Pa Kua diagram corresponded with the central axis of the practitioner's own body. When analyzing the movement associated with the pivot step, the center of the diagram is placed at the axis of rotation of the pivot, namely the ball of the pivot foot. This point will usually be located somewhere between the central axis of the practitioner's body and the central axis of the opponent's body. Many times, but not always, this point will correspond with the first point of contact between the practitioner's body and the opponent's body.

While the *Pa Fang Ken Pu* steps are typically utilized in offensive maneuvers when moving the center of one's body in towards the center of the opponent's body, the pivot steps are defensive maneuvers the practitioner will utilize to quickly move the center of his or her body out of the opponent's line of attack. Again, the degree which the practitioner's center will rotate away from the opponent's direct line of attack will depend on the opponent's movement in relation to both direction and velocity. In partner practice the student will work to gain experiential knowledge of correct timing and optimum angle of the pivot in the pivot step application.

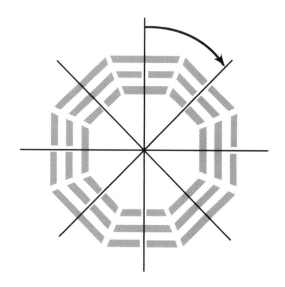

Angular Rotation Around a Central Axis

Circle Walking

Practitioners who have studied Pa Kua Chang for any length of time, are no doubt familiar with Pa Kua Chang's circle walking practice. Walking the circle is the cornerstone of the art, all major systems of Pa Kua Chang (even those who practice straight line sets) practice this method and thus "walking in a circle" has become Pa Kua Chang's trademark. However, even though the circle walking practice is common to all major systems, a student who has studied the art from a variety of different teachers can quickly become

frustrated when trying to investigate exactly how circle walking practice is performed.

There are at least a dozen different walking techniques and each teacher seems to have their own detailed criteria for practicing these techniques. Investigating the art of circle walking, one may run across some of the following: the lion step, the dragon step, the chicken step, the tiger step, the snake step, the crane step, the rippling step, the mud walking step, the shake step, the stomp step, the hesitation step, the continuous step, the sliding step, the digging heel step, the gliding step, and even steps such as the camel step and the elephant step. Some of these are different names describing the same step and others are steps used only for specific leg strength training. One will also encounter Pa kua Chang schools who walk the circle painstakingly slow and others who walk very fast. Then one may also encounter the lower, middle, and upper basin position along with a wide variety of upper body postures one might assume while walking. To the beginning student who simply wants to know how to walk the circle, all of this may seem very confusing.

Natural and Comfortable

Park Bok Nam's approach to teaching the beginning student the circle walk practice is very straight forward and simple. His guidance to the beginner is to walk at a natural walking pace (not too slow and not too fast) with a natural heel-toe walking gate (lion step). Primarily, Park wants the student's body to feel natural and comfortable when walking the circle. If the practitioner feels natural and comfortable, less fatigue will be experienced and the practitioner can practice longer. Important points which Park stresses to the beginner are all aimed at allowing the body to feel relaxed and comfortable while maintaining certain structural alignments.

The upper body posture is exactly like the dragon posture described previously, however, the hips are rotated in towards the center of the circle (about 45 degree off the path of the circle),

The Standard Circle Walking Posture

the forward (upper) palm is facing the center of the circle, and the eyes are looking towards the center of the circle through the index finger and thumb of the upper hand. The lower hand is held 3 to 5 inches below the elbow of the upper arm. The shoulders are relaxed and allowed to drop down, the back is slightly rounded. The elbows are bent slightly and allowed to sink down. How much do you bend the elbow? As an example, Park will tell the student to first hold the upper arm out with the elbow locked all the way and stiffen the arm. From this position, he will then tell the student to relax the arm. The elbow will drop down into a natural, comfortable position, but it will not be bent too much. This is the correct elbow position for the upper arm.

The head is positioned so that the eyes are looking straight (not up, down, or to the side). The head and neck position is critical to avoid stress and strain in the neck and eyes after walking for an extended period of time. If the eyes are not looking straight and the neck is not held erect, the eyes and/or neck can become tired or stiff after 10 to 15 minutes of walking. When muscles become tired or stiff, *ch'i* does not circulate properly and becomes stagnant in that area. When *ch'i* becomes stagnant in the head and around the eyes, it can be dangerous. Park refers to this as *shang ch'i* (rising *ch'i*). *Shang ch'i* can build up pressure in the head and cause severe headaches which may last for weeks.

If any area of the body experiences fatigue after 10 to 15 minutes of circle walking practice, the posture is not correct. If the body alignments are correct and the body is relaxed, one should be able to walk the circle for hours without feeling a great deal of muscle fatigue. If the student can learn to walk while feeling comfortable and relaxed for a period of 20 to 30 minutes and practice everyday, the circle walking practice will improve considerably. Park states that it takes approximately one year of circle walk practice for one hour everyday to begin to understand correct circle walking. With each successive year of practice, the understanding of this Pa Kua Chang component will deepen.

After Park had been practicing the circle walk for an hour everyday for over a year, he told his teacher that he now had an understanding of the

circle walk practice. Lu Shui-T'ien simply laughed and told him to keep practicing. After another year of practicing the circle walk for one hour a day, Park told his teacher, "You were right Sifu, last year when I thought that I understood the circle walk, I really did not. Now after another year of practice, I can understand this method." Lu laughed at him again and told him to keep practicing. Park now says that with every passing year a new element of the circle walk practice will reveal itself. Park, after 32 years of practicing Pa Kua Chang, still practices walking the circle for one hour every day.

Making the Body Light

The number one priority after feeling natural and comfortable in the circle walk practice is to make the body feel light. In order to accomplish this, Park tells the student to imagine that he or she is walking on thin ice. Additionally, when walking, the practitioner's feet should not make any noise when contacting or leaving the ground. Working to make the body feel light when walking the circle will help increase the mobility and speed in all footwork.

Lu Shui-T'ien was fond of having his students play a game in order to practice walking quietly. This game required one student to sit with his eyes closed in the center of a circle while two other students walked around him. When Lu said stop, the two students walking would stop in place and, without opening his eyes, the student sitting in the middle was required to point to where each student had stopped and identify the student. This game required the two students who were walking to be very quiet in their stepping to try and fool the student in the middle. The student in the middle improved his awareness skills by having to listen for any sound which would identify the students who were walking.

The knees should be bent when walking, but they are not bent too deeply when first practicing the exercise. The deeper the practitioner bends the knees, the better for leg conditioning, however, they are not bent so much that the practitioner cannot walk for at least 30 minutes without fatigue. Beginners will start off walking in a relatively high posture for the first few weeks and then gradually bend the knees a little more as leg strength

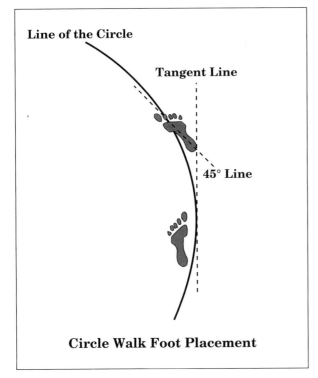

Circle Walk Foot Placement

improves.

When applying the circle walk tactics in combat the practitioner will employ a mid-level, comfortable stance throughout the majority of any encounter. Although there are applications for the low posture, this posture is only assumed for those specific applications, not in general footwork application. Walking too low will be sluggish. In combat nimble and swift footwork is the priority.

Park teaches that the knees should be bent so that the body is comfortable and relaxed. If the body is too upright, balance, stability and quickness of motion will not be optimal and the *ch'i* will not sink to the *tan t'ien*. If the knees are bent too much, movement will be sluggish.

When practicing the circle walk, the foot placement should be as shown in the illustration above. The outside foot (foot furthest from the center of the circle) cuts in approximately 45 degrees to an imaginary line which is tangent to the circle. The inside foot steps relatively straight ahead (parallel to the line which is tangent to the circle). Angling the outside foot helps the practitioner circumnavigate the arc of the circle. The exact angle of the outside foot will depend on

the size of the circle, however, as stated above, this foot will usually angle in approximately 45 degrees.

When walking the circle, the body should not bob up and down, sway side-to-side, or rock back and forth. The upper body should be stable and motionless. Tactically, if the head and upper body are not stable and steady with every step it is easy for the opponent to predict when the practitioner is going to move. For instance is the practitioner's head bobs up and down with every walking step the opponent can detect this pattern and use it to his advantage. When the head bobs up the opponent knows that the practitioner is going to take a step and thus he is "telegraphing" his movement.

A key element in basic circle walk practice for the purpose of *ch'i* development is to keep the *tan t'ien* stable and calm. If the body bobs up and down or rocks back and forth or wobbles side to side, the *tan t'ien* area will expand and contract with the movement. Park likes to have the student walk around an object such as a pole or tree which has a line drawn on it at eye level. This helps to maintain a focus while walking and gives a point of reference to help maintain a steady upper body position.

Having a consistent central focus point will also aid in cultivating the meditative aspects of the circle walk practice. The circle walk practice should not be seen as solely a physical exercise designed to increase balance and stability while walking. It is also a practice which helps the practitioner improve concentration and focus while remaining relaxed and in constant motion.

Circle Walk Practice

Park will have the beginning student walk the circle keeping the above mentioned guidelines in mind for at least one year before further instruction is given. Park's philosophy is that the only way to learn how to walk the circle is by walking the circle - working to obtain a "body knowledge." His approach is, "Don't talk about it, don't think about it, just do it."

Intellectual examination of the circle walk practice will not be of much assistance. Really the only way to improve the circle walk practice and deepen the understanding of this method is to spend *a lot* of time walking the circle. If the student adheres to the above mentioned guidelines, the technique will be correct, questions will be answered, and improvement through hours of practice will be inevitable.

Why should one practice walking in circles so much? Aside from the fact that the circle walk practice will help improve concentration and focus, develop strong legs, aid in *ch'i* development, and improve physical and respiratory stamina, this practice helps the practitioner develop the ability to remain relaxed, integrated, stable, and rooted while in constant motion. This ability is vital when applying Pa Kua Chang as a fighting art.

Walking around a central object such as a Pole or Tree helps maintain focus.

The basic circle walk practice is typically performed while the practitioner is holding one posture (the dragon posture) or a series of static upper body positions as demonstrated in the *ch'i kung* circle walking form presented in Chapter 6 of this book. Holding these static upper body postures enables the practitioner to develop his or her body and forge strong structural connections and alignments. This practice is similar to the *chan chuang* standing meditation practiced performed by many Hsing-I, I-Ch'uan, and Shaolin schools, however, in Pa Kua the practitioner does not stand still while holding these postures, he walks. Maintaining structural integrity and root while constantly walking is the first stage of learning how to apply powerful strikes to an opponent while remaining in constant motion. As discussed previously, this ability is characteristic of Pa Kua Chang.

The Dragon Step

After practicing the circle walk utilizing the heel-toe "lion step" for a considerable length of time, Park will teach the student how to walk using the "dragon step" (also referred to as the "snake step" or "mud walking step"). In the dragon step the heel is only brought up off the ground slightly when stepping and as the foot is brought forward, the bottom of the foot remains parallel to the floor and hovers just slightly above the floor. When the foot has come forward and is ready to step down, it is placed on the ground such that the entire foot lands flatly on the ground at the same instant. There is no heel-toe rolling motion as in the lion step. The dragon step is a bit more difficult to perform than the natural heel-toe walk of the lion step, however its advantage is that it helps bring *ch'i* down to the legs and feet and thus it is a good method to employ in *ch'i kung* circle walking practice.

Park Bok Nam divides his Pa Kua Chang forms training into two categories; *ch'i kung* forms and combat forms. While all forms should be consistent with the body alignments and principles associated with a full *ch'i* flow, the *ch'i kung* forms are practiced with *ch'i* awareness and development as a focus. The *ch'i kung* forms are not as complex as the fighting forms and the postures and movements are more "open" or stretched out

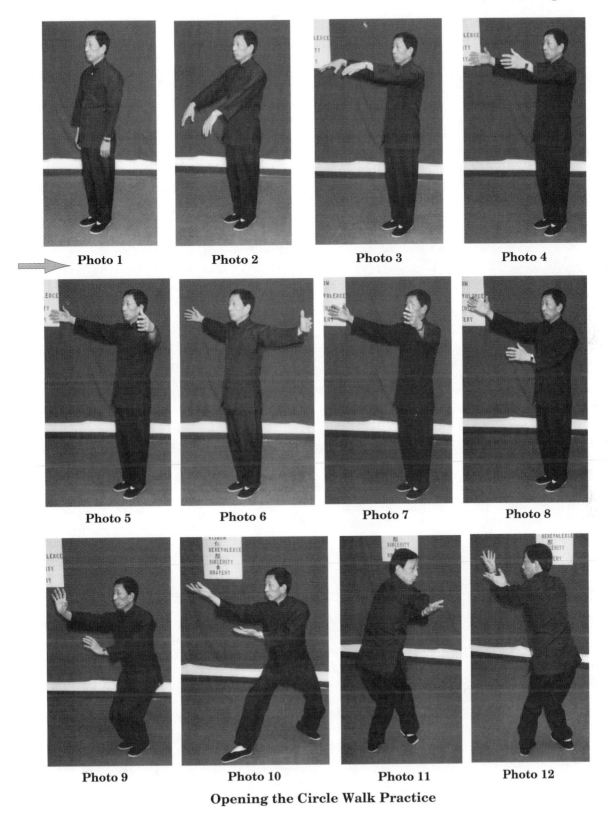

Photo 1   **Photo 2**   **Photo 3**   **Photo 4**

Photo 5   **Photo 6**   **Photo 7**   **Photo 8**

Photo 9   **Photo 10**   **Photo 11**   **Photo 12**

Opening the Circle Walk Practice

Photo 13   **Photo 14**

than those of the combat forms. Park states that a rule of his Pa Kua Chang method is, "When practicing for *ch'i* cultivation the body is "open," when practicing for fighting, the body is "closed." Additionally, the *ch'i kung* forms will be used by the beginning and intermediate students to help obtain and maintain a strong *ch'i* flow in the body. At the advanced stages the practitioner should be able to maintain a full body *ch'i* feeling during all maneuvers regardless of their complexity.

The intermediate student in Park's school will practice the dragon step while executing the *ch'i kung* circle walking forms, however, the lion step is always used in the combat forms. Park's number one priority when performing Pa Kua movements is that they feel natural and comfortable. When executing the quick, evasive footwork of Pa Kua Chang the steps must be light, quick, and natural.

Why isn't the dragon step used in combat? Park has two answers. First, he points out that there is no animal in nature that walks with their feet sliding out in front of them and no human being naturally walks this way. It is not a natural step. Like many other of Pa Kua's circle walking methods, this step is a training step used for a specific training purpose.

The second reason Park feels that the dragon step is not to be used in combat is that it is not suitable for rough and rocky terrain. The fighting surface will not always be smooth and even. The Pa Kua combat circle walking step is executed very

quickly and is frequently executed around very small circles, executed while changing directions rapidly, and executed on all kinds of terrain. From Park's experience, and the experience of his teacher, the best step to use in all of these situations is the lion step.

While Park Bok Nam only teaches two different stepping techniques associated with the circle walk practice, he is quick to admit that this does not mean these two methods are the only methods available. Park's philosophy is that whatever walking method a practitioner uses is good as long as the practitioner has a good reason for using that method, and they can demonstrate how the method can be employed effectively.

Park is adamant that his students know why every part of his Pa Kua Chang system is practiced and how it is applied. He thinks that if someone were to ask one of his students why they practice in a certain manner and that student cannot answer the question with anything better than, "That is the way my teacher told me to do it" then his teacher's Pa Kua Chang method will "lose face." Park loves for students to ask "Why?"

Opening the Circle Walk Practice

The standard opening sequence of movements performed prior to beginning the circle walk practice will vary from one school to the other. Just as in the circle walk stepping itself, no one can say that one school is correct and the other is incorrect. Whenever someone asks Park Bok Nam what he thinks about the way another Pa Kua Chang school executes any movements or techniques, Park's answer will always be, "If there is a good reason why they do that and they can show that it works, then it is good." The standard opening sequence executed in Park's school before the circle walk practice is described below and demonstrated in the photographs on the previous page.

1) To begin the circle walk practice the practitioner will stand with the center of the circle directly to his or her left. The feet are together and facing forward. The practitioner should be facing the Northern direction and thus the center of the circle is West. The practitioner is relaxed. The first

move executed is a toe-out with the left foot 45 degrees (in towards the circle's center). As the foot turns out, the body also turns 45 degrees so that the practitioner is now facing Northwest. Facing Northwest is the standard starting direction in many schools of Pa Kua Chang because in the Later Heaven arrangement of the trigrams the trigram *Ch'ien* (Heaven) resides in that position (see photo 1 on the page before last).

2) The arms slowly raise up straight out in front of the body. The arms and shoulders remain relaxed (photos 2 and 3).

3) The arms slowly move out to the sides of the body. The body remains relaxed, do not allow the shoulders to raise up (photos 4, 5 and 6).

4) The arms move back towards the center of the body (photo 7). As the arms move back in, the left hand comes under the right elbow and the right hand is held up at eye level. This hand posture is exactly like that held in the dragon posture described at the beginning of this chapter. Both hands are along the body's center line. The knees bend as the arms move toward the center. The eyes look through the space between the index finger and thumb of the right hand as if peering through a gun sight (photos 8 and 9).

5) The left foot toes out slightly as the right foot steps forward. Both hands turn over so that the palms face up. The left hand is held near the right elbow. The feet are in the *pai pu* position, the weight is distributed equally (photo 10).

6) The left foot steps into *k'ou pu*. As the left foot steps, the left arm comes under the right. The right palm is facing down, the left palm is facing up. The practitioner's back is to the center of the circle (photo 11).

7) The body turns back to face the path of the circle as the left hand comes up and out in front of the face. The right hand is positioned below the left elbow. The practitioner is now in the "dragon" posture (photos 12 and 13).

8) The practitioners steps off with the rear foot and begins to walk the circle holding the dragon posture. The eyes look into the center of the circle (photo 14).

Changing Directions on the Circle

Park teaches the beginning student a very simple and straight forward technique for changing directions on the circle while executing the circle walk practice. When desiring to change directions, the practitioner will first *k'ou pu* (*k'ou pu* is described later in this chapter) with the outside foot (see photo 2 on the next page). The weight transitions to this leg as both palms begin to transition to *yang* palms (facing up). The lower palm comes up under the elbow of the upper arm as in the straight *fan chang* maneuver described in the next chapter (see photo 3).

As the wrist of the lower palm slides up the forearm of the upper arm, the body swivels around its center and the inside foot (which is about to become the new outside foot) pivots on the heel. Therefore, as the palms pass the "wrist-on-wrist" position, the feet are both facing opposite the direction the practitioner was originally walking (see photos 4 and 5). The practitioner will now step-off in the other direction with the back foot (inside foot) and begin walking as the palms slowly change to *yin* palms once again (see photos 6 and 7).

When the practitioner executes the *k'ou pu* and the palms begin to change, the intention, or focus, is shifted from the old upper palm to the palm that will be the new upper palm. The focus is shifted when the palms reach the wrist-on-wrist position. The palms change slowly as the practitioner walks so that the "*ch'i* feeling" will not be lost and the palms will remain full of *ch'i*. If the beginner turns the palms over too quickly, he or she will loose the full feeling of *ch'i* in the palms that was generated during the practice.

As the student in Park's school becomes more familiar with the circle walk practice and the basic directional change, more complex direction changes will be taught. When the combat forms are practiced the changes become even more complex and are executed rapidly. This basic change of direction outlined above forms the basis for further study as the student learns to change smoothly without a break in body connection or loss of *ch'i*.

Photo 1   Photo 2   Photo 3   Photo 4

Photo 5   Photo 6   Photo 7

Changing Directions on the Circle

Completing the Circle Walk Practice

When completing the circle walk practice session, the practitioner in Park's school will not end the practice haphazardly. While walking the circle the practitioner has maintained a high degree of focused concentration and an increased level of *ch'i* flow through the body, especially in the palms. In order to increase the awareness of *ch'i* in the body and begin to forge a mind/body/nervous system connection, the practitioner will transition smoothly out of the focused attention and heightened state of awareness built during the circle walk practice. Concentration on the mind/body/nervous system connection will serve

the practitioner well when the need arrises in combat or health building to elicit this mind and body state rapidly.

While continuing to walk the circle and focusing into the center of the circle, the practitioner will allow the bottom hand to move out to the side while the upper palm remains in position as shown in the series of photographs on the next page (photos 1 through 3). While the bottom palm is moving, both palms remain in the yin palm position. When the bottom hand has been fully extended out to the side, the palms turn up and the arms begin to move upward (photos 4 through 6). Then the hands move overhead, the palms turn down and the hands are brought down

94

Photo 1

Photo 2

Photo 3

Photo 4

Photo 5

Photo 6

Photo 7

Photo 8

Photo 9

Photo 10

Completing the Circle Walk Practice

the front of the body (photos 7 through 9). When the hands have reached a natural and relaxed position resting by the sides of the body, the practitioner stops walking and turns in to face the center of the circle (photo 10). The practitioner continues to walk while the arms are moving, the walking stops when the hands reach the relaxed position by the sides (photo 10). (The photos do not depict continuous movement due to the difficulty of shooting a sequence of photos while the practitioner walks in a circle.)

The practitioner will remain standing in a comfortable posture with the hands resting down by the sides of the body for several minutes. Attention is focused on the palms and the *ch'i* that has gathered there. After practicing any exercise which is designed to bring *ch'i* to the palms, Park recommends that the student allow the hands to hang loosely by the sides, relax all of the body's joints, and place the concentration on what Park calls the "*ch'i* feeling." Typically this "*ch'i* feeling" will first manifest itself in the hands as fullness, heat, and/or tingling.

When the practitioner has obtained this *ch'i* feeling during the execution of any exercise, he or she will want to relax for several minutes and concentrate on this feeling after the exercise has been completed. By concentrating on the feeling, a mind/body/nervous system connection associated with this feeling will develop. The more developed this connection becomes, the easier it will be for the practitioner to bring *ch'i* to the palms. With continued practice, the student will be able to produce this effect just by thinking about it. Later, increased amounts of *ch'i* will flow to the palms naturally, when it is needed, without conscious thought.

One goal in practicing Pa Kua as a self-defense art is to be able to move *ch'i* very rapidly to the palms (or any other part of the body) when striking. When the mind/body/nervous system connection has been fully developed, as soon as the body moves the *ch'i* will be there and the movement of *ch'i* to the palm will be rapid and spontaneous. Forging the mind/body/nervous system connection during and after the circle walk practice will help the practitioner reach this goal.

Park also recommends that after the circle walk

practice has been concluded the student maintain a relaxed body state and not lift anything heavy or perform vigorous exercise for 30 to 45 minutes. In Park's school the basic circle walk practice is always the last exercise performed in any training session.

Park suggests that if the practitioner desires to walk the circle for 30 minutes a day, it is better to walk for 30 minutes at one time rather than walking 15 minutes in the morning and 15 minutes in the evening. When practicing the circle walk, it is best to walk a minimum of 15 minutes after every training session. Therefore, if the student works out twice a day, he or she might walk 30 minutes after the morning session and 15 minutes after the evening session if there is little time available. Of course, the more circle walking the better. One hour is optimal.

When Park was training with Lu Shui-T'ien, his teacher would take him to a local park and tell him to walk the circle for an hour. Lu would then go for a walk and return an hour later. The first time this happened, Park became bored with the circle walk and practiced some other things while his teacher was gone. When Lu returned he walked over to Park and put one hand on Park's chest and another hand on his back. After Park took one breath, Lu hit him with the hand that was on his chest and dropped him to his knees. Lu exclaimed, "You did not practice walking the circle for the whole hour, your *ch'i* is not strong enough!"

Park had to admit that he had not walked the circle for the entire hour and so Lu sat down on a bench and Park had to walk the circle for a full hour while his teacher watched to make sure he did it. Park states that Lu could walk the circle for hours at a time. Even when he was in his seventies, Lu could walk the circle longer than any of his students.

Lu, who always felt that practicing in a natural environment was best, would always practice his circle walk outside on a dirt surface. He would wear a hat and heavy coat when traveling to the practice area and then take the hat and coat off when practicing. Immediately after finishing his practice he would put the hat and coat back on to keep his body warm and conserve the *ch'i* he had developed during the practice.

Circle Walking Patterns

The standard circle walking practice in Park's school consists of walking continuously around a single circle of a consistent diameter for a desired period of time, changing directions, and then walking around the circle in the opposite direction for the same period of time and continuously repeating this pattern for as long as desired. Beginning students should walk at least 15-20 minutes at a time. More advanced students should walk even longer. The longer the better.

The change of direction used by the beginner is as described in this chapter, however, as the student gains experience and ability the change of direction will become more complex. While walking the practitioner will build a strong, balanced *ch'i* feeling throughout the body. The change of direction facilitates a movement and readjustment of the *ch'i* that has been brought to the practitioner's awareness while walking. The simple change of direction readjusts, or moves the *ch'i* in a simple manner. Once the student develops an awareness and connection with this simple *ch'i* movement, the practitioner is taught slightly more complex changing gestures so that the *ch'i* is directed differently. The more complex changes are taught in a progressive manner so that the student eventually learns how to direct and control the *ch'i* while performing any of Pa Kua Chang's complex movements.

The student in Park's school will spend a lot of time with standard circle walk pattern, however, this practice is only one of many circle walking patterns which are contained in Lu Shui-T'ien's method. The second pattern which the student in Park's school will practice is modeled after the *t'ai chi* diagram and is shown in the illustration at right. The arrows indicate the walking pattern. The palm change in this pattern is executed as the practitioner transitions through the middle of the circle. As the practitioner steps off the line of the circle along the line which goes through the circle's center, he or she begins to perform the basic straight *fan chang* maneuver (as described in the next chapter).

Other circle walking patterns, which the student in Park's school will practice, involve combining large circles with smaller circles and walking in

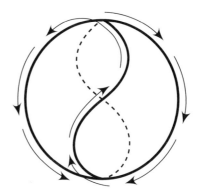

Yin Yang Circle Walking Pattern

different spiralling patterns. Pa Kua Chang footwork, as it is applied in self-defense, can become very complex. The practitioner sometimes walks in large circles and sometimes in very small circles. The small circles change instantly to larger circles and the large ones rapidly change to small depending on the technique applied and the reaction of the opponent. Through the practice of a large variety of circular walking patterns the student can become accustomed to maintaining root, *ch'i* awareness, and full body coordination while walking very tight circles or changing circular patterns quickly.

Since this book is designed to only cover the fundamentals of Park's Pa Kua Chang method, the additional circle walking patterns and their associated palm changes will not be explained in any detail in this book. However, examples of a few of the other circle walking patterns are shown on the next page. Each of these patterns are practiced separately at first and then the student learns how to combine the patterns. The student also learns the *when's*, *how's* and *why's* of the each different pattern's applications.

Circle Walking and the Pa Kua Diagram

Since the *Pa Fang Ken Pu* steps exemplified linear movement along eight directions, and the pivot step is associated with angular rotation around a central axis, it is not hard to guess that the circle walking technique is the physical employment of the principle associated with

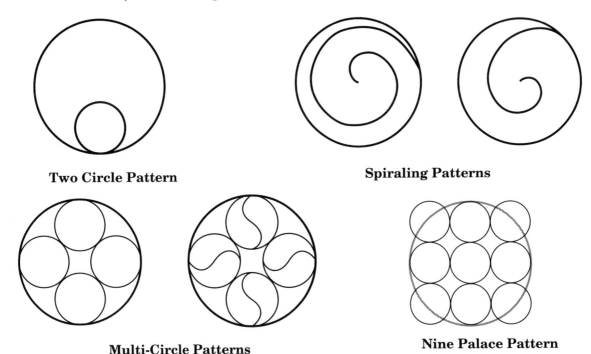

Two Circle Pattern

Spiraling Patterns

Multi-Circle Patterns

Nine Palace Pattern

circular movement around a central axis. Whereas the center of movement in the *Pa Fang Ken Pu* steps is the practitioner's own body center, and the axis of angular rotation in the pivot step is a point in-between the practitioner and the opponent (the ball of the practitioner's pivot foot), the central axis in the circle walk practice is usually the central axis of the opponent's body, although in some instances it can be located at the point of contact between the practitioner and the opponent.

While the *Pa Fang Ken Pu* steps are characteristic of one being in the center and focusing outward, the circle walking practice lends the opposite perspective of being on the outside and focusing in toward the center. However, there is also another principle of movement which is associated with the Pa Kua diagram depicted at right which entails the practitioner being in the circle's center and focusing outward while moving in circular patterns. This principle is extremely important in Pa Kua Chang body movement and is characteristic of movements the practitioner performs with the shoulders and hips rotating around the his or her central axis. This principle will be discussed in detail in the next chapter.

As the reader can see from the various circle walking patterns described in the last section, the circle's center can change rapidly and the circles can be large or small or change rapidly from large to small as in the spiraling pattern.

A theoretical explanation of how all of the patterns associated with the Pa Kua Chang diagram are combined in forming a complete arsenal of Pa Kua Chang stepping techniques will be discussed later in this chapter. However, first we will describe Pa Kua's characteristic *k'ou pu* and *pai pu* footwork.

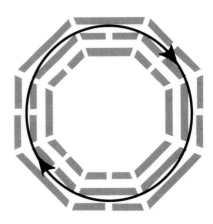

Circular Rotation Around a Central Axis

K'ou Pu and *Pai Pu* Stepping

Like the *Pa Fang Ken Pu* steps, the pivot steps, and the circle walking, *k'ou pu* (hooking step) and *pai pu* (swinging step) stepping help build the base of Pa Kua Chang footwork and mobility. Anyone who has practiced any Pa Kua Chang form is no doubt familiar with the *k'ou pu* and *pai pu* footwork. Typically these foot movements are utilized to change direction when walking the circle and are integral parts of most of the familiar palm changes of the popular Pa Kua Chang forms. The most familiar utilization of *k'ou pu* and *pai pu* is shown in the illustration on the next page. While walking the circle, the practitioner will first toe-in with the outside foot (illustrations 1 and 2) and assume the *pa* (eight) stance. This movement is called *k'ou pu*. The stance is called the "eight stance" because the feet form a pattern similar to the Chinese character for the number eight (see illustration and photographs below). When in the eight stance, the weight is distributed evenly.

A slight variation of the *k'ou pu* "eight" stance is also common. This variation is called the *k'ou pu* "T" stance. In this stance the feet form a "T" shape (imaginary lines extending from each foot will cross and form a "T") as shown in the photograph on the next page. In the "eight" stance, both feet turn in approximately 45°. In the *k'ou pu* "T" stance one foot turns in more than the other.

The *K'ou Pu* Step

K'ou　　　**Pu**

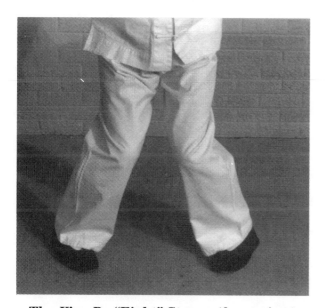

The *K'ou Pu* "Eight" Stance (front view)

The *K'ou Pu* "Eight" Stance (back view)

The *K'ou Pu* "T" Stance

The *k'ou pu* movement is typically followed by *pai pu* when changing directions on the circle (see illustration and photos on the next page). Although there are a number of various arm movements associated with the *k'ou pu* and *pai pu* footwork, the hand movements which Park uses most frequently in conjunction with these steps are described later in the book.

From the *k'ou pu* or the *pai pu* foot movement, there are many follow-on steps a practitioner can execute, it all depends on the function, associated upper body movement, and the response of the opponent. Many times in the popular Pa Kua Chang forms, the *pai pu* will be followed by another *k'ou pu*.

In the illustration at the bottom of the page, we show a typical *k'ou pu pai pu* sequence used when changing directions on the circle. While walking, the practitioner will first *k'ou pu* with the outside foot (illustration #2). The practitioner will now be facing the center of the circle. The next step is a *pai pu* in the opposite direction from the original walking direction (illustration #3). From this position, the practitioner can step off and walk the circle as we described in the circle walking section of this chapter. However, in this series of illustrations we have the practitioner executing another *k'ou pu*. The practitioner is now facing away from the center of the circle (illustration 4). From here the practitioner will execute another *pai pu* and then step off to walk the circle in the other direction (illustrations #5 and #6). There are a great number of different palm techniques that can be executed with this footwork sequence. However, we will not address these changes in this book.

Because of the frequency at which the *k'ou pu* and *pai pu* stepping maneuvers are executed in Pa Kua Chang forms and because these maneuvers are highly functional when used in conjunction with a large variety of palm techniques, Park will have the student become very familiar with these steps by practicing an exercise executing only

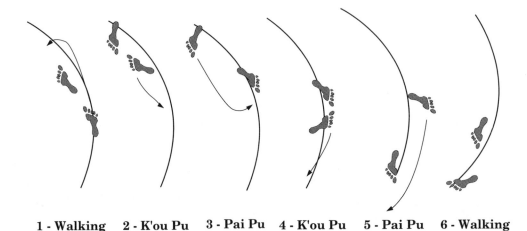

1 - Walking   2 - K'ou Pu   3 - Pai Pu   4 - K'ou Pu   5 - Pai Pu   6 - Walking
CCW   CW

Typical *K'ou Pu Pai Pu* Stepping Applied to a Basic Palm Change

Pai   Pu

The *Pai Pu* Step

Pai Pu (front view)

Pai Pu (side view)

successive *k'ou pu* and *pai pu* steps until these steps are executed correctly and the movements become natural.

Basic *K'ou Pu Pai Pu* Exercise

In this *k'ou pu pai pu* exercise, the student will move along a straight line as shown in the illustration below. From the *pai pu* stance, the practitioner will first execute *k'ou pu*, then *pai pu*, then *k'ou pu* again repeatedly.

This exercise utilizes what is called the "90 degree" *k'ou pu* because when the practitioner steps, the body is facing the direction 90 degrees away from the starting direction. The standard *k'ou pu* as shown in the circle walking illustration can be a "45 degree" *k'ou pu* or a "90 degree" *k'ou pu*. In the "45 degree" *k'ou pu* the practitioner

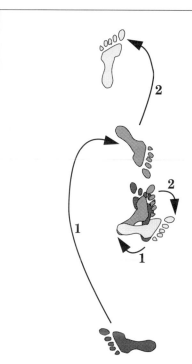

**Step 1 - Pivot on ball of lead foot
and k'ou pu with back foot**

**Step 2 - Pivot on heel of back foot
and pai pu with lead foot**

90 Degree *K'ou-Pai* Stepping Pattern

101

takes the *k'ou pu* step without pivoting on the front foot and thus the body is facing 45 degrees from the direction of original travel. In order to execute the 90 degree *k'ou pu*, the practitioner will allow the lead foot to pivot slightly as the rear foot comes forward and toes-in (see illustration at right).

When practicing this exercise, the practitioner works to make the movements crisp and exact while maintaining balance, root, and alignment. In Park's school, the *k'ou pu* and *pai pu* footwork are primarily used when executing tight turning movements and/or quick change of direction. Unless the student has spent a considerable amount of time practicing the basic *k'ou pu* and *pai pu* steps, advanced footwork application will be difficult.

K'ou Pu Variations

After the student is comfortable with this exercise, Park will add a slight variation which requires the student to pivot farther on the front foot as the *k'ou pu* step is being executed. Instead of the body ending up facing the 90 angle to the path the student was originally facing, the body pivots 180 degrees during the *k'ou pu* step and the student now faces directly opposite the direction he was originally facing. This step is referred to as the "180 degree" *k'ou pu* (see the illustration at right).

This practice modifies the simple *k'ou pu* and *pai pu* footwork in accordance with the principle of angular rotation around a central point and thus is, in a sense, combining the *k'ou pu* step with the pivot step. Following this theory, there are many different pivoting angles that one can practice and utilize in fighting while executing the *k'ou pu* and/or *pai pu* steps. The illustrations at right show the 45, 90, and 180 degree *k'ou pu* steps. Employment of each of these stepping maneuvers, or variations thereof will be dictated by the movement of the opponent.

Pai Pu Variations

Just as the *k'ou pu* maneuver can be varied and adjusted as the situation dictates, the *pai pu* maneuver can be similarly modified. The "swinging out" motion of the *pai pu* step can be varied to fit any angle between 0° and 180°. The

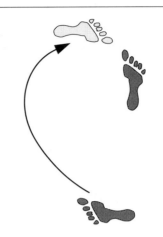

45 Degree K'ou Pu Stepping

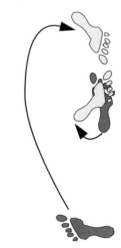

90 Degree K'ou Pu Stepping

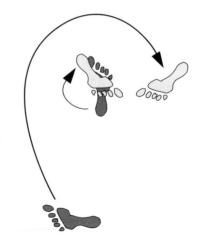

180 Degree K'ou Pu Stepping

180 Degree *Pai Pu* Step

pai pu maneuver shown on the previous page could be referred to as a 90° *pai pu* as the feet are roughly at 90° angles. This is the most common *pai pu* stepping angle, however, this step can easily be executed at various other angles as the situation dictates. Another common *pai pu* angle is 180° as shown above. We will refer to this step as a 180° *pai pu* as the toes of each foot face directly away from each other. This step is employed in tight turns and changing of direction and is considered to be an advanced maneuver because it should not be practiced until the student has gained a considerable amount of flexibility in the hip joints. In execution of this step, the hips must be able to open so that there is no torque experienced in the knee joints. If the practitioner's hips are not sufficiently loose, there is danger of damaging the knees. If the student cannot keep the knees facing the same direction as the toes, this maneuver should not be practiced.

Intermediate *K'ou Pu Pai Pu* Exercise

Once the student has developed enough hip flexibility to practice the 180° *pai pu* properly, Park will teach another *k'ou pu pai pu* stepping exercise. This exercise consists of successive *k'ou pu* and *pai pu* steps executed in a circular pattern as shown in the illustration on the next page.

Starting in the *k'ou pu* position facing the center of the circle, the student will execute a *pai pu* of approximately 135° with the right foot. The left foot will then step into *k'ou pu*. The practitioner

will now be facing away from the circle's center. Now the practitioner will execute a 135° *pai pu* with the left foot followed by a *k'ou pu* with the right foot. The practitioner is now in *k'ou pu* facing the center of the circle once again. He or she will continue this pattern over and over. The pattern followed by this repetitive stepping pattern is a circle as depicted in the illustration.

Combining the Stepping Methods

By applying the Pa Kua diagram geometric principles to *k'ou pu* and *pai pu* stepping, these two stepping patterns can be explored far beyond the typical functions which they serve in most popular Pa Kua Chang forms. When the practitioner combines the *k'ou pu* and the *pai pu* footwork with *Pa Fang Ken Pu* steps, pivot steps, and circle walking in various patterns and sequences, he or she can learn to double or triple their knowledge of stepping maneuvers.

Park encourages his students to experiment with various combinations of all the basic stepping patterns to see which ones work well. The student will first imagining that an opponent is continuously attacking and practice working out stepping patterns to avoid the attacks and set up for counterattack. In examining the best footwork solution available in avoiding an attack, the student will research beyond a simple "get out of the way" solution. In researching any component of Pa Kua Chang the student should always think about the linking aspect or " What comes next?"

When an evasive technique is employed it should be executed so that the practitioner evades while simultaneously placing his or her body in the optimum position for counterattack *and* in such a position that it would be difficult for the opponent to continue his attack. When any research is conducted, the student always considers the follow-on possibilities and how they might be handled in the most efficient manner.

After researching stepping methods with an imaginary opponent, the student practices the stepping with a partner in two-person stepping exercises. Park firmly believes that the only way a student will develop the ability to fight is to engage in hundreds of hours of partner work. Like all aspects of Park's training system, partner work starts out very simple and progresses gradually.

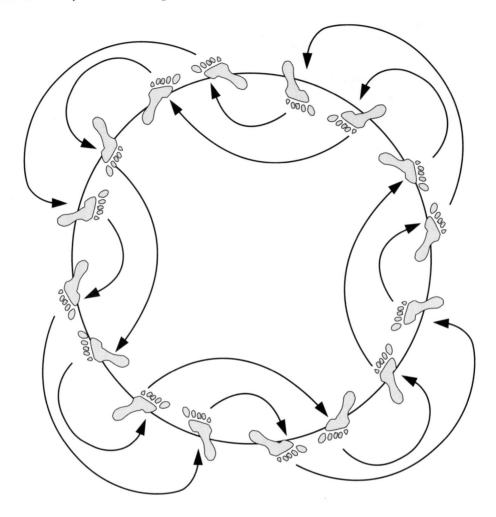

Intermediate *K'ou Pu Pai Pu* stepping Pattern

Each partner exercise builds upon the last until finally the partners are engaging in all out free style sparring.

Having the knowledge and experience to take any one technique out of any Pa Kua Chang form and research variations to get a feel for how that technique might be applied in any given situation is a skill that Park demands of his students. With a thorough knowledge of Pa Kua Chang footwork and palm striking fundamentals (which are based on the theories of *yin/yang*, the five phases, and the eight trigram circle) this skill is not so hard to obtain.

The next section of this book will explore some of the relationships between the footwork described above and the theories of the eight trigram circle.

Combining the Pa Kua Chang Footwork Techniques

Thus far in this chapter we have introduced the reader to a variety of Pa Kua Chang's basic stepping techniques as taught by Park Bok Nam. The student in Park's school will spend many hours practicing each one of these stepping techniques in isolation, however, practicing the stepping exercises by themselves is only the first level of learning how to apply the stepping movements in a self-defense situation.

After developing basic skills with each separate Pa Kua Chang footwork technique, the practitioner in Park's school must learn how to combine the techniques so as to move naturally, swiftly, and fluidly from one stepping technique to another. The combinations of stepping methods a practitioner uses in combat should arise spontaneously in response to any of the opponent's movements. This ability requires an innate "body knowledge" of the stepping techniques and how to best apply them. When practicing two-person stepping drills with Park, the student is constantly frustrated because no matter where he or she moves, Park has either moved in behind the student or has a knee in the student's groin.

Reaction Drills

The first exercise Park will have a student practice in order to learn how to combine stepping techniques is a reaction drill in which a partner or group leader will randomly call out a series of stepping techniques and the students will execute the techniques as they are called out. This exercise is a good tool to use in order to test the student's ability to assume the correct posture upon completion of each stepping maneuver. If the correct posture is not assumed immediately after executing a step, the next step cannot be executed rapidly. Park also uses this exercise to check how much a student has been practicing. When Park calls out a stepping technique, if the student hesitates, has to think about the step before

executing it, or steps incorrectly, he knows that the student has not spent enough practice time with the basic footwork drills.

Typically this exercise is used in conjunction with the *Pa Fang Ken Pu* steps combined with the pivot steps, however, circle walking and *k'ou pu pai pu* can be easily added to the sequence of steps called out by the group leader. Developing the ability to change immediately to either the jump step or pivot step while circle walking, or to change to circle walking after executing any of the other steps, will greatly improve the practitioner's ability to apply Pa Kua Chang footwork in combat.

The ability to move rapidly from the circular footwork to the linear footwork and back again is a vital skill. In many instances, researching these combinations is accomplished using the five phase model. The circular pattern of the creative cycle and linear pattern of the destructive cycle models are applied directly to the footwork in this instance.

Researching Combinations

Park states that after practicing the stepping exercises and drills, the student needs to research the principles of the stepping patterns he or she has learned and discover how the steps can be combined most efficiently. After researching the stepping combinations, the student will then practice the combinations which seem to work well. The majority of the stepping combinations are practiced in accordance with the theory of combinations outlined in the pivot step section of this chapter. Once the student finds an attack/ defense stepping combination which works well, he or she will practice all of the possible combinations of the particular stepping sequence. An example of how an attack/defense/attack sequence is practiced given the jump step as an attack and the pivot step as a defense was outlined in the pivot step section of this chapter. Many other combinations of stepping patterns can be practiced in this manner.

Park will generally teach a few basic combinations to get the student started, however, he feels that the student should not be "spoon fed." Once the student has an experiential understanding of the basic steps and basic patterns, Park feels that the student should research further combinations based on the theory of the Eight Trigrams, *Yin* and *Yang*, and the Five Phases. Park will check the student's progress and lend advice, but it is the student's job to work out the combinations on their own. He feels that if the students discover the combinations on their own, the combinations will not be forgotten and the students will have a better understanding of how to apply Pa Kua Chang footwork as a result of the research. Park feels that without this kind of "homework" the student's ability to really understand how Pa Kua Chang is used in self-defense will not grow to its full potential.

In conjunction with researching combinations and patterns, the student is encouraged to use his or her imagination and "shadow box" with an imaginary opponent by using the stepping patterns and combinations to avoid attack and seek optimum angles of counter-attack. Park emphasizes that this is a very important step in the training process. By brainstorming and developing "what if" scenarios to work out against an imaginary opponent, the student can get a feel for what stepping patterns will work and then practice how to best vary those patterns in hypothetical situations. Also, working against an imaginary opponent will add a degree of realism to the practice and thus the student will not fall into the trap of becoming too mechanical in performing repetitive movements.

The final phase in training Pa Kua Chang footwork combinations is to actually apply the stepping movements while working with a partner. Park will first teach his students a basic two-person stepping exercise which will help the students get a feel for working jump step and pivot step combinations against an opponent. Following this exercise, the students will practice a "freestyle" stepping exercise. These two exercises are described below.

The Guard Stance Posture

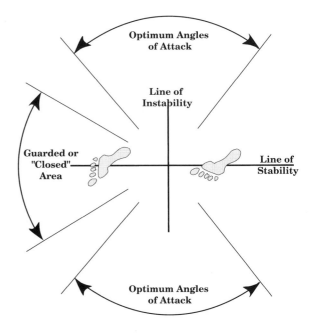

Line of Stability and Instability in the Guard Stance Posture

106

Basic Two-Person Stepping Exercise

Theoretically, when a martial artist assumes a stance, there are lines along which that stance is strong and stable, and there are lines along which the stance will be weak. By "lines" we are referring to lines, or angles, along which outside force could be applied. For instance, if someone were to assume the guard stance posture shown in the photograph on the previous page, the lines of greatest stability and instability would be as shown in the illustration. Obviously, if someone were to attack a person standing in this posture, the attack would best be directed along the line of instability. Not only is the stance less stable along this line, but the opponent's body is "open." With this concept in mind, the first basic two-person exercise, and the follow-on freestyle exercise, are practiced so that the student learns how to utilize footwork in order to position his or her body along the line of instability of the opponent while keeping the opponent from maneuvering to a position along his or her line of instability.

The basic two-person stepping exercise consists of each partner utilizing a jump step and pivot step combination in succession to alternately attempt to pivot to a position along the partner's line of instability and then jump step along that line through the partner's body. When the first partner attempts to perform the jump step, the second partner will pivot step out of the way (90 degree pivot). This sequence is shown in the illustration at right and the photographs on the next page.

When this exercise is first practiced the students will maintain the jump step/pivot step combination in order to help develop a feel for the timing involved when moving out of the way of an opponent's direct attack and subsequently launching a quick counterattack. Once each partner feels comfortable with this exercise, they will then move on to a similar freestyle exercise which combines all of the Pa Kua Chang footwork.

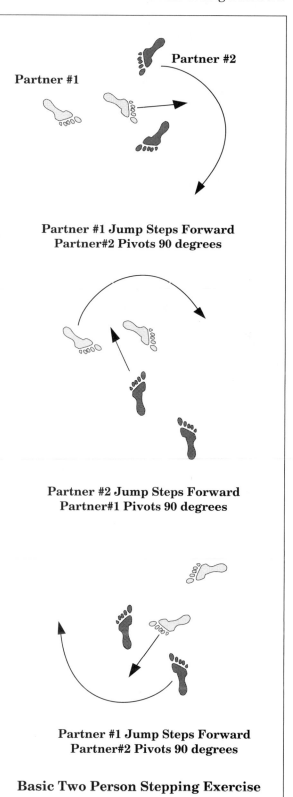

Partner #1   **Partner #2**

**Partner #1 Jump Steps Forward
Partner #2 Pivots 90 degrees**

**Partner #2 Jump Steps Forward
Partner #1 Pivots 90 degrees**

**Partner #1 Jump Steps Forward
Partner #2 Pivots 90 degrees**

Basic Two Person Stepping Exercise

**Partner #1 Jumps
Forward**

Partner #2 Pivots

**Partner #2 Jumps
Forward**

Partner #1 Pivots

The Basic Partner Exercise

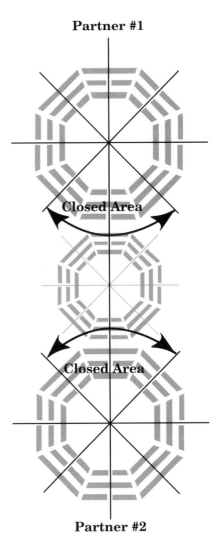

Freestyle Two-Person Stepping Exercise

Earlier in this book, and in the preceding sections of this chapter, we briefly discussed the combinatorial theory which is inherent in the *I Ching* and the three geometric principles of movement which Park interprets from the Pa Kua Diagrams. Additionally, we also discussed the theory of *yin* and *yang* and the *yin yang* representation in the *T'ai Chi* Diagram. When researching stepping combinations in individual training and in the freestyle two-person exercise,

students discover how these fundamental principles of Pa Kua Chang apply directly to the application and training of Pa Kua Chang footwork. While the freestyle stepping exercise is performed as a game to see which partner can uproot, or unbalance the other, it is also a learning experience and should be approached as such. If both partners work together to investigate the direct applications of theoretical concepts to the physical footwork training in Pa Kua Chang, they will better understand how one might use these theories to research and further develop the art.

While examining the principles of movement which are symbolized by the arrangements of the Pa Kua diagram in the proceeding sections of this chapter on Pa Kua Chang footwork, we have explained that there are generally three principles of movement and three axes of rotation. The principles of movement are circular movement around a central axis, angular rotation around an axis, and linear movement in eight directions. The three axes of rotation are: the central axis of the practitioner's body, the central axis of the opponent's body, and a vertical axis formed at the point (or points) of contact between the two opponents.

If we represent the opponent's body, the practitioner's body, and a central point in-between the two bodies by the center of three separate Pa Kua diagrams, we get the representation shown in the illustration on the previous page. Using these three diagrams in relation to each other and the steps associated with the geometry of each, the practitioner can better understand how stepping combinations work.

While it is interesting to contemplate these three diagrams as representations of the principles associated with Pa Kua Chang stepping, the models will not be of any use unless the steps are practiced physically. In teaching, Park does not place emphasis on the diagram representation, his emphasis is on the performance of the physical movements. The real research is done with physical practice against real partners, not on the drawing board with the diagrams. Knowing the theory simply aids the practitioner's research and development efforts in practice.

In the previous section of this chapter, we discussed optimum angles of attack in conjunction with a basic partner exercise. The next level of this exercise is to practice "freestyle." Each partner can use any combination of stepping patterns in an attempt to offset the other partner. This exercise is practiced with the footwork alone. The arms are held behind the back. One partner will offset the other by "stepping through" the partner's body at an optimum attacking angle and knocking him or her off balance.

Park feels that it is extremely important that students practice two-person drills using footwork alone for a significant amount of time before adding hand and arm movements. Once the hands and arms come into play, the student tends to lose concentration on the footwork. All of Pa Kua Chang's applications involve positioning the body optimally before, during, and after technique execution by utilizing skillful footwork methods. If students first work to develop the footwork component fully and make the stepping principles reflex actions in the body, the hand, arm and leg techniques become much easier to learn and apply.

This exercise proves to be a "testing ground" for all of the stepping combinations that the student has practiced and researched on his or her own. Up to this point in the training program the student has only practiced pre-set combinations and patterns and combinations researched through the "shadow boxing" practice. Now is the time to put those patterns and combinations to the test against a real partner and see which ones work and which ones are not so effective. Again, this is a laboratory, not a field of competition. If one partner easily offsets another, both partners should analyze what happened and why. In this manner both partners learn from the other's mistakes. Each partner takes note of what works well and what doesn't. When each student returns to his or her individual practice, they know exactly what they need to work on.

Pa Kua Chang Footwork - Conclusion

Spending hours stepping up and down the length of a room may seem like a laborsome task, but in order to condition the body properly and develop a "muscle-memory" of the stepping movements, this kind of labor is required. Anyone who has watched Park apply these movements in a self-defense demonstration is immediately convinced of their effectiveness and necessity.

By "putting in the hours" with the stepping exercises, researching the patterns, visualizing imaginary partners, and working with real opponents, the practitioner will eventually develop an innate feel for how to move his or her feet optimally in a combat situation. When the practitioner can naturally respond to an opponent's movements with skill, little effort, and no thought, they will have embodied the principle of *wu-wei* and thus will have achieved a high level of internal boxing skill.

Park Bok Nam firmly believes that the most important component to learn thoroughly before attempting to apply Pa Kua Chang as a combat art is Pa Kua Chang footwork. Learning how to get out of the way of an opponent's attack while simultaneously placing one's self in the optimum position for counterattack is the first step in learning how to fight. It is an extremely important step, and one that many practitioners tend to ignore. Footwork is not glamorous, it is not much fun, and it is not easy. However, in Pa Kua Chang as taught by Park it is extremely important. No matter how powerful an opponent's strike, if the practitioner is not there when it lands, all the opponent's effort has been wasted.

The Pa Kua Chang practitioner is a footwork specialist. Walking in circular patterns is the trademark of his art, however, the extent of his footwork arsenal extends far beyond circular stepping. He circles, pivots, moves straight in, pivots again, changes direction and then continues to circle. His footwork is constantly adapting and changing in response to the opponent's movements. His ability to initiate one technique and then change rapidly keys off of his constantly changing footwork.

Footwork is the foundation for all of Pa Kua Chang's applications and special techniques - even Pa Kua *chin na* and throwing techniques are executed through the footwork. Pa Kua practitioners are well known for their evasive maneuvers. Without an extensive experiential knowledge of Pa Kua Chang footwork, the practitioner will have difficulty grasping the essence of this art. Park believes that unless the Pa Kua Chang student has a thorough experiential knowledge of footwork, he or she will never be able to thoroughly understand how Pa Kua Chang is used as a fighting art.

In summary, we will use mathematical type equations to list all of the components of Pa Kua Chang footwork that have been discussed in this chapter. The first equation lists the major footwork components outlined in this book.

Pa Kua Chang Basic Footwork = Eight Directions Rooted Steps + Pivot Step + Circle Walk + K'ou Pu Pai Pu

Next we will break down each of these components into their main sub-components:

Eight Direction Rooted Steps = Jump Step + Full Step + Full Step with a Jump + 90 Degree Step + V-step

Further sub-components of this equation include practicing all of these steps on the right and left sides and moving both forward and backward.

Pivot Step = Front Foot Pivot + Back Foot Pivot

Further sub-components of this equation include practicing these pivot steps on both the right and left side and pivoting through all pivoting angles.

Circle Walk = Circle Pattern + T'ai Chi Diagram Pattern + Spiral Pattern + Multi-Circle Patterns

Further sub-components of this equation include practicing all of the circle walk patterns at varying speeds (slow, medium, fast) and in high, middle, and low stances and employing both the lion and dragon steps.

K'ou Pu Pai Pu = 90 degree + 180 degree

Further sub-components of this equation include practicing all stepping angles associated with these two maneuvers.

Each of the main sub-sub-components of Pa Kua Chang's footwork sub-components might be detailed as follows:

Jump Step = Forward Jump Step (Left and Right) + Backward Jump Step (Left and Right)

Full Step = Forward Full Step (Left and Right) +

Backward Full Step (Left and Right)

Full Step with a Jump = Forward Full Step with a Jump (Left and Right) + Backward Full Step with a Jump (Left and Right)

90 Degree Step = Forward 90 Degree Step (Left and Right) + Backward 90 Degree Step (Left and Right)

Front Foot Pivot Step = 45 Degree Pivot + 90 Degree Pivot + 135 Degree Pivot + 180 Degree Pivot

Rear Foot Pivot Step = 45 Degree Pivot + 90 Degree Pivot + 135 Degree Pivot + 270 Degree Pivot

By starting practice with the lowest level of sub-components and building gradually towards the combination of all footwork components, the Pa Kua Chang practitioner in Park Bok Nam's school develops a complete and well integrated set of footwork fundamentals as a foundation to further study in Pa Kua Chang.

Chapter 4
Pa Kua Chang Body Training

Chapter 4
Pa Kua Chang BodyTraining

Two important aspects of any Chinese martial art system are flexibility and leg strength. Without building these two components early on in the training program, the student will always have problems with relaxation, correct body alignment, and the mechanics of correct movement associated with the art. In this chapter we will introduce exercises which are designed to help increase both leg strength and body flexibility.

Park Bok Nam's Training Program

When a new student enters Park Bok Nam's Pa Kua Chang school, Park will first evaluate the student's level of flexibility, coordination, balance, strength, and general health to determine the student's strengths and weaknesses. Based on this evaluation, Park will develop a training program

Park Bok Nam demonstrates his high degree of flexibility

which will be uniquely designed for that student in order to prepare his or her body for the study of Pa Kua Chang. Students who enter the school with a low level of physical skill, or in poor health, will start out slowly with basic conditioning and flexibility exercises. Students who have had some background in internal martial arts and have developed some skills previously will skip the very basic exercises and will be taught at a much faster pace.

The student with some martial arts background and a body which is in good physical shape will usually start with the material which is contained in this book. If the student practices hard and shows progress, everything in this book is taught within the first 6 to 8 months. Within the first week of practice, the student will be shown the basic *Pa Fang Ken Pu* steps, the circle walk, the breathing and *ch'i kung* exercises described in the *ch'i kung* chapter of this book, the *tou chang* exercise described in the palm exercise chapter, and the *fan chang* (overturning palm) exercises which are described in this chapter.

Once a student has been taught most of the material which is contained in this book, he or she will then learn a series of eight Pa Kua *ch'i kung* movement exercises which serve to increase overall body flexibility, especially in and around the spine and the body's joints, in order to improve the body's overall physical condition and increase the student's *ch'i* awareness, feeling, and circulation to distal points of the body. The movements in this exercise set are a bit more complicated than anything we have described in this book.

This *ch'i kung* exercise set is followed by a series of eight Pa Kua palm training exercises (not related to the eight mother palms) which develop internal striking mechanics. Eight elbow exercises and eight kicking exercises are also taught in conjunction with the palm training exercises. Additionally, the student will learn eight "straight line" Pa Kua Chang sets which consist of a series of tactical fighting techniques practiced repeatedly while moving in a straight line.

All of the exercises listed above are designed to increase flexibility in the hips, spine, and shoulder joints, train the proper mechanics associated with internal arts movement, and increase coordination and stability while moving rapidly and applying power. Additionally, these exercises develop the practitioner's *ch'i* feeling (sensitivity) and generate the ability to move *ch'i* through the whole body (improve distal circulation). All of this material is taught prior to any Pa Kua Chang tactical circle walking form sequence. The student who practices hard would typically learn all of this material within the first 10 to 12 months of practice.

In conjunction with the material listed above, the student will learn a basic *ch'i kung* circle walking form (as shown in the *ch'i kung* chapter of this book). This form consists of eight "animal" static upper body postures which are held while walking the circle. When the student first learns these postures, the changes in-between the postures are simple. After the student can change smoothly and maintain a constant feeling of *ch'i* throughout the body while working with the simple changes, more complex changes are taught.

In conjunction with the *ch'i kung* form, Park's students learn eight exercises which prepare the student's body for the first eight changes of the first of four Pa Kua Chang combat forms. Park's circular combat forms are taught in progressive stages. The eight preliminary exercises contain movements which are found in the eight kuas of the first form. The student will practice these exercises as repetitive training drills before practicing them in conjunction with walking on the circle. The student will typically learn the first combat form within the first 12 to 14 months of training. Once the student can demonstrate the ability to move smoothly through the first combat form, the second combat form will be taught.

Each progressive stage of combat forms which Park teaches builds on the changes that were trained in the previous form so that when the student learns the 64 changes of the final open hand form, all of the movements will be familiar and natural and the student will have a full knowledge of the form's applications. In addition to the combat circle walking forms, Park also teaches his intermediate students an eight-section, or eight "road", "straight line" combat form.

While learning the combat forms in progressive stages, the student will also begin to learn basic training exercises with the staff and the broad sword. In Park's school the student will eventually learn how to use a multitude of Pa Kua Chang weapons. Park's favorites are the staff, the spear, the straight sword, the broad sword, and the short knives.

Park's approach to teaching all aspects of Pa Kua Chang - form, fighting, palm striking, *ch'i kung*, breathing, meditation - is very systematic, allowing the student to develop gradually and fully so that there are no weak areas, missing pieces, or bad habits. He strongly believes that students should start out with very simple movements and exercises and work with them until basic skills are developed before moving on to anything more complex.

Park believes that before a student can learn Pa Kua Chang forms, he or she needs to have a body which is ready to learn Pa Kua Chang forms. This "Pa Kua Chang body" is developed beyond normal levels of flexibility (especially in the hips, spine, and shoulder areas), coordination (which includes maintaining proper body connections and structural alignments when moving), balance, leg strength, endurance, and *ch'i* awareness.

In Parks school, development of flexible hips, spine, and shoulders in conjunction with full body movement is initiated with the first of several introductory palm changing drills. We will discuss a few of these introductory exercises in this chapter. The first set of exercises, the *fan chang* (overturning palm) set, will not only help to loosen up the hips, spine, and shoulders, but will teach the basic movements and mechanics utilized in the *tan huan chang* (single palm change) maneuver. *Fan chang* is also combined with the stepping maneuvers of the *Pa Fang Ken Pu* when the arm movements are combined with the steps.

Park teaches three versions of *fan chang* - straight *fan chang*, circle *fan chang*, and *t'ien* (heaven) *fan chang*. We will discuss these three exercises in this section. The *fan chang* section will be followed by an exercise called "Scooping the Moon from the Sea Bottom."

The *Fan Chang* Exercises

Rotation is extremely important to the Pa Kua Chang practitioner. The ability to rotate the body around its central axis in a coordinated, integrated fashion is necessary if the practitioner hopes to develop the striking power inherent in Pa Kua Chang's movements. Rotating the shoulders and hips in unison around the central line of the torso (line running from the crown of the head to the perineum), rotating the arms around their central line (the bones of the arms) and rotating the legs around their center (the bones of the legs) all with the correct coordination and timing is where much of the power in Pa Kua Chang movement is initiated. The majority of all Pa Kua Chang's techniques involve rotating or twisting the torso and the four limbs. The twisting of the legs drives the twisting of the body, the rotation of the body drives the movement of the arms, and the rotation of the arms helps supply power to the palms.

The ability to rotate the four limbs and the body around their respective centers is enhanced when the hips, shoulders and spine are loose and flexible. One of the first exercise sets a student in

Fan   **Chang**

Park's school will learn is designed to insure that the hips, shoulders and spine are loose and can rotate fully and that the legs, torso, and arms move in a coordinated and integrated fashion. The first exercise of this set, called straight *fan chang*, is introduced below.

Straight *Fan Chang*

This first exercise, straight *fan chang*, is simply an introduction to the basic mechanics of the palm movement. Although the movements of this exercise may seem simple, correct performance of the *fan chang* maneuver is vital as the "overturning palm" mechanics form the basis for many of the Pa Kua palm changes and help to

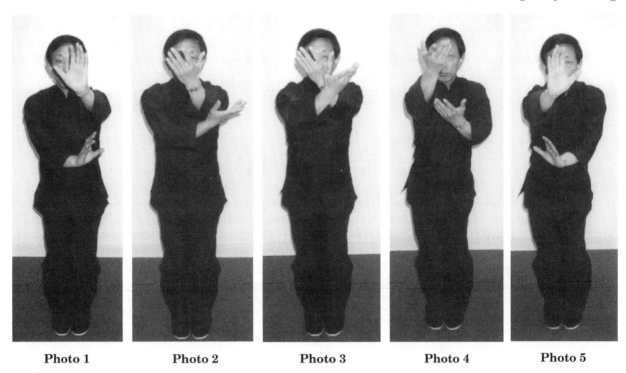

Photo 1   Photo 2   Photo 3   Photo 4   Photo 5

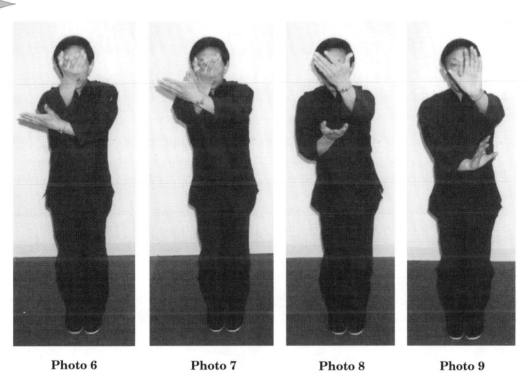

Photo 6   Photo 7   Photo 8   Photo 9

The Straight *Fan Chang* Exercise

develop the mechanics of correct Pa Kua Chang movement.

To begin the exercise, the arms are held in the "guard stance" position (described in the previous chapter). The forward hand is held at nose height and the eyes look straight ahead, using the space between the thumb and index finger as a "gun sight" (see photo # 1 on the previous page). The lower hand is held just below the elbow of the upper arm (3-5 inches) . The hips and torso are angled comfortably (about 45 degrees). The shoulders are in line with the hips and thus the shoulder on the side of the upper arm is angled forward of the body's central axis, while the shoulder on the side of the lower hand is slightly behind the body's central axis (see shoulder and hip alignment diagram below). In this exercise, the body's central axis remains vertical.

The back is rounded slightly as if the spine were a hinge and the two sides of the back moved forward around the spine. The scapula move out to the sides slightly, however the practitioner does not allow the scapula to ride up. When the back is rounded in this manner the shoulders will ride forward slightly, however, do not pull forward from the shoulder, simply round the back. If the student allows the shoulders to project too far forward, he or she will lose the proper shoulder/hip alignment. Both shoulders and both elbows are dropped down. When the shoulders drop down and the back is rounded slightly, the body's center line is protected and the lungs move to the back to facilitate ease in breathing.

The lower hand is held under the upper elbow to help close the body's center line. In addition, when the lower hand is close to the upper elbow the practitioner can quickly execute the *fan chang*

maneuver. Tactically, this move, as it is described below, will serve to clear an opponent's attempt to engage or grab the outstretched upper arm.

Fan chang is also typically executed in conjunction with the *k'ou pu* and *pai pu* footwork when the practitioner is changing direction. If the lower hand is held too low or too far away from the upper elbow, the center line of the body will be open and the speed and accuracy needed to properly execute a tactical palm change will be inhibited. In the correct position, the lower hand is held close enough to the upper elbow to facilitate rapid execution of the *fan chang* maneuver and at the same time it is held far enough from the body so it can rapidly intercept a low punch or kick.

In this exercise, the feet, ankles, and knees are held together comfortably (no need to press them together), and the toes are facing forward. For ease of explanation, the movement will first be grossly defined and then we will follow up by discussing the subtleties, connections, and body relationships in more detail. We will start by defining the arm movement, but keep in mind, in all Pa Kua Chang movement the arms do not move independently of the body. We start by explaining only what the arms are doing for ease of explanation.

From the starting position, both palms begin to turn over as the lower hand moves up and out to the side (under the elbow of the upper arm) and the practitioner begins to inhale. As the lower palm begins to turn, the index finger runs along the back of the elbow of the upper arm. The palm continues to move out to the side as it turns so that by the time the palm is facing up, the wrist of the lower hand is touching the area of the upper arm just behind the elbow (see photo # 2). By the

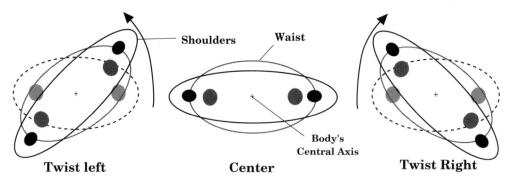

Shoulder and Hip Alignments in Straight Fan Chang Execution

time the bottom hand reaches this position, both palms should be facing up (*yang* palm). (Note: In Pa Kua Chang parlance when a palm is facing up it is referred to as being *yang* and when the palm is facing down it is called *yin*. We will utilize this terminology in the remainder of this book.) The upper palm remains extended and at nose height so that the face will remain covered during the move.

Next, the lower hand moves up along the upper arm with the wrist remaining in contact with the forearm of the upper arm as it moves. If the lower hand is not extended out to the side such that the wrist is in contact with the forearm of the upper hand, the practitioner will not have the mechanical advantage necessary to clear away an opponent who has grabbed the forward hand or arm.

Once the lower palm reaches the height of the upper palm (wrist on wrist - see photo # 3), the upper palm begins to move down, the palms begin to turn and the practitioner starts to exhale. The lower palm becomes the upper palm and the arms fall into the "guard stance" position on the other side (see photos 4 and 5). With this movement the shoulder and hip on the side of the new upper hand will be forward of the body's central axis because the hips are angled approximately 45 degrees (see illustration on the previous page). Once the palms have changed, the practitioner will change the palms back by executing the same sequence of maneuvers (see photos 6 through 9).

In Pa Kua movement, the hands and arms do not move independently of the body. Now that the reader has a basic idea of what the hands and arms are doing, we will investigate the straight *fan chang* maneuver in order to examine what the entire body is doing.

When performing *fan chang*, the entire body will swivel back and forth around the body's central axis with the changing of the palms. The central axis of the body is defined by the imaginary line drawn from the crown of the head down through the perineum (in acupuncture terminology the line would be drawn from the *pai hui* through the *hui yin*). The entire body will move as one integrated piece around the central axis, but the motivation for the movement will

come from the ground up. The hips and shoulders will always move together and remain aligned (see illustration on previous page).

When practicing this exercise, the practitioner should feel the upper body movement being motivated from the heels and up through the muscles of the inner thighs. Each leg rotates around its respective center and this leg rotation in turn rotates the hips and body. The knees should not move, they should remain facing forward and thus the leg rotation primarily applies to the thighs.

In Pa Kua Chang, the movement of what the Chinese call the *yao kua* is very important. The *yao k'ua* includes the areas of the body we in the West refer to as the inner thighs, hips and waist. Too often beginning practitioners will only twist the waist when executing a maneuver. If one only turns the waist, the proper hip and shoulder alignments will suffer. The practitioner should develop the ability to be able to twist the body from the thighs so that the hips and waist twist and the shoulders and hips always remain in alignment. The *fan chang* series of exercises will help the practitioner loosen the muscles in the inner thighs, buttocks, and hips so that the necessary degree of flexibility is attained and proper alignments can be maintained.

In the straight *fan chang* exercise, the body swivels back and forth around its central axis as the palms change. The head remains facing the front. The practitioner works to perform the exercise so that the body's central axis remains stationery, the body does not bob up and down nor wobble back and forth - it swivels around its center. The shoulders are relaxed, and the palm movement is smooth.

The practitioner should rotate the hips to the full 45 degree position with each change of the palms. The hips and shoulders should always remain aligned. The illustration at the bottom of the previous page illustrates the hip and shoulder positioning for this exercise.

The timing of the palm change is also important. The palms do not start to turn over until after the arms are at the wrist-on-wrist position shown in photo #3 on page 117. In the starting position the hips and torso are facing a 45 degree angle from the forward position (where the

Photo 1

Photo 2

Photo 3

Photo 4

Photo 5

Straight *Fan Chang* Partner Exercise

eyes are looking). The turning of the hips back towards the center initiates the arm movement. As the hips reach the position facing squarely forward, the hands are at the wrist-on-wrist position of photo #3 on page 117. As the hips continue to rotate the palm extends forward of the wrist-on-wrist position until the arm reaches its full extension and then the palm turns over smoothly as the hips reach their full rotation.

Straight *Fan Chang* Partner Exercise

To get a feel for the proper timing of the palm changing from *yang* to *yin*, one can practice the straight *fan chang* drill with a partner. In this exercise, both partners face each other in the dragon stance posture with the wrist of the forward arm resting on each other (see photo #1 above).

The back of one partner's upper palm is against the back of the other partner's upper palm. Both partners execute the straight *fan chang* exercise at the same time (see photo #2). As each partner reaches the wrist-on-wrist position (see photo #3), the changing bottom palms start to engage each other. As the movement continues, the wrist of the new upper palm should be in contact with the wrist of the partner's new upper palm (see photo #4) and then the palms turn over. The first repetition is complete (see photo #5 above).

Students practicing this exercise will notice that if both partners turn the palms over at the right time, the palms will both stay in the center line of the body. However, if one partner turns the palm over at the wrong time, his or her palm will be moved out to the side slightly by the partner's changing palm. If this occurs, then the student knows that his or her palm change was not executed at the proper time. When practicing this partner drill, the students should not use force or arm strength to press against the partner's arm. As in all Pa Kua Chang techniques, positive results are obtained through the execution of correct mechanics of the movement and alignments of the body, not gross muscle strength.

The straight *fan chang* exercise is strictly an exercise designed to train the mechanics of the *fan chang* maneuver. The practitioner should not try to put excessive strength or power into the movements, concentration is on being fluid and relaxed. Errors typically made by beginners are: allowing the shoulders to rise up, not turning the hips far enough, not maintaining the shoulder/hip alignments, not turning the palm over at the proper time, and not keeping the upper hand high enough during the change to protect the face. Remember, the upper hand does not start to move until the lower hand is up to the wrist-on-wrist position. This way the face is always protected.

Circle *Fan Chang*

The circle *fan chang* exercise employs the same basic palm movements as the straight *fan chang* exercise, however, the palm changes are more gradual and the torso twists so that the conclusion of the change occurs with the head and palms facing 180 degrees from the starting position. During the course of each palm change the head and upper torso will rotate 360 degrees, the palms gradually change during the course of the body rotation. Although the upper body rotates through the circumference of a circle, the feet and knees always remain pointing in the same direction. This exercise is the first in a series which help to really stretch and open up the hips, spine, upper and lower back, and shoulders.

The student begins this exercise facing forward in the guard position (starting with the left palm as the upper palm as in straight *fan chang,* see photo #1 on the next page). The student then begins to inhale and executes the first *fan chang* as in the straight *fan chang* exercise. Once the bottom palm has reached the wrist-on-wrist

position, the student begins to exhale as the torso starts to turn (to the right) and the upper (left) palm begins to slide down the inside of the forearm of the right arm with the palm still facing up (*yang*). The torso continues to twist towards the right. The palms remain in the *yang* orientation (insure upper palm is up high enough to protect the face) until they reach the 90 degree position straight out to the body's side (see photo #4). From this position the palms start to turn as the body continues to twist. When the practitioner has completed the 180 degree rotation, the palms have changed to *yin* (guard position), and the practitioner is facing directly behind the direction he or she started from (see photo #6).

From this position the student begins to inhale and executes the *fan chang* once again as the body twists back to the front (see photo #9). When facing back towards the front, the palms are both facing up (*yang* position) and the right wrist is on top of the left wrist (see photo #10). From here the student begins to exhale and the body continues to twist to the other side and execute the same maneuver (see photos 11-13). During the exercise the eyes always look in the direction of the upper palm and the body should rotate around its central axis. The practitioner does not let the body wobble side-to-side when twisting.

To help the student remember the positioning of the palms while they transition through the 360 degree turn, Park uses an analogy to the times of day. The position directly in front of the practitioner (i.e. the direction the toes are pointing) is referred to as noon and is the supreme *yang* position (both palms are facing up). The position directly behind the practitioner is midnight, or the extreme *yin* position (both palms are angled facing down in the guard position).

If the practitioner is circling to the right (as shown in the illustration on page 123) the *fan chang* begins at the midnight direction with the palms in the *yin* position. As the practitioner begins to twist the body and inhale, the palms begin to change from *yin* to *yang*; this is analogous to sunrise. By the time the hips are facing forward (same direction as the toes) the palms are at the mid-day position, and have changed to the *yang* palms. As the body continues to twist to the right the practitioner begins to exhale and the palms

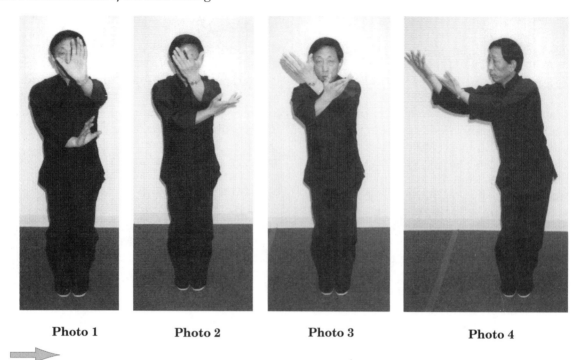

Photo 1   Photo 2   Photo 3   Photo 4

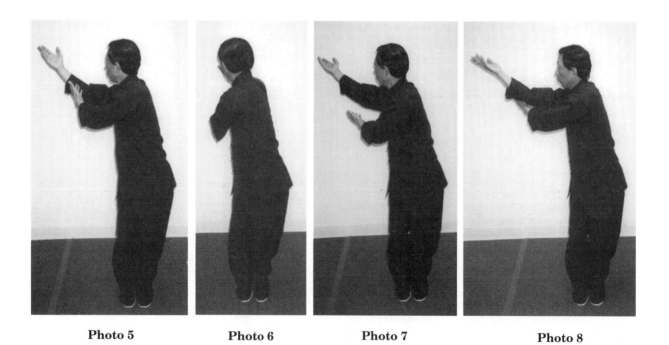

Photo 5   Photo 6   Photo 7   Photo 8

Circle *Fan Chang* Exercise

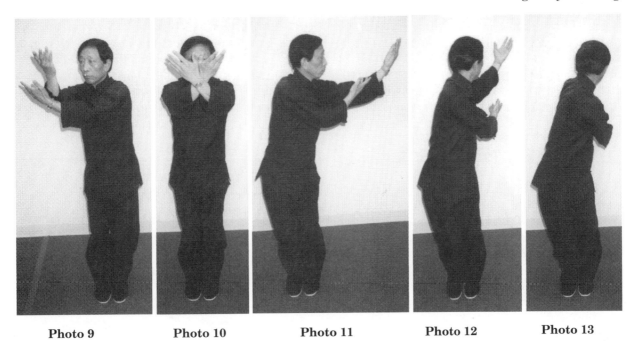

| Photo 9 | Photo 10 | Photo 11 | Photo 12 | Photo 13 |

Circle *Fan Chang* Exercise (continued)

start to change again, transitioning from *yang* to *yin*. This change is analogous to sunset. When the body has twisted to the maximum extent (palms facing rear or midnight position), the palms are back in the *yin* position. At this point the practitioner starts to inhale and twists the body back to the left and thus the sun rises again.

The Chinese believe that the energy of the day is strongest when *yin* is changing to *yang* (sunrise) and when *yang* is changing to *yin* (sunset). This theory carries over to the changing of the palms. The palm movements are most powerful when the *yin* palm is changing to the *yang* palm and when the *yang* palm is changing to a the *yin* palm. Typically the *yin* changing to *yang* will be used in conjunction with a defensive maneuver, such as a parry or to free one's self from a grab, and the *yang* changing to *yin* will be used in conjunction with an offensive strike.

The circle *fan chang* exercise will not only increase flexibility in the hips, spine and shoulders, but it also serves to train equilibrium, balance, coordination and the ability to rotate the body, from the feet up, around its central axis. Careful attention to precise movement and positioning of the palms will also ingrain habits that will serve one well when practicing Pa Kua forms or fighting.

Both of the *fan chang* exercises outlined above are also excellent training tools used in developing the ability to concentrate *ch'i* in the palms and move *ch'i* from one palm to the other. When practicing the exercises, the practitioner should

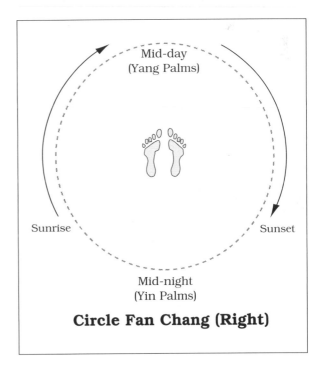

Mid-day
(Yang Palms)

Sunrise

Sunset

Mid-night
(Yin Palms)

Circle Fan Chang (Right)

insure that the palm movements are smooth and a continuous "*ch'i* feeling" is maintained in the palms. The practitioner's intention should be focused on the upper palm. When executing the change, as the lower palm replaces the upper palm the intention switches to the new upper palm.

T'ien Fan Chang

T'ien fan chang is similar to the circle *fan chang* exercise introduced previously, however, it works to develop more flexibility in the upper back and neck. This exercise is typically practiced after executing a number of repetitions of the circle *fan chang* exercise and thus in the beginning posture of this exercise the palms and eyes are facing 180 degrees from the direction the feet are pointing (see photo #1 on the next page). From this position, the exercise proceeds just as the circle *fan chang*. First, the lower (left) and upper (right) palms begin to overturn as the body twists back towards the front. As the palms are overturning, the left palm comes up underneath the right elbow (see photo #2). Now, as the torso continues to twist back towards the front, the left palm begins to follow the right forearm and comes straight up over the head as the palms change (see photo #3). Then the left palm moves up and directly over the head (see photo #4). The palms face down and the eyes look at the left (upper) palm.

The body continues to twist and the palms overturn; the palms then come straight down into the same posture the practitioner started with, but on the other side (see photos 5 and 6). From here the steps are repeated going back in the other direction (see photos 7-11). As the palms come up over the head, the practitioner does not lean back. The head simply tilts back to look at the palms as they are going over the head.

During the execution of this exercise the practitioner will inhale as the palms go overhead (photos 1 through 4) and exhale as the body twists and the palms are directed towards the rear (photos 4 through 6). During the position shown in photo 4, the practitioner transitions from inhale to exhale.

Combining the Three Fan Chang Exercises

The straight *fan chang*, circle *fan chang*, and *t'ien fan chang* exercises can be practiced together as one continuous exercise set to help increase flexibility, build leg strength, and ingrain proper palm changing mechanics. Additionally, each exercise helps to bring *ch'i* to the palms.

When first starting to practice these *fan chang* exercises, the beginning student will probably experience stiffness and lack of mobility in the hips, waist, back, and shoulders and thus the *ch'i* flow to the hands may not be felt to a strong degree. However, once the student has practiced for several months the hips, back, and shoulders will begin to loosen up and he or she will feel more comfortable and relaxed executing the movements. When the spine and surrounding muscles become supple, "energy gates" which are located along the spine begin to open. As the entire body becomes more flexible and these energy gates begin to open, *ch'i* flow to the palms will increase dramatically and will be more noticeable. When the student reaches this stage of training, the intent of the exercises can be changed and the exercises can be used as powerful *ch'i* circulation exercises.

To facilitate maximum *ch'i* development, each repetition of each of the three exercises is practiced slowly and deliberately with the intention focused on the lead, or forward, palm. After the student's body has reached a sufficient level of flexibility, Park will teach the student to practice these three exercises together as a complete set. The set begins with straight *fan chang* which is repeated for as many repetitions as desired. It is best to execute at least 15 repetitions on each side. After executing the straight *fan chang* exercise for at

T'ien   Fan   Chang

Photo 1   Photo 2   Photo 3   Photo 4   Photo 5   Photo 6

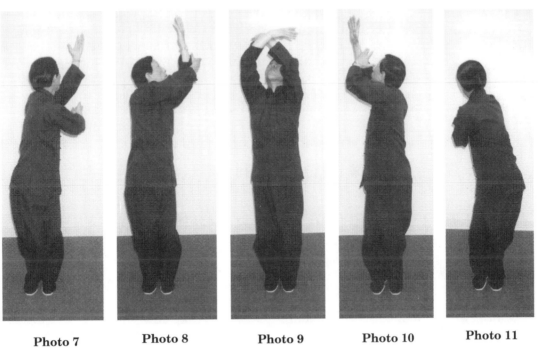

Photo 7   Photo 8   Photo 9   Photo 10   Photo 11

The *T'ien Fan Chang* Exercise

least 15 repetitions, the practitioner will transition directly into the circle *fan chang* exercise and execute it at least 15 times on each side. After the last repetition of circle *fan chang*, the practitioner will go directly into the *t'ien fan chang* exercise. When at least 15 repetitions of *t'ien fan chang* exercise have been executed, the practitioner will switch back to the circle *fan chang* exercise once again.

After executing at least 15 repetitions of the circle *fan chang* exercise, the practitioner will once again execute the straight *fan chang* exercise. Upon completion of the second set of straight *fan chang*, the practitioner will then allow the hands to slowly fall down by his or her sides and stand for a few moments to allow the *ch'i* to settle.

After any exercise which is designed to bring *ch'i* to the palms, one should allow the hands to hang loosely by the sides and concentrate on what Park calls the "*ch'i* feeling." Typically this feeling will first manifest itself in the hands as fullness, heat, and/or tingling. When the student has obtained this feeling during the execution of a *ch'i* circulation exercise, he or she will want to relax for several minutes and concentrate on this feeling after the exercise has been completed.

By concentrating on the "*ch'i* feeling," the student will begin to develop a mind/nervous system/body connection associated with this feeling. The more developed this connection becomes, the easier it will be for the student to bring *ch'i* to the palms. With continued practice, the student will be able to produce this effect just by thinking about it. Later, increased amounts of *ch'i* will flow to the palms naturally, when it is needed, without conscious thought.

One goal in practicing Pa Kua as a self-defense art is to be able to move *ch'i* very rapidly to the palms (or any other part of the body) when striking. When the mind/nervous system/body connection has been fully developed, as soon as the body moves, the *ch'i* will be there. The movement of *ch'i* to the palm will be rapid and spontaneous. Forging the mind/nervous system/body connection during and after the *fan chang* exercises will help the practitioner reach this goal.

Throughout the entire *fan chang* set, the awareness is focused on maintaining the "*ch'i* feeling." With continued practice, this feeling

should be experienced throughout the entire body. The *ch'i* feeling is typically felt in the hands first, however, this feeling will eventually be sensed in the arms, shoulders, torso, and legs as the practitioner's body awareness improves. As the *ch'i* feeling is experienced moving up the arms and to the rest of the body, the student will also experience the *ch'i* moving deeper into the body.

In terms of *ch'i* circulation, Park speaks of three areas of concern: the skin, the nerves, and the bones. By "circulation of *ch'i* in the skin" Park is referring to circulation through the meridians and channels defined in traditional Chinese medicine. This would include circulation in the major meridians and channels as well as the smaller network of collaterals, or *lo*. The sensation of *ch'i* and blood circulation at the skin level will typically be the first the student will experience. If the student has practiced *ch'i kung* or internal martial arts for any length of time he or she is most likely familiar with this sensation.

Circulation of *ch'i* in the nerves is slightly more advanced and will usually be experienced after the student has been practicing *ch'i kung* for a fairly long time, although it will vary from person to person. The student will typically experience a sensation in the hands, or other part of the body, like an electrical shock or current when *ch'i* begins to circulate at this level. This feeling can be somewhat uncomfortable at first.

Feeling the *ch'i* circulation in the bones is usually experienced at the more advanced stages of practice. This sensation is experienced within the bones themselves. Again, the exact sensation will vary from person to person. When a student begins to feel *ch'i* circulation at the nerve or bone level, Park will modify their training program to help bring the student to still higher levels of experience. See the chapter of this book on *Pa Kua Ch'i Kung* for further details about Park's *ch'i kung* system.

The *fan chang* exercise sequence is one of many exercises that comprise the *ch'i* circulation component of Park's *ch'i kung* system. The other components of his *ch'i kung* system include breathing exercises and meditation exercises. Although, at the beginning levels of practice, all three of these components are practiced separately in specific exercises designed to develop one particular component, not including one of these components in a training program will seriously hinder development of the other components. Park feels that if a student only practices moving *ch'i kung* exercises and/or form routines without also practicing breathing and meditation exercises, the student will reach a plateau in their development.

When Park teaches *ch'i kung* seminars he will ask students what experiences they have had with feeling *ch'i*. Most will indicate that after a number of months of training they experienced the heat, fullness, and/or tingling sensations in their hands and various other parts of their body. Since the first experience with this *ch'i* sensation, most students have gradually felt stronger degrees of these same sensations, but have not had any other drastically different experiences. In Park's view, these students have reached a plateau in their training and have not progressed because they have not had adequate breathing and meditation training in conjunction with their other practices. Park states that once a certain level is reached, the breathing practice changes in order to take the student to higher levels. To Park, breathing training is a very important part of practice. Since Park teaches breathing and meditation methods by prescription only, his complete breath training system will not be discussed in this book.

An eventual goal of training to maintain a full body *ch'i* feeling during the execution of relatively simple training drills, such as the three *fan chang* exercises, is to be able to maintain the full body *ch'i* feeling while executing the complex turning, twisting, and coiling movements associated with Pa Kua Chang. This is not an easy task. The training must progress gradually and flexibility is an important aspect of this progression. The more flexibility, relaxation, and suppleness the practitioner can develop in his or her muscles, joints, and tendons, the easier it will be to generate strong, balanced *ch'i* flow and maintain a full body *ch'i* feeling.

After a student can maintain a full body *ch'i* feeling while executing the simple *fan chang* sequence, Park introduces the student to a more complex set of body movements. This exercise set consists of a preliminary, or warm-up, exercise followed by eight other exercises designed to increase flexibility and balance the *ch'i* flow in the body. The warm-up exercise to this set is the circle *fan chang* exercise and the first of the eight *ch'i kung* exercises is the *t'ien fan chang* exercise. The next seven exercises are more complex and thus the practitioner should have a strong foundation with the *fan chang* exercises before attempting the full *ch'i kung* set. Once this set is practiced for a sufficient amount of time, the student will then graduate to a simple Pa Kua Chang circle walking *Ch'i Kung* form.

Through a progressive methodology, starting with very simple exercises and working gradually to more complex exercises, the student's development will be complete. The *fan chang* series of exercises are taught to the beginner to help build the fundamental martial art requirements of flexibility and leg strength, but additionally these exercises will help the student obtain a muscle memory of proper palm changing mechanics and help develop strong *ch'i* circulation while executing these movements.

Scooping the Moon from the Sea Bottom

The "Scooping the Moon from the Sea Bottom" (*Hai Ti Lao Yue*) exercise is one of the most physically demanding of the basic body conditioning exercises taught in Park's school. While this exercise will certainly help the practitioner develop a great amount of leg strength and flexibility, it is also designed to help the student learn how to rotate the body around its central axis on an inclined plane. While learning how to rotate the body around its center in an upright posture with the legs together was relatively simple in the *fan chang* exercises, it becomes much more difficult in this exercise because the body is in an extended "bow" stance. Rotating the hips correctly in this position requires a greater degree of hip flexibility and thus maintaining full body integration and coordination becomes more difficult. This exercise is executed as follows:

1) To begin the exercise the practitioner will assume the "guard" stance described in the previous chapter and as shown in photograph #1 on the next page.

2) Next the practitioner toes-out with the rear leg as the weight shifts back. The lower hand moves in towards the body's center with the palm up and the upper hand hooks in so the fingers are facing the body as shown in photo #2.

3) The upper (right) palm then turns over and circles to the right side of the body as shown in photo #3. The left hand remains in front of the chest with the palm facing up as shown in photo #3.

4) From here the body begins to drop down on the left leg as the right palm slides down the right side of the body. The palm is still facing up. The left palm is still facing up and held close to the chest as shown in photo #4.

5) The body continues to drop down on the left leg and the right palm continues to slide along the right side of the body until is has extended out past the right foot as shown in photo #5.

6) From this position, the practitioner pushes off the left leg and the weight begins to transition to the right. As the weight transitions and the body begins to come up on the right side, the right palm turns over 360 degrees. Both palms are now still facing upwards and the right palm performs a scooping motion as if "scooping the moon from the sea bottom" as shown in photos #6 and #7.

7) The left leg continues to push until it has fully extended and the right palm has also extended out fully and is held up at eye level. Both palms are still facing up as shown in photo #8. Notice that the feet have pivoted on the heels and are now facing 45 degrees from the frontward orientation.

8) From this position the left palm pierces straight upward underneath the right arm and continues upward until it is fully extended as shown in photos #9 and #10.

9) Now the right palm pierces straight up and out underneath the left arm as shown in photos #11 and #12 and then again the left palm pierces straight up underneath the right palm as shown in photos #13 and #14. The palms remain facing up throughout these three consecutive piercing maneuvers.

When executing the three upward piercing movements with the palms, the practitioner concentrates on making this a full body movement.

Hai   Ti   Lao   Yue

Photo 1   Photo 2   Photo 3   Photo 4

Photo 5   Photo 6   Photo 7   Photo 8

Photo 9   Photo 10   Photo 11   Photo 12

Photo 13   Photo 14   Photo 15   Photo 16

The "Scooping Moon From Sea Bottom" Exercise

Photo 17   **Photo 18**   **Photo 19**   **Photo 20**

Photo 21   **Photo 22**   **Photo 23**   **Photo 24**

Photo 25   **Photo 26**   **Photo 27**

The "Scooping Moon From Sea Bottom" Exercise (continued)

The body rotates in its entirety around a line that is drawn from the back heel up through the crown of the head. The back leg rotates around its center from the ankle up to the hip. The hips rotate around the center of the pelvis and the shoulders move in unison with the hips. Beginners will typically move only the shoulders and arms when executing this movement. This is incorrect. The shoulders and hips remain aligned and thus to execute this movement correctly, the hip joints must be very loose and flexible.

10) After the left palm has pierced the second time, the left wrist bends and the fingers of the left palm point in towards the left armpit and the left palm descends down the left side of the body as shown in photos #15 and #16. The movement is then repeated on the other side as shown in photo #16 through #27. The full exercise (both sides) is repeated for at least 10 to 20 repetitions.

Except for the 360 degree rotation of the palms when scooping up on one side or the other, the palms remain facing upwards throughout the exercise. Park recommends that students imagine that they are holding something in the palm during execution of the exercise as this imagery will help bring *ch'i* to the hands.

At first these movements are executed slowly. The student will want to concentrate on the correct body alignments and hip rotation. Later, the exercise can be performed at a greater speed with the piercing movements of the palms being executed very rapidly.

"Scooping Moon From Sea Bottom" Variation

Another version of the "Scooping Moon From Sea Bottom" exercise can be practiced which is executed in the same manner, however, the practitioner does not bend down low when transitioning from one side to the other. This version is demonstrated in the photographs below and on the next page.

Instead of bending down into the low posture and then transitioning up into the extended bow stance as in the previous exercise, the practitioner performing this exercise will twist from one side to the other in the standard dragon posture stance. The footwork for this exercise is executed exactly as discussed in the footwork chapter when the "turnaround" footwork maneuver was presented.

From the dragon posture (photo 1) the practitioner will begin to hook the lower hand around the front of the body as in the previous exercise. However, instead of allowing the hand to turn under towards the armpit right away, the practitioner leads this movement with the elbow as shown in photo 3 below. One can imagine this movement blocking an attack to the ribs.

After the elbow comes back to the rib area, the hand then turns and curls under the armpit as shown in photo 4. From this position, the hand spears straight out as if to attack the opponent's armpit (see photo 5). The practitioner now executes the "turnaround" footwork while simultaneously allowing the palm to overturn as the feet change (see photo 6).

The practitioner will now execute the three piercing palm maneuvers as they were executed in the previous exercise (see photos 7 through 11). After executing three consecutive piercing palms, the practitioner transitions to the other side and repeats the exercise as shown in photos 12 through 21 on the next page.

Photo 1   Photo 2   Photo 3   Photo 4

Photo 5   Photo 6   Photo 7   Photo 8

The "Scooping Moon From Sea Bottom" Exercise Variation

Photo 9   Photo 10   Photo 11   Photo 12

Photo 13   Photo 14   Photo 15   Photo 16

Photo 17   Photo 18   Photo 19

Photo 20   Photo 21

The "Scooping Moon From Sea Bottom" Exercise Variation (continued)

The Circle Principle

When teaching students Pa Kua Chang's circle walking exercise, Park is quick to point out that the circle walking footwork is but a small piece of Pa Kua Chang's overall "circle principle." We have already seen that, in relation to the circular arrangement of the Eight Trigrams, there are a number of ways to utilize circular geometry in relation to Pa Kua Chang movement. The equation Park uses to describe the circle principle is as follows:

Circle Principle = *Circular Stepping* + *Body Circle* + *Hand Circle*

In this equation the "body circle" sub-component not only refers to the three principles of movement of circular movement around a central axis, angular movement around a central axis, and linear movement in one of eight directions, which are associated with the Pa Kua diagram as discussed in the footwork chapter, but also refers to the body's rotation around its own central axis, which we have discussed in this chapter.

One might define the body's rotation around its center as the movement associated with different parts of the body moving angularly, or circularly around the body's center and therefore, if we place a Pa Kua diagram at the body's center, this fourth movement principle is consistent with the three described earlier. What the equation shown above says is that all four of the ideas which relate to the circular geometry of the Pa Kua diagram will apply equally to foot movement, body movement, and hand movement in Pa Kua Chang application.

The circular movement concepts which relate to the footwork were described in the footwork chapter of this book. The "body circle" and "hand circle" components are discussed here briefly.

Body Circle

"Body circle" can include any one of a number of different circular or rotational articulations as follows:

1) Part of the body rotating around its central axis. The central axis of the torso is the centerline of the body. The central axis of any of the body's limbs would be the bones of those limbs.

2) Part of the body rotating or circling around a central point. These central points are usually located at the body's joints. Any one of the body's joints can pivot or rotate around many of the other joints. For instance the hand (finger joints) can circle using the wrist, the elbow, the shoulder, or the hip as central points of rotation.

3) The pivoting or circling of the whole body around points such as the front foot, the back foot, the opponent, or the point of contact between the practitioner and the opponent.

Typically, in Pa Kua Chang, many of these circular and rotational motions are occurring simultaneously in any given movement or technique.

Hand Circle

The "hand circle" sub-component of this equation can refer to such movements as:

1) A sweeping circular motion of the hand (through very small or larger arcs).

2) A wrapping type motion of the hand like a snake wrapping around a tree limb.

3) The rotation of the forearm around its central axis such as that occurring when the practitioner changes from *yin* palm to *yang* palm or vice-versa.

If one were to place an imaginary Pa Kua diagram in the air, the four components of movement discussed above all apply to the hand, or the elbow. The hand can move linearly in one of eight directions from a central point; the hand can move in a circle around a central point (which would include spiraling and wrapping); the hand can move in an angular rotation around the wrist joint, around the elbow joint, around the shoulder joint or even around the central axis of the body (hip joints) as in the circle *fan chang* exercise; and the hand/forearm can move around the central axis of the forearm. Just as the theory of the Pa Kua diagram's geometry is applied to the stepping and body movement, it can also be applied to the hand movement to research optimal ways of combining and executing techniques.

Hand + Body + Step

In Park's view, the equation shown for the "Circle Principle" not only depicts that the three elements of Circular Footwork, Body Circle, and Hand Circle are all basic components of the principle, it also indicates that all three of these components should be present together in any technique. Park uses the simple example of an opponent throwing a straight punch at his chest.

In the first photo shown below, an opponent throws a punch at Park's chest and Park uses a *yin* palm changing to *yang* palm technique to block the punch (Hand Circle). This technique will work fine in some instances, however, if the opponent is very fast, or has a very powerful punch, the strike could break through this defense and thus the technique is incomplete.

In the second photo, Park combines the *yin* and *yang* turning of the hand with the pivoting of the body around its central axis (Body Circle +

Hand Circle) to defend against the attack. In this instance, if the opponent's strike were to get past the hand technique, the body will no longer be in the direct path of the strike. The turning of the body solves the problem of the first strike, however, Park is now in a vulnerable position because the body is not aligned with the stance and thus the opponent's next attack could mean trouble.

In the third photograph Park executes the hand technique (changing from *yin* to *yang* and back again with the step) with the turning of the body and circular footwork in the form of a pivot step around the front foot (Circular Stepping + Body Circle + Hand Circle). With this technique, he has not only completely moved out of the way of the first strike, but he has placed himself in a position where he can easily counter-attack. Executing the Circular Stepping in conjunction with the Circular Body movement and Circular Hand movement will always provide the most complete technique in either attack or defense.

All Pa Kua Chang movement contain elements of circular motion - the twisting, rotating, and circling of the various parts of the body and palms are movements which help define Pa Kua Chang and thus there is much more circling in Pa Kua than just the circle the practitioner will walk around.

Hand Only
(Without Body and Step)

Hand + Body
(Without Step)

Hand + Body + Step
(Complete)

Combining the Palm Work with Pa Kua Stepping

All technique application in Pa Kua Chang involves a combination of footwork, body movement, and hand movement. In Park Bok Nam's school, after the student has worked on the footwork, body work, and hand work which has been described in this book thus far, he or she will then combine these components so that all footwork drills will involve an integrated full body movement in conjunction with simple hand techniques.

It is important to keep in mind that when we discuss combining hand, body, and footwork that there will always be full body coordination, integration, and connection. When the hand, body, and feet move together, they should always be properly aligned and structurally connected. Practicing the basic footwork drills in conjunction with simple hand techniques will help the student forge these connections.

Hand + Body + Step

Bringing together the hand, body, and stepping movements is not difficult if the student is familiar with the "Guard" or "Dragon" Posture, the *Pa Fang Ken Pu* stepping patterns, the pivot step, and the hand and body movements associated with the *fan chang* exercises. From the guard stance, the simple rule of thumb to follow is: if the practitioner changes the lead foot when stepping (as in the "full step" movement), he or she will execute straight *fan chang* at the same time. This movement is demonstrated in the photos below (sequence goes from right to left).

Full Step + *Fan Chang*

The *fan chang* maneuver is executed with the full step, the full step with a jump, and the 90 degree turning step movements that were discussed in the footwork chapter of this book. The photographs on this page and the next page demonstrate these hand/step combinations.

The full step with fan chang is executed as follows: From the guard stance position (photo 1), the practitioner will begin to execute *fan chang* in order to block an opponent's strike or clear his arm away if the opponent has grabbed (see photo 2). As the palms change, the practitioner will step forward with the rear foot (photo 3). When the forward step has been completed, the palms have changed and the practitioner is back in the guard stance on the other side (opposite foot and hand are forward - see photos 4 and 5).

| 5 | 4 | 3 | 2 | 1 |

The full step executed with the *fang chang* maneuver

The full step with a jump executed with the *fang chang* maneuver

The 90 degree turning step executed with the *fang chang* maneuver

When executing this move in a fighting situation, there is a strike (application of internal power) incorporated in the *fan chang* maneuver, however, this should not be practiced until the student learns the mechanics of an internal strike so that the application of the technique will be properly executed. When this move is first taught the student works to make the movement smooth, relaxed, and fluid. The "power" will be added after the student has spent a sufficient amount of time with the palm exercises described in the palm training chapter of this book.

The student should practice the straight *fan chang* maneuver in conjunction with the full step, full step with a jump, and the full step with a 90 degree turn until the movements can be executed fluidly, smoothly, and naturally. The changing of the palms and the conclusion of the step should always coincide. In execution of these maneuvers, shoulder and hip alignment should always be maintained.

When changing the palms in conjunction with the full step with a 90 degree turn, the practitioner will insure that the palms always stay in front of the face. Turning the palms to the 90 degree angle before turning the face and/or body will leave the face unprotected. The same is true if the body and face turn to the 90 degree angle before the palms. The turning of the palms and body should coincide as shown in the photo sequence on the previous page.

The practitioner should be able to execute the hand and body movement simultaneously and end up back in the perfect guard stance posture after the movement has been executed with no adjustments or additional movements required. This hand/step combination is first executed slowly and deliberately so that the student can concentrate on the correct body mechanics. Later, the student can practice moving faster. Eventually the student will add power to the changing of the palms so that the overturning lead palm is employed as a striking palm. Adding power to the palm movement in combination with stepping maneuvers will be described in a later chapter of this book.

Changing Step Partner Exercise

Once the student becomes familiar with the full step and *fan chang* combination, he or she can practice this combination with a partner. Earlier in this chapter we discussed a two person straight *fan chang* drill. This next partner drill is executed in the same fashion, however, a full step forward and subsequent full step back is added with the changing of the palms. The exercise is executed as follows:

1) Both partners assume the dragon stance posture and face each other as shown in photo #1 on the next page.
2) Both partners begin to execute the *fan chang* maneuver as shown in photo #2.
3) As the bottom hand begins to slide up the forearm to the wrist-on-wrist position partner A executes a full step forward and partner B executes a full step back. Notice that in photo #3 both partners have reached the wrist-on-wrist position and they have both executed a full step.
4) The *fan chang* maneuver continues (photos #4 and #5). As we discussed when explaining the straight *fan chang* partner exercise, both partners will remain guarded and protected if they both execute the *fan chang* properly.
5) At the conclusion of the *fan chang*, both partners will begin to execute *fan chang* again (photo #6).
6) As the bottom hand begins to slide up the forearm to the wrist-on-wrist position partner B executes a full step forward and partner A executes a full step back (photo #7). The *fan chang* maneuver continues to completion (photos# 8 and #9).
7) The partners continue executing this stepping/palm changing exercise repeatedly.

Yin Yang Changing Palm with Jump and Pivot Steps

In the execution of Pa Kua Chang footwork, if the practitioner does not change the lead foot when stepping, as in the "jump step" and "pivot step" maneuvers, he or she will not execute *fan chang*, however, the palms will change from *yin* palms (facing down) to *yang* palms (facing up) and back again as the step is executed. The lead palm

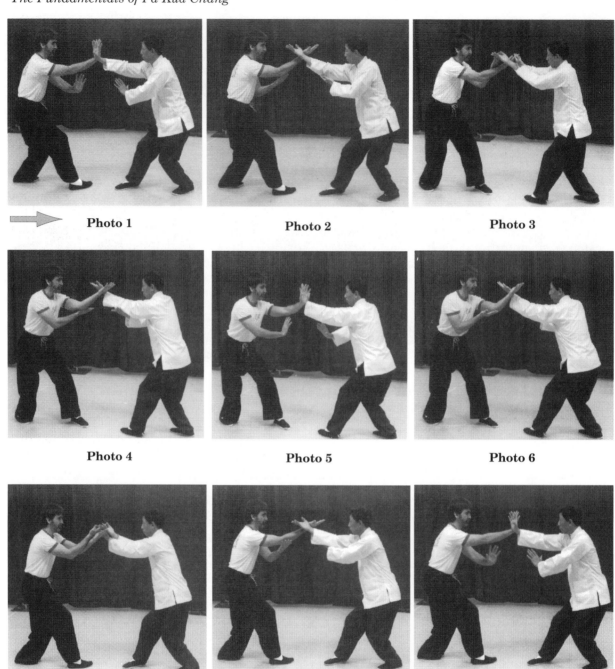

Photo 1

Photo 2

Photo 3

Photo 4

Photo 5

Photo 6

Photo 7

Photo 8

Photo 9

Changing Step Partner Exercise

| Photo 1 | Photo 2 | Photo 3 |

Changing *yin* palm to *yang* palm and back again

stays the same, it simply turns over and turns back as the practitioner steps. This palm movement sounds very simple, however, it is important to remember that the palm does not move independently of the body. The movement of changing a palm from *yang* to *yin,* or vice-versa, is driven by the rotation of the hips around the body's central axis. The mechanics of this movement are discussed below. We will first describe how to turn the palm from *yin* to *yang* and back again while standing still and then

explain how this is accomplished in conjunction with the jump step and the pivot step footwork.

Changing *Yin* to *Yang* and Back Again

If the practitioner assumes the dragon posture and desires to change the palms from *yin* to *yang,* the first motion of the body is for the hip on the side of the upper palm to pull back (see photo #2 above). The motion of the hip pulling back will cause the shoulder to pull back also as the

| 5 | 4 | 3 | 2 | 1 |

Execution of the Jump Step with the Overturning Palms

5   4   3   2   1

Execution of the Pivot Step with the Overturning Palms

practitioner retains the hip/shoulder alignments. As the shoulder pulls back, the palm turns from *yin* (facing down) to *yang* (facing up). In a sense, the body is simply turning around its center and the palm moves with it. As the palm moves, the forearm rotates and the palm changes.

When changing the palm from *yin* to *yang* it is essential that the practitioner maintain correct body alignments. As the hips and shoulders rotate the shoulders should remain relaxed and dropped down. The student should not allow the shoulders to ride up. Also, the shoulder/hip alignment should be maintained. There is a tendency in beginners to let the shoulder on the side of the upper palm pull back too far. Additionally, the knees should not wobble from side to side as the hips turn. The knees should remain facing the same direction as the toes.

In order to change the palms from *yang* back to *yin*, the practitioner will simply rotate the hips back to the original position. As the hips and shoulders rotate, the forearms rotate and the palms overturn.

Executing the Jump Step with the *Yin Yang* Changing Palms

Once the student has practiced changing the palms from *yin* to *yang* in the static dragon posture, it is easy to add the mechanics of the *yin yang* changing palms to the jump step maneuver. From the dragon stance posture, the practitioner will pull back the hip on the side of the upper palm to change the palms from *yin* to *yang* as described in the last section (see photos 1 and 2 on the bottom

of the previous page). As soon as the palms have changed from *yin* to *yang*, the practitioner will jump step. As the jump step is executed, the body will rotate around its center so that the hip and shoulder which were pulled back rotate forward during the jump and the palm changes from *yang* back to *yin* (see photos 3 through 5). After the jump has been executed the practitioner is back in the perfect dragon posture.

Executing the Pivot Step with the *Yin Yang* Changing Palms

Like the jump step, the pivot step maneuver is also executed with the *yin yang* changing palms hand gesture. When executing the pivot from the guard stance, as the body pivots around the front foot, the palm changes from *yin* to *yang* as shown in the sequence of photographs as the top of this page. Because the pivot step is primarily a defensive technique and is typically followed by an immediate offensive attack, the practitioner will not change the palm back from *yang* to *yin* at the conclusion of the pivot maneuver. As depicted in the photo sequence above, the palm will remain in the *yang* palm position at the end of the pivot step and will change back to *yin* as the follow-on attack step is executed. A defense/attack sequence is described in the next section.

Defense + Attack + Defense

Since the pivot step is primarily a defensive maneuver and is always used in combination with an offensive attack, we will now discuss the

5   4   3   2   1

10   9   8   7   6

Defense + Attack + Defense Sequence

yin to *yang* changing palms used in conjunction with the pivot step by describing the " defense + attack + defense" exercise addressed in the last chapter, only this time we will include the hand movements.

In the "defense + attack + defense" sequence, the first move which is executed is the pivot step as described in the last section (as shown in photographs 1-5 above). After the pivot step is executed, the practitioner will immediately execute a jump step attack and the palm will change from *yang* to *yin* (see photos 6 and 7 above). Immediately after the jump step is executed, the practitioner performs the next pivot step, the palms change once again from *yin* to *yang*. This combination sequence is repeated over and over so that the practitioner gains a body knowledge of the pivot step/jump step combination.

While all eight of the possible three-element combinations as discussed in the footwork chapter can be practiced with the hand work as described above, Park will usually have the student concentrate on the following combinations:

$$D + A + D$$
$$A + D + A$$
$$A + A + D$$
$$D + A + A$$

When practicing the "overturning palms" maneuver in conjunction with the stepping, the student works to make the palm changes smooth and the stepping quick and light. When the practitioner moves, the footwork and hand movements are performed together so that the hand maneuver is completed at the same time as

Photo 1   **Photo 2**   **Photo 3**   **Photo 4**

Photo 5   **Photo 6**   **Photo 7**

**Circle walk change of direction utilizing the mechanics
trained in the circle *fan chang* exercise**

the footwork. At the conclusion of the movement, the practitioner should end up back in the perfect "guard" posture; the hand and foot movement having reached completion simultaneously. All movements should be smooth, fluid, and relaxed.

At this point, in the training process the student does not try to put power into the palm work (as if striking someone) - this component will be added later.

Fan Chang and Walking the Circle

The circle *fan chang* exercise is designed to prepare the student for changing direction while walking the circle. When executing *fan chang* in conjunction with the *Pa Fang Ken Pu* steps, the hands are out in front of the body and change along the direction of movement. When the practitioner walks the circle, the hands are facing into the center of the circle and the direction of movement is along the path of the circle, thus the torso is twisted slightly to the side (about 45 degrees). While walking the circle and executing a simple change of direction facing inside the circle (*nei chang*), the practitioner will *k'ou pu*, turn, and then step off in the other direction as demonstrated in the footwork section of this book. When executing this footwork, the practitioner will simultaneously execute the *fan chang* maneuver with the palms.

When this change of direction was discussed previously, a simple straight *fan chang* maneuver was executed, however, there is a variation which employs a wider upper body turning radius and thus the mechanics trained in the circle *fan chang* exercise are employed. During the execution of this change, the direction the palms are facing transitions from one side of the body to the other in a wide turning radius as shown in the photos on the previous page. This is only a 180 degree change in direction, however, the 360 degree body turning executed in the circle *fan chang* exercise will help loosen the body and train the mechanics associated with this movement.

The full 360 degree turning motion of the circle *fan chang* exercise helps to loosen the hips and stretch the adductor muscles of the inner thighs so that the body twisting motion executed in conjunction with the Pa Kua Chang circle walking and associated palm changes can be executed properly. A common mistake beginning practitioners make in alignment when holding the circle walking dragon posture is to twist at the waist, not the hips. This is incorrect. The practitioner wants to always maintain the hip and shoulder alignment. If the practitioner twists at the waist, the hips and shoulders are not aligned and the chain of power will be broken at the waist.

In order to twist the body correctly the practitioner should turn the body at the hips, not the waist. Turning at the hips requires a flexible waist and strong, flexible inner thigh muscles. The circle *fan chang* exercise helps to train this component and thus the circle walking posture and change of direction become easier for the student to execute.

The basic circle walk change of direction variation which is taught in Park's school after the student has become familiar with the circle *fan chang* exercise is shown on the previous page.

Hand Movement with *K'ou Pu* and *Pai Pu*

The *k'ou pu* and *pai pu* foot maneuvers have numerous arm positions which may be executed in conjunction with the footwork, however, in this section we will introduce a few of the most common arm positions utilized in Park Bok Nam's school when executing the *k'ou pu* and *pai pu* footwork.

The arm position the student in Park's school will first learn to execute with the *pai pu* footwork is referred to as the "giraffe" posture. This posture is traditionally referred to as the "unicorn" posture, however, Park calls it "giraffe" because the execution of the movement resembles a giraffe whipping its neck. This hand posture is shown in the photograph below. Both palms face upward (*yang* palms). The forward palm is at eye level and the rear palm is held close to the elbow of the forward palm.

Pai Pu	*K'ou Pu*
Giraffe Posture	**Snake Posture**

Execution of K'ou Pu and Pai Pu Stepping with the Hand Work

K'ou Pu
"Hiding Flower Under Leaf" Posture

The arm position associated with the *k'ou pu* footwork can be either the "white snake" posture or the "hiding flower under leaf" posture. These two postures are shown in the photographs on page 143 and above, respectively. The reader will notice that the only difference between the two postures is that in the snake posture the bottom palm is facing down and the practitioner looks at the upper palm and in the "hiding flower under leaf" posture the bottom palm is facing up and the practitioner looks at the lower palm. Although the palm one looks at will depend on which palm is the "active" palm and thus is situational, looking at the upper palm in the snake posture and the lower palm in the "hiding flower" posture is a general rule Park will give to beginners.

Another rule for beginners when executing these two *k'ou pu* postures is that if the practitioner is stepping into *k'ou pu* and he or she is facing the center of the circle, the snake posture is executed. If the practitioner is stepping into *k'ou pu* and he or she is facing away from the circle's center, the "hiding flower under leaf" posture is executed. When executing a simple change of direction on the circle, execution of the 90 degree *k'ou pu* will orient the practitioner so that he or she is facing

the center of the circle and thus the snake posture is executed. The "hiding" flower posture is typically used in more complex changing maneuvers.

In the snake posture, which is traditionally called "white snake coils its body," Park uses the snake analogy to help the student understand the alignments in this posture. He states the upper hand is the snake's head and the lower hand is the snake's tail. In most applications involving this posture, the upper hand is the active, or striking hand and thus the practitioner watches the snakes head. The arms and upper back form the body of the snake. The forearms are held approximately parallel to the ground. The upper hand, or snake's head, extends beyond the elbow of the lower arm and the lower hand, or snakes's tail, extends out beyond the elbow of the upper arm. The lower hand is tucked in closer to the body than the upper hand. In other words, the lower hand is closer to the armpit than the upper arm is to the shoulder. These alignments are simple to remember if one envisions a snake coiled up and ready to strike.

Lu Shui-T'ien explained to Park that in China the white snake was known for it ability to crush whatever it wrapped its body around. This particular breed of snake was known to have been strong enough to wrap its body around the bottom of a horses leg and break the horse's ankle. Lu said that he remembers throwing large pieces of bamboo near the white snake and watching the snake wrap its body around the bamboo and crush it.

In the "hiding flower under leaf" posture the practitioner will rotate the hips as far as possible and watch the bottom hand so that the entire spine and neck will twist and stretch. The twisting primarily occurs in the thigh and hip area (*yao k'ua*). Even though the practitioner is twisting as far as possible, the hips and shoulders should still be aligned. If the practitioner cannot maintain proper hip and shoulder alignment, he or she should not twist quite as far. Beginning students tend to allow the waist to turn farther than the hips and thus the shoulder and hip alignment is lost.

Pa Kua Chang Body Training - Conclusion

In the last chapter we emphasized the importance of Pa Kua Chang footwork, however, as important as the footwork is, unless the practitioner can learn to move the body in a coordinated, integrated fashion with the stepping maneuvers, the results of effective stepping will not reach fruition. In this chapter we have discussed the basics of Pa Kua Chang body movement through the mechanics of the *fan chang* exercises and the "Scooping Moon From Sea Bottom" exercise. As simple as these exercises might seem, the student who practices them on a regular basis will reap great benefits in terms of proper Pa Kua Chang body movement. With a strong foundation forged in these simple exercises, the student will be ready to effectively handle the more complex body movements associated with Pa Kua Chang.

The body rotations which were discussed in this chapter are vital to effective Pa Kua Chang application. When these body rotations are used in conjunction with Pa Kua Chang stepping techniques, the Pa Kua practitioner can easily find openings in the opponent's defense and rapidly destroy an opponent in a situation which calls for such action.

Park Bok Nam tells a story about a time when his teacher met an Aikido instructor who was a friend of Park's. Lu Shui-T'ien, Park and his friend went on a walk and discussed martial arts. At one point in the conversation the Aikido instructor grabbed Lu Shui-T'ien's arm. Lu quickly changed his palm from *yin* to *yang* as he shook his body and allowed the palm to whip out as it overturned. The Aikido instructor was thrown to the ground. Lu kept walking.

Later, Park asked his teacher, "Why were you so mean to my friend?" Lu said, "He is an internal martial artist. I do not know how skilled he is with his *ch'i* and I do not know his intentions in grabbing me. He should not touch me unless he asks."

The story exhibits how the correct body rotations applied at the proper angles and with the correct timing can be very effective. These connections are trained through hours of practice with simple exercises such as the *fan chang* set.

Lu Shui-T'ien's use of the body movements of Pa Kua Chang in combination with Pa Kua Chang stepping was so effective that he could immediately enter the weak spot in any opponent's defense and he passed this skill on to Park. Park said that Lu told him, "If you have a container of water and that container has a hole in it, the water will leak out of that hole no matter how small a hole it is." Lu said that similarly, a Pa Kua Chang practitioner finds the opening in an opponent's defense no matter how small. As soon as the opening presents itself, like water running out of a hole in a plastic bag, the Pa Kua practitioner is flowing through that hole.

In this chapter basic body movements were presented and then these movements were combined with Pa Kua Chang stepping techniques. When first combining the hand, body, and foot movement the student in Park's school will strive to execute these movement smoothly and fluidly while remaining relaxed and comfortable. In the beginning stages of this training "power" application is not a concern of the student.

The student in Park's school does not apply striking power to the "foot + body + hand" movements until he or she has spent a considerable amount of time practicing palm striking exercises so that the he or she can learn how to develop the mechanics of applying power prior to having to worry about how to apply powerful strikes in conjunction with the steps. The next chapter discusses the basics of power development using Pa Kua Chang palm exercises as a vehicle.

氣　眼　身
與　與　與
力　手　步
合　合　合

Ch'i Coordinated with the Strength

Eyes Coordinated with the Hands

Body Coordinated with the Steps

Chapter 5
Pa Kua Chang Palm Training

Chapter 5

Pa Kua Chang Palm Training

Although a Pa Kua Chang practitioner in combat will strike with the fist, the palm, the wrist, the elbow, the shoulder, the hip, the knee, the heel, the foot, the head and multiple combinations thereof, this art has become famous for its development of devastating palm strikes. A skilled practitioner of Pa Kua Chang can deliver a powerful palm strike from any distance, at any angle, at any time, and from any direction. Thunder Palm, Hurricane Palm, Lightning Palm, Crushing Palm, Vibrating Palm, Splitting Palm, call the variations what you will, the end result is usually the same - devastation of the opponent in combat.

In Park's method, there are two important components which the practitioner must develop in order to begin to achieve an effective internal palm strike. First, the mechanics of physical movement and the physical body alignments must be correct. Second, the practitioner must be able to move *ch'i* from the *tan t'ien* to the palm instantaneously. The second requirement is discussed in the Pa Kua *Ch'i Kung* chapter of this book. The first requirement, palm mechanics, is outlined in this chapter. However, before the palm mechanics are explained, we will discuss Park's interpretation of what is meant by "internal power."

Internal Power vs. External Power

Park Bok Nam does not like to talk much about the details of energetics, anatomy, and physiology which are involved in the application of an "internal" strike. All of Park's teaching is very direct and is focused on the student being able to actually accomplish the task rather than understand in intricate detail how the task was accomplished. When it comes to "internal" striking, if the student has never experienced an internal strike, Park will first give them a taste of what it feels like and then teach them exercises designed to learn how to develop it. Park feels that it is better for the student to practice an exercise that will develop the skill rather than talk about how it is done.

When teaching internal striking mechanics, Park prefers to perform the technique and have the student feel Park's body while the technique is being performed. He feels that by having the student feel what is going on with his body the student will develop a much better sense of what is happening than if he were to try and explain it in words.

There are two things that a student will immediately notice when Park gives them a small taste of an internal strike. The first thing observed is that Park does not have to move very much in order to deliver an incredibly powerful strike. A small, quick shake of Park's body is enough to knock a big man off his feet. Secondly, the student will notice that the strike penetrates very deep inside the body and stays inside the body. These are two of the main characteristics of an internal strike: it can be delivered through very small body articulations, and it penetrates deep inside the body of the person on the receiving end. This is much different than the effects commonly connected with an external strike.

150

Park defines "external power," in an equation form, as follows:

External Power = Speed + Distance + Mass

Anyone who has taken high school physics will notice that this equation looks very similar to the familiar equation: force = mass times acceleration (f=ma). The application of external force is effective when a mass (the fist, foot, etc.) is moved with accelerated speed through a distance. The greater the mass, the faster the movement, or the greater the distance traveled at an accelerated speed, the greater the damage on impact. Makes sense, right? If a big guy takes a big swing at someone and hits them with a large meaty fist, it is going to hurt. At this point in the lecture, Park usually shows the class how skinny his arms are and then asks the biggest guy in class to come up to the front of the room. He places his palm on the big guy's chest, and without pulling his palm off the guy's chest at all, Park shakes his body slightly, the guy's knees buckle and he hits the floor.

Park explains that internal power is much different than external power. When applying internal power, one does not need mass, does not need distance, and the person on the receiving end does not feel damage on the surface of his body as he would in an external strike, he feels it inside. There are no bruises, contusions or other external signs of being hit. The damage is done deep inside the body. Lu Shui-T'ien was well known in Korea for his ability to hit a watermelon with a palm strike and turn the insides into liquid. The external watermelon rind would not be broken at all, yet when someone cut the melon open the meat of the watermelon looked as though it had been blasted with a shotgun.

This description of internal power is not news to people who have been practicing internal martial arts. The desire to develop this kind of power is probably why many people are interested in the "internal styles." But how do you develop this power? Some like to profess that it requires years and years of practice with "secret" training methods. Park doesn't feel this way. Development of this ability does take work, however, there is no big secret and there is no "magic." It just requires

a lot of dedication to the practice of proper mechanics and correct *ch'i kung* and there can be no missing pieces. This is why Park's training program is so systematic and why he requires precision in the performance of basic exercises before students are allowed to progress. He does not believe that the practitioner will get there by just practicing choreographed form routines.

Park defines "internal power," in an equation form, as follows:

Internal Power = Internal Striking Mechanics + Ch'i Movement

Where:

Ch'i Movement = Mind (Intention) + Fluid and Relaxed Body Movement + Breathing

Analyzing these equations, it is easy to see why this striking method is called "internal." The development of internal striking mechanics requires the student to start with exercises which condition the muscles, joints, tendons, and ligaments to work in a coordinated, integrated fashion while the body remains relaxed, supple, and structurally aligned. Once development along these lines has occurred through the practice of large body movements, the student will work to refine the movements so that the same result can be obtained through smaller and more subtle movements. The student is taking large physical movements and "internalizing" them.

In addition to the physical mechanics involved in the development of an internal strike, the practitioner will work to develop the *ch'i* component as well. This training involves breathing exercises, meditation, and nonspecific body movement exercises all focused on improving distal circulation of *ch'i* in the body, balancing the *ch'i* in the body, unifying the body's strength, and focusing the mind. The focus of much of this training is turned inward and thus it is easy to see why this component adds to the "internal" aspect of the strike.

If the student spends a few hours every day training the components of internal striking in a progressive manner, internal striking power is attainable. In Park's system, *ch'i* development is trained through a series of progressive meditation, breathing, and *ch'i kung* exercises. In the beginning levels of training the student will practice these components separately (i.e. when first practicing *ch'i kung* body movement exercises, the beginner will not worry about a specific breathing pattern but instead concentrate on obtaining the "*ch'i* feeling"). Each component is developed to some extent separately and then the pieces are brought together so that the meditation, breathing, and *ch'i kung* movements are practiced simultaneously. (A complete description of Park's basic Pa Kua *ch'i kung* training is included later in this book.) After this stage of development, these components are then combined with striking mechanics to develop internal striking skill.

Striking mechanics are developed in Park's school while practicing a series of eight palm striking exercises followed by a series of eight elbow striking exercises. These are then followed by a series of "speed combination" exercises. The speed combinations combine the palm and elbow strikes and teach the student how to apply multiple strikes rapidly. Park's teacher, Lu Shui-T'ien, required him to train each one of the eight palm striking exercises for one hour each day for a period of six months before the next palm exercise was taught. At this rate, it took Park 48 months before he learned all eight of the palm exercises and thus Park refers to this training sequence as "48 month palm." Park does not require his students to practice each palm for such a long time before teaching the next exercise in the sequence, however, he recommends that if the student really wants to develop exceptional striking power, he or she practice as it was traditionally taught.

The Basic Palm Exercises

Before being introduced to the "48 month palm" exercises the student in Park's school will learn two preliminary palm striking exercises - the first is called *tou chang* (shaking palm) and the second is the "dragon back" exercise. The *tou chang* exercise begins to develop the student's ability to relax the body and extend power from the heels up to the palm while rotating the hips and shoulders around the body's central axis. Concentration is focused on completely relaxing the arm, shoulder, and back so that the power is generated from a full body motion and there are no tense areas to block the flow of energy or chain of continuous motion. In this section we will describe these two fundamental exercises and then we will describe the first two of the "48 month palm" exercises.

Tou   Chang

Tou Chang

The goal in developing the first stages of internal striking power in Pa Kua Chang is to cultivate an unbroken chain of fluid movement which extends from the feet all the way up through the palm. To avoid broken links in this chain, the entire body must be loose and flexible, especially in and around the joints. If there are tight or restricted areas, there will be a kink in the chain. Because the chain of movement is from the ground up, Park starts the student training the mechanics from the palm down. The rationale here is simple. If the practitioner trains the mechanics that will develop power initiating in the hips or lower back before having developed proper movement, flexibility, and softness in the upper back, shoulders and arms, the power being generated from the hips and lower back will become restricted when it reaches the upper back, shoulder, or arm and this can cause injury. Thus, although the striking force is coming up from the ground and channeled through the rotation of the hips and shoulders around the body's central axis, the

Photo 1

Photo 2

Photo 3

Photo 4

Photo 5

Photo 6

Photo 7

The *Tou Chang* Exercise (slow set - front view)

focus of the *tou chang* exercise is to relax the arm, shoulder and upper back while training the mechanics of proper motion in these areas.

Park came to his Pa Kua Chang teacher after having studied a Korean "hard style" for a number of years. When his teacher first taught him the *tou chang* exercise, Park's upper body movement was very stiff and mechanical. To help remedy the situation, Lu Shui-T'ien had Park do nothing but follow and observe two cats which lived at Lu's house. Lu told Park to carefully watch the way these cats walked, ran, jumped, pounced, played, and hunted. Everyday for two weeks when Park came to practice he was told, "Go watch the cats." Lu's message was that the only way Park would learn how to properly move his body in Pa Kua

Chang was to learn how to be as flexible, smooth, supple, fluid, light, and quick as the cats.

The *tou chang* exercise is executed as follows:
1) Stand in a "horse" stance with both palms face up and resting by the sides of the rib cage. See photo 1 front view (above) and photo 1 side view (on the next page).
2) One palm moves straight out and rises up at approximately a 45 degree angle. See photo 2, front view and photo 2, side view.
3) The palm continues to rise up until it reaches approximately eye level. The extension of the palm is motivated by the hips and shoulders moving in unison around the central axis of the body. The body's central axis is the imaginary line which extends from the crown of the head down

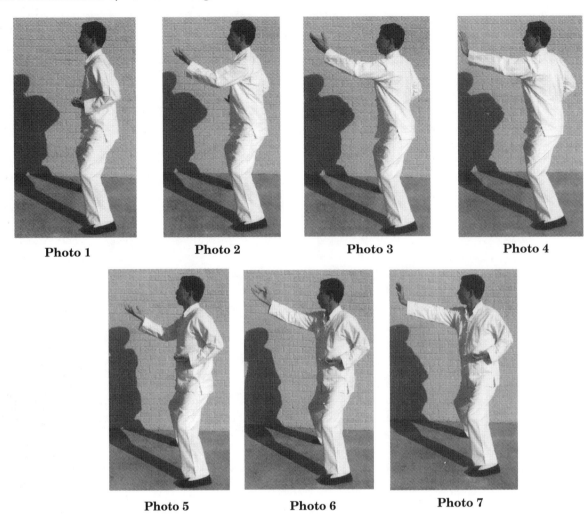

Photo 1 **Photo 2** **Photo 3** **Photo 4**

Photo 5 **Photo 6** **Photo 7**

The *Tou Chang* Exercise (slow set - side view)

through the perineum (in acupuncture terminology the line would be drawn from the *pai hui* through the *hui yin*). See photo 3, front view and photo 3, side view.

4) As the hips and shoulders reach the full extension of their rotation, the palm changes from *yang* (facing up) to *yin* (facing down, or out away from the body). The knees remain facing forward. Do not allow the knees to wobble or sway with the twisting of the hips. See photo 4, front view and photo 4, side view.

5) Repeat steps (1) through (4) with the opposite palm. The palm that was just thrown moves back to the original position beside the rib cage as the next palm is thrown out (see photos 5 through 7 front view and side view).

When executing the *tou chang* maneuver it is important to keep the palm facing up until just before the hip and shoulder reach the point of maximum rotation and the strike is applied.

The Chinese view the energy of the day as being strongest when *yin* is changing to *yang* (sunrise) and when *yang* is changing to *yin* (sunset). This theory carries over to the changing of the palms as well. The palm movements are most powerful when the *yin* palm is changing to the *yang* palm or when the *yang* palm is changing to a the *yin* palm. Typically the *yin* changing to *yang* will be used in conjunction with a defensive maneuver, such as a parry or when freeing one's self from an opponent's grab, and the *yang*

154

changing to *yin* will be used in conjunction with an offensive strike.

Training Stages

As stated in the footwork chapter, Park encourages his students to train any exercise that he teaches in several progressive stages. First the exercise is executed very slowly with concentration on the proper body alignments and the correct mechanics of the movements. The student works the exercise slowly until it can be executed with exactness and fluidity. During the *tou chang* exercise the mind is focused on the striking palm. By focusing intently on the striking palm the student begins to form a mind/body/nervous system connection. The mind intention is what leads the energy movement in the body, if the intention is keen, the energy movement is full, complete, and rapid. Park often explains this principle through an example. He states that if a person was to put a healthy arm in a sling for a week and not use that arm at all, when the arm came out of the sling it would be stiff and hard to move even though it was healthy when it went into the sling. It is stiff because it was not used and therefore the mind did not think about moving the arm. Because the mind did not send signals for the arm to move (place intent in the arm) the energy and nerve impulse travel to that arm was minimal. Although the muscles in the arm are healthy they do not operate properly without continual stimulation from the mind and nervous system.

When the body moves slowly and the intention is focused on that movement, more energy, blood, and nerve impulse moves into the areas of the body where the intent is focused. Because the body is moving slow, more muscle control is

1   2   3   4   5

6   7   8   9

The *Tou Chang* Exercise (fast set)

required. When more muscle control is required and the intention is sending more nerve impulses to the muscles, more muscle fibers are activated and thus the muscles are trained more completely. Additionally, because the practitioner strives to relax the major muscle groups while in motion, secondary muscle groups, which may not usually be under conscious control, come into action to help move the body and thus there is a more complete muscle development in the execution of the movement. When the muscles are trained in this manner and the intention is focused, a seemingly unnatural amount of strength can be developed. This component is trained very fully in T'ai Chi Ch'uan and I-Ch'uan practice.

The next step is to execute the exercise with power. The power in the *tou chang* exercise is generated by a quick and aggressive rotation of the hips and shoulders moving in unison around the body's central axis. When this stage is executed, the upper body, shoulders, and arms are very relaxed. The arm is thrown out in a movement similar to the cracking of a whip. The intention, alignments, mechanics, and muscles are conditioned properly during the first, or slow movement, stage. This second stage takes these components and brings them all together in a quick burst in order to develop "short" or "shock" power. The difference between "long" or "heavy" power and "short" or "shock" power will be explained later in this chapter. The photo sequence on the previous page demonstrates this exercise executed with power.

The third stage of execution of any exercise in Park's system is to execute the exercise with power and speed. In the *tou chang* exercise the element of speed is added by executing left/right striking combinations in rapid succession. The left palm is thrown with power and then this strike is immediately followed by a quick powerful strike with the right hand. This exercise enables the practitioner to develop the ability to move the upper body quickly around the body's central axis. During the exercise, the student should concentrate on keeping the body vertical and stable. There should be no bouncing up and down, shifting of weight from one leg to the other, or swaying back and forth. The body simply rotates quickly around its center.

The fourth stage of execution is to combine the palm exercise with Pa Kua Chang footwork. This stage is divided into two "sub-stages." The first sub-stage is to practice the footwork and hand work in combination through slow deliberate movements as described in the previous chapter. The second sub-stage is to add power into the striking and stepping combination. Adding powerful strikes in combination with the stepping movements will be described later in this chapter.

In the fifth stage of training any exercise the student will work to refine the movements of the exercise so that large movements become very small. After training the *tou chang* exercise for a sufficient amount of time the practitioner should be able to lay his or her palm on an opponent's body and, without pulling the palm back off of the body at all, apply a very powerful strike with a quick "shaking" of the body around its central axis. The power from this "shaking" of the body is similar to that achieved by a dog shaking water off of its wet coat.

The sixth stage of training these exercises is to work on linking continuous combinations of the palm strikes with elbow strikes and footwork. In Park's system this component is trained by first executing a variety of "speed combination" drills while standing in a static posture and later executing the same combinations together with stepping maneuvers.

Breathing

Correct breathing in conjunction with proper body motion is critical in the development of the internal strike. The mechanics of correct breathing during the execution of a strike will significantly enhance the movement of *ch'i* in the body. Rapid movement of *ch'i* from the *tan t'ien* to the palm is a crucial component of the internal striking ability. In order to develop this ability fully, specific *ch'i kung* breathing methods are practiced so that the *tan t'ien* and the *ch'i* are developed in a progressive manner. The basics of this process are outlined in the *ch'i kung* chapter of this book.

While executing the basic palm exercises which are described in this book, the practitioner will exhale forcefully through the nose in unison with the striking motion. The practitioner will

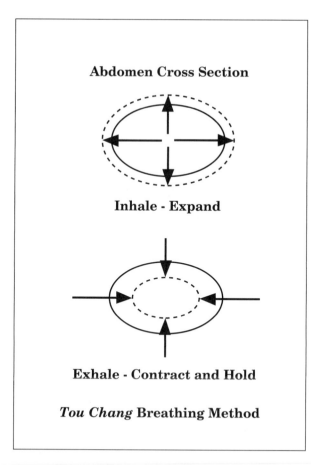

Abdomen Cross Section

Inhale - Expand

Exhale - Contract and Hold

***Tou Chang* Breathing Method**

abdominal development exercises are outlined in the *ch'i kung* section of this book.

After inhaling fully, the practitioner will exhale by physically contracting the lower abdomen and thus applying pressure on all sides of the *tan t'ien*. Making the audible "grunt" with the exhale will help the abdomen contract properly. When the abdomen has been fully contracted the practitioner will not relax the abdominal muscles, but will still maintain a slight tension in the lower abdomen as if to hold the *tan t'ien* slightly compressed until the next inhale. The exhale is short and sharp. The compression on the lower *tan t'ien* will help "pump" the *ch'i* throughout the body. With the intention and correct body motion guiding the *ch'i*, it will naturally be directed to the palm.

Beginning students should not concentrate too much on the breathing mechanics. The audible exhale will be enough to allow the lower abdomen to contract. Beginners should focus on the proper physical mechanics of the *tou chang* movement and on keeping the body relaxed. After the student has been properly trained through a correct series of Park's "prescription" breathing exercises, the lower abdominal breathing will be developed and the student can work to integrate the breathing with the palm striking exercise in a more complete manner.

Because the *tou chang* breathing method, combined with the relaxed body, vigorous whipping motion of the body around its center, and focus intention on the palms, helps to stimulate the flow of *ch'i* and blood in the entire body, Park recommends that even students who are not interested in learning how to defend themselves practice this exercise. Park has a number of students who come to study with him in order to improve their health. He will devise a unique training program for each individual which will allow the body's health to improve in a safe, gentle manner. When the student's body has progressed to the stage where they can properly execute the *tou chang* exercise, Park will have them practice this exercise in order to allow the body to further loosen and relax while the pumping of the *tan t'ien* and the whipping motion of the exercise stimulate *ch'i* flow in areas that are obstructed.

also audibly "grunt" as the air is passing out of the nose. The exact sound of the "grunt" at this point is nonspecific.

In order to help propel *ch'i* from the lower abdomen to the palm when executing the palm strike, the inhale and exhale are executed in a specific manner. When the practitioner inhales, he or she allows the entire lower abdomen to expand. There should be expansion in both the forward and backward directions as shown in the illustration above. The practitioner should work to allow the expansion to occur in the lowest portion of the abdomen (in the pelvic region, below the belly). Remember that the *tan t'ien* is located approximately three inches below the navel and thus expansion of the *tan t'ien* occurs much lower than the belly.

Development of correct abdominal breathing is trained in Park's school through a series of progressive breathing exercises. The basic breathing exercises which are taught prior to the

Photo 1   Photo 2   Photo 3

Photo 4   Photo 5   Photo 6

The Dragon Back Exercise (slow set)

By simply working diligently with the *tou chang* exercise everyday, the practitioner can develop an incredible amount of striking power. Lu Shui-T'ien told Park that when he was in China, traveling on horse back, a farmer saw him on the road late one night and invited him to take his night's rest at his home. When the farmer found out who Lu was, he asked if he could teach him something about martial arts before he left the next day. In gratitude for the farmer's kindness in giving him a place to sleep for the night, Lu taught him the *tou chang* exercise.

Two years later Lu happened by the same area of the country and stopped to see the farmer. Lu had not expected the farmer to have practiced the exercise, however, the farmer told him that he had indeed practiced everyday. The farmer was proud of the ability he had developed and wanted to give Lu a demonstration. He brought out one of his sheep and struck it with his palm. The sheep let out a cry and was stunned for a moment but then walked away as though nothing had happened. Lu congratulated the farmer on his practice and was surprised that he had practice so hard for two years on this one exercise. "What's the point?", one might ask. Nothing happened to the sheep, right? The next day when they went outside, the sheep was dead. When they cut it open they saw that it had bleed to death internally.

Dragon Back

After the student has developed flexibility, fluidity of motion, and the proper mechanics associated with the *tou chang* exercise, Park will teach another preliminary exercise which is practiced prior to learning the first of the "48 month palms." This exercise trains the back and spine to perform what Park calls the "dragon back" movement.

The "dragon back" movement is a segmented whipping of the spine to produce a "whip cracking" effect at the palms. The whipping of the spine is executed in this exercise through a large range of motion so that the muscles of the upper and lower back which surround the spine become loose and supple. Suppleness along the spine will not only help the practitioner in the mechanical execution of this component of striking, but will also encourage the flow of *ch'i* from the *tan t'ien*, along the spine and out to the palms. As in the *tou chang* exercise, once the muscles have been trained by executing the exercise through a large range of motion, the motion is refined so that the effect is achieved while the body movement is minimal, or in many cases, undetectable to an untrained observer. Park can execute this spine rippling mechanic so subtly that it is undetectable to the eye, however, if one were to place their hand on his spine when he is striking, the slight rippling motion of the spine can be felt.

A verbal explanation of this exercise is very difficult and photos are not much help, this is one reason why this book comes with a companion video in which the exercises are demonstrated by Park himself. The mechanics of this motion are very similar to those used in cracking a whip, but now the whip is the practitioners spine. The

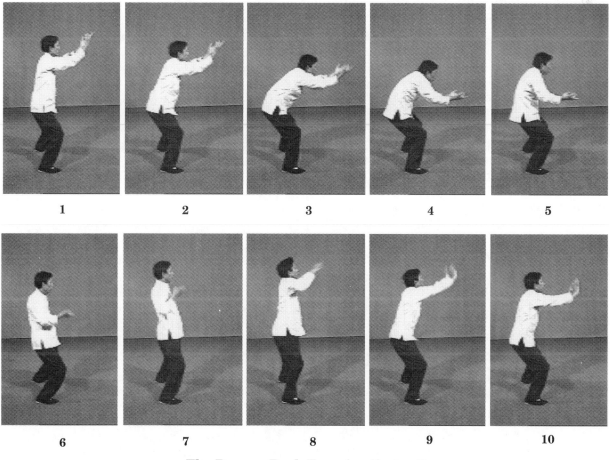

The Dragon Back Exercise (fast set)

"dragon back" exercise is executed as follows:

1) The practitioner assumes a "horse" stance with the palms facing up and extended out in front of the body as shown in photo 1 on the previous page. The shoulders are relaxed and held naturally.

2) The coccyx is tucked under while the area of the lower back known in Chinese medicine as the *ming men* (located between the second and third lumbar vertebra) is pulled back. The palms remain facing up and extended out slightly. The shoulders remain relaxed. See photo 2.

3) The middle back arches like a cat getting ready to pounce. The transition from step (2) to step (3) should be smooth, fluid, and continuous. The shoulders remain relaxed and dropped down even though the upper back is arched. The palms remain extended. See photo 3.

4) As the "ripple" or "wave" continues up to the upper part of the back, the lower back, which has been tucked under, flattens out to prepare for the next undulation, resembling the snapping motion executed when cracking a whip. The practitioner has now rippled a wave all the way up the spine and is back in a position similar to that shown in photo 1 (see photo 4). The motion the practitioner has executed so far is similar to the motion used when drawing back a whip right before executing the quick cracking motion. This first wave is executed slowly and with relatively large movements (a big wave).

5) From the position in step (4) the practitioner will tuck the coccyx under once again, however, this time it snaps quickly and sends another wave, which moves much more rapidly than the first, back up the spine (photo 5). The practitioner will allow this small, fast wave to extend out the arms and as the wave reaches the end of the arms the palms turn over (see photo 6). This "cracking" wave is much more subtle than the first "wind-up" wave.

During the execution of this exercise the entire upper body remains relaxed and the movement is motivated by the pelvis rocking forward, then rocking back, and then snapping forward. The shoulders should remain relaxed and dropped down throughout the entire exercise. If the shoulders and arms are not relaxed sufficiently, the snapping motion of the spine will create a small whiplash-like effect in the neck and head

which may cause discomfort. If the shoulders and arms are relaxed, all the power generated in the back will travel out to the palms and thus will not go up to the head.

This exercise is demonstrated at full speed in the sequence of photos shown on the previous page. This sequence should give the reader a better understanding of the mechanics involved.

Single Palm Change Exercise (*Tan Huan Chang*)

After having practiced the *tou chang* and "dragon back" exercises for a sufficient amount of time, Park will then teach the student the first of the eight "48 month" palms. In this first palm exercise, *tan huan chang* or single palm change exercise, the practitioner will learn to combine the "dragon back" mechanics with the rotation of the body around its central axis which was practiced in the *tou chang* exercise. When the performing these mechanics correctly and combining them with the *ch'i* component, a tremendous amount of power can be generated with very small, subtle movements.

While producing a great amount of power through small, subtle movements is an eventual goal in internal arts practice, before small movements can be used effectively, the body is trained through practice with larger movements and the use of force which is not so subtle. Although this force is applied while the practitioner maintains a relaxed body, it is still *ming ching*, or obvious power, which is being applied during the initial training stages. The practitioner starts the training process with large movements so that the muscles, joints, tendons, bones, and ligaments can be properly stretched, loosened, and otherwise developed. The practitioner can only move on to small, subtle movements after the body has been

Tan   *Huan*   *Chang*

Photo 1　　Photo 2　　Photo 3　　Photo 4

Photo 5　　Photo 6　　Photo 7　　Photo 8

Photo 9　　Photo 10　　Photo 11　　Photo 12

The Single Palm Change (*Tan Huan Chang*) Exercise (slow set)

1   2   3   4

5   6   7   8

9   10   11   12

The Single Palm Change (*Tan Huan Chang*) Exercise (fast set)

The Single Palm Change (*Tan Huan Chang*) Exercise (fast set - con't)

fully developed. Thus, while the movements in the *tan huan chang* exercise are large at first, they become very small and are executed quickly in actual application.

The *tan huan chang* exercise is executed as follows:

1) The practitioner assumes a dragon stance posture with the arms held as shown in photograph 1 on page 161. Both palms are facing up. The upper palm is held at eye level and the lower palm is held near the elbow of the upper palm.

2) The practitioner steps out in an extended "bow" stance while maintaining the same upper body position (see photo 2).

3) From the posture above, the practitioner begins to execute the "dragon back" motion with the back while simultaneously twisting at the

hips and pulling back the hip which is on the side of the striking hand (see photo 3). The body and hand movements are greatly exaggerated when the beginner first starts practicing this exercise. Remember, at this stage it is a body conditioning exercise. When these striking mechanics are applied in combat, the movement is so small it is barely apparent to the observer.

4) The practitioner continues with the dragon back movement. As the second wave is whipped out, the hip which was pulled back is also thrown forward with the palm strike. As in the previous two exercises, the palm does not turn over until just before the hip reaches its full extension. The full extension of the hip is timed to occur simultaneously with the second whipping motion of the dragon back body action. See photos 4 and 5.

5) From this position the practitioner will draw the front leg back and assume a "cat" stance with the majority of the weight on the back leg. While the forward leg is drawing back, the practitioner executes the *fan chang* maneuver. See photos 6 and 7.

6) Now the practitioner begins the dragon back motion again in order to prepare to throw the other palm (photo 8). As the back arches, the hip on the side of the striking hand also pulls back.

7) As the second wave of the dragon back cracks, the hip is thrown forward and the palm is thrown (see photo 9).

8) The practitioner executes *fan chang* once again while stepping forward into the extended bow stance posture in preparation for the next repetition of the exercise. See photos 10 through 12.

The fast set sequence is shown on the previous two pages.

Double Palm Change Exercise (*Shuang Huan Chang*)

The next exercise in the "48 month" palm series is known as the "double palm change exercise." In this exercise, the practitioner will perform the double palm striking movement which was executed in the dragon back exercise, however it is now performed from the dragon stance posture instead of the horse stance. This

Photo 1   Photo 2   Photo 3

Photo 4   Photo 5   Photo 6

The Double Palm Change (*Shuang Huan Chang*) Exercise (slow set)

The Double Palm Change (*Shuang Huan Chang*) Exercise (fast set)

Shuang   Huan   Chang

exercise is depicted as a slow set in the photographs below and as a fast set in the photographs on the opposite page.

In performing this exercise the practitioner will start from the dragon stance posture with the palms held out at eye level, both palms facing up (see photo 1 on page 164). From this position the practitioner will execute the dragon back movement as practiced in the dragon back exercise. This movement is best displayed in the fast set series on the opposite page (photos 1 through 8). The slow set is performed in the same manner as the fast set, however, in the slow set the focus is on stretching the spine and maintaining the proper mechanics while in the fast set the focus is on getting power to the palms.

After the strike has been thrown, the practitioner will drop the hands down by the sides (as shown in photo 4 of the slow sequence), bring the hands up and out to the sides (see slow sequence photo 5, fast sequence photos 10 through 12), and then the hands come over top and back to the starting position (see photos 12 through 14 of the fast set).

The practitioner will practice this set for as many repetitions as desired and then switch to the other side by stepping back and allowing the opposite foot to be forward.

Through diligent practice of the *tou chang* and "dragon back" exercises, the follow-on "48 month" palm exercises, and the *ch'i kung* associated with these palm methods, the Pa Kua Chang practitioner in Park's school learns to develop an extremely powerful palm strike which, eventually, will require very little body motion to execute. Because the Pa Kua Chang practitioner can apply his palm strikes at close range and at any angle with little or no "pull-back" or "wind-up" and because these palm applications are combined with the evasive

footwork and snake-like body movements characteristic of Pa Kua Chang, these palms seem to appear out of nowhere and are delivered with an unbelievable amount of power.

Controlling the Power

Once the student in Park's school has practiced all of the "48 month" palms for a sufficient amount of time, Park will then teach the student how to control the power that the student can now generate. Through practice of the "48 month" palms in conjunction with the breathing and *ch'i kung* exercises taught in Park's school, the student can generate a tremendous amount of power in a strike. Unless the student learns how to control this power, it can be very dangerous when the student is learning how to spar with training partners. In addition to learning how to control the power in terms of magnitude of force, the student will also learn how to focus and direct the power in this stage of training.

Park tells a story about one of his students in Korea who loved to practice the "48 month palms." Everyday when the student came to practice, the palm exercises where the only thing he would perform. He spent hours everyday working with these exercises. One day the student had to go to his employer's house to pick up something for his boss. When the student approached the front door, his boss' dog came running at him and leapt towards him. The student smacked the dog to stop him. The dog yelped and then ran away. The next day the dog was dead. When the vet opened the dog up to see why it had died, he saw that the dog's internal organs had been ruptured and the dog had bled to death internally. This student had not learned to control his power and had inflicted unnecessary damage on the dog.

Park speaks of many exercises that his teacher taught him in order to learn how to control, focus, and direct the power he had developed while practicing the "48 month" palm exercises. Each of the "48 month" palms has a separate series of follow-on training exercises which involve striking various types of objects and apparatus. These exercises are designed to develop the practitioner's ability to control the amount of power in a strike and also control where the force of the strike is directed and to what degree the force of the strike will penetrate the body which is being hit. The majority of these exercises are designed to learn how to control what Park calls the "shock" power. Some also refer to this expression of force as "short" energy.

"Shock" vs. "Heavy"

There are generally two types of power application which Park speaks of in the internal martial arts. The first, which he calls "heavy *ch'i*", is also referred to as "long energy" or "long force." This application of force is exemplified in a T'ai Chi push. When this kind of technique is applied, the opponent, when thrown or pushed, will generally travel a long distance, as if being picked up and carried away. When a "long" energy technique is executed the practitioner's force is applied over a relatively long period of time (long meaning a few seconds). Someone who is very good at applying long energy can apply it so smoothly and subtly that the opponent is not even aware it is occurring; he or she suddenly finds themselves airborne without knowing how it happened. Usually long, or heavy, energy is a smooth application of power and although the opponent is thrown a long distance, they are generally not damaged internally.

The application of what Park calls "shock *ch'i*" (also referred to as "short" energy) is quite different. In terms of time vs. power, all of the power in a pure shock technique is applied instantaneously (see "time vs. force" illustration). If the strike is executed correctly, the energy from this strike will penetrate deep into the opponent's body and stay there.

The force of the shock strike is not comparable to that of the "battering ram effect" which plows through the opponent, the "hammer effect" which inflicts damage topically, or the "axe effect" which seems to cut through the opponent. The force of this strike penetrates the opponent's body and reverberates inside that body. A person on the receiving end of this strike does not feel as if he or she were pushed, smacked, yanked, or slammed; they feel as though they were "shocked" or otherwise severely rattled from the inside out.

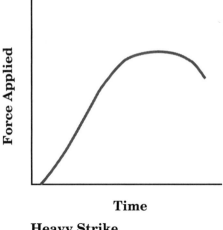

Heavy Strike

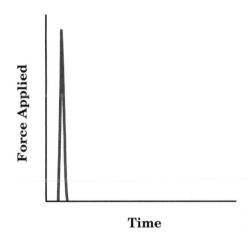

Shock Strike

(Time vs. Force Applied graphs suggested by Ken Fish)

In most instances the force of the "shock" strike is not applied until after the practitioner's hand is on the opponent's body. When the strike is applied, the subtle whipping of the body through segmented articulations of the joints expresses a powerful force initiating from the ground and traveling up and out to the hand. The shaking of the body which accompanies the whipping force results in this force being applied for only a fraction of a second. This extremely short, focused expression of force produces a concussive effect in the opponent's body. The effect of this explosive force being applied and then instantaneously taken away causes the opponent's body to collapse on itself as muscles will go into spasm in reaction to the force. Primary targets for induction of spasm are the heart and lungs of the opponent.

This "shock" application is very dangerous as it can cause the opponent's internal body tissue to rupture and tear or it can induce severe secondary muscle spasm. A person hit with pure shock energy will not be thrown back at all, they will simply drop where they are standing or double over in pain. If the opponent is thrown back, the technique was not purely applied. The goal is to get all of the energy and force of the strike to remain inside the opponent's body, not travel through the opponent. This occurs when the tremendous force is applied for an instant and then taken away.

If a martial arts practitioner applies power quickly and the opponent is thrown backward, the power application is not true "shock" power, it is lies somewhere between the "shock" power and the "long" or "heavy" power. If one were to consider the "shock" power as being *yang* and the "long" power as being *yin*, the relative nature of the *yin* and *yang* analogy would tell us that there would be a continuum of power application variations based on a mixture of "shock" and "long" power. Part of the control aspect of learning how to strike involves controlling the percentages of these two striking components in any given strike. In some instances a practitioner will want to apply a pure "shock" strike, while in other situations a "heavy" strike would be better employed. In many other situations a strike containing a mixture of these characteristics is appropriate.

Training how to "shake" the body as a dog shakes when throwing water of its coat by learning how to rapidly rotating the hips and shoulders in an explosive manner around the body's central axis is initiated through practice of the "*tou chang*" exercise. Training how to "whip" the striking arm by generating power through segmented joint articulations was initiated through practice of the "dragon back" exercise. Becoming skilled at these two exercises forms the first stage of learning how to apply "shock" power. As the mechanics are continually trained and the movements become more and more subtle, a quick shaking motion of the body is all that is required to deliver a deadly

striking technique. When this power is applied correctly, there is literally a whiplash like effect inside the opponent's body. A short shock wave enters the opponent's body and reverberates.

Controlling the "Shock"

When Park first began to train how to control the "shock" strike, he was living in his teacher's home. His teacher hung a medium size bag full of saw dust in the bathroom doorway. Every time Park entered or left the bathroom he had to strike this bag with full force and the bag was not to swing. If the bag moved laterally when it was struck, the shock strike was not applied purely. The bag could shake or bounce when it was hit, but not swing or sway.

One important point worth mentioning; when Park was trained he spent a few years working with only the *tou chang* and dragon back exercise before he was taught the first "48 month palm" exercise. Subsequently he spent 4 years practicing the 8 palms of the "48 month palm" method. It was only after all of that training that he was taught any palm striking methods which involved hitting an object or apparatus. Like the exercises described in this chapter, all of the "48 month palm" exercises first involve striking into the air without hitting an object. Obviously if one is training to defend themselves and strike people, it would be wise to obtain a feeling for what it would be like to hit solid objects by doing so in training. Hitting a solid object, such as a person, is much different than just hitting air.

The reason Park insists that a student not hit a solid object until the student has spent a long time practicing the "48 month" palm exercises is simple. When practicing the correct mechanics of an internal "shock" strike, if the student hits a solid object before the body is conditioned fully, it is very easy to cause damage to the body. The mechanics of the movement, structural alignments, and fullness of *ch'i* to the palm and arm must all be in place before Park will allow a student to hit a solid object. If this type of strike is applied incorrectly, it is very easy for the "shock" which is applied to come back into the practitioner's arm and cause damage. Even when a student in Park's school begins training to hit objects, the objects are never too solid or heavy and always have some "give" to them.

Another method that Park used to train "shock" power was to hit and break a board which was floating in water. In order to be able to break the board, all of the force from the strike must stay in the board. If too much force moves beyond the board, the board will simply bob up and down in the water and will not break.

In order to learn how to make the shock of this strike penetrate, Lu Shui-T'ien had Park practice another method which involved a large bucket of water. However, this time instead of keeping the energy on the surface in order to break a board, the "shock" of the strike had to penetrate the water and break a cake of tofu that was placed in the bottom of the bucket. Park states that his teacher could slap the top surface of the water without hardly any water being splashed and the cake of tofu in the bottom of the bucket would explode.

A third method trained Park's ability to control the depth and direction of the force. This method involved hitting a watermelon. The rind of the water melon could not be damaged by the strike, however, the inside of the watermelon would be destroyed. Lu Shui-T'ien could call out which part of the watermelon's insides would be damaged before he hit the melon. He would say, left side, right side, middle, bottom, or top, and whatever he called, when they cut the melon open, that was the part that was damaged. Park was required to learn to perform this same exercise.

Lu Shui-T'ien's ability to direct and control his power was phenomenal. Park said that one day he was outside of Lu's house practicing and he heard Lu arguing with his son. Lu got so mad at his son that he shot the tip of his cane within inches of his son's head and it penetrated the middle of a window glass pane. The spearing of the cane through the window pane had been so fast and powerful that the window pane did not shatter. The cane's tip simply knocked out a "bullet hole" in the center of the window. Lu's son ran outside after his father had almost hit him with the cane. Lu Shu-Te looked at Park and said, "Did you see what he did! I know my father is mad at me, but I am so proud of him. I don't think many people in the world could ever do that."

Why Strike with the Palm?

We mentioned at the top of this chapter that the Pa Kua Chang style of Chinese martial arts has become famous for its employment of devastating palm strikes. One might ask why a fighting art would focus on the development of a palm strike when so many other martial styles and pugilistic sports employ the fist as the primary weapon.

Park states that in striking with the palm, the practitioner gains a greater amount of control over the force which is produced from the striking mechanics associated with the Pa Kua Chang movements. It is easier to produce the implosion force of the "shock" strike inside the opponent's body if the palm is used as the striking weapon and it is easier to control the direction of that force. Because of the way the joints are articulated in producing the "shock" force, the palm allows for a more refined control of both the physical force and the *ch'i* that is expressed in this strike.

Intermediate Palm Training Methods

As we have mentioned previously, after the student in Park's school has become proficient in the *tou chang* exercise and the dragon back exercise he or she will then start training the "48 month" palm exercises. The first two of those palm training exercises are the single palm change (*tan huan chang*) exercise and the double palm change (*shuang huan chang*) exercise. The remaining six of the eight "48 month" palms will not be presented in this book, however, since Park will be presenting these palm training skills in the future in video format and in his seminars, we list their names here in English and Chinese for reference:

The "48 month" palms

1) Single Palm Change
   (*tan huan chang*)

2) Double Palm Change
   (*shuang huan chang*)

3) Throwing Palm
   (*shuai chang*)

4) Slapping Palm
   (*p'u chang*)

5) Lifting Palm
   (*t'o chang*)

6) Chopping Palm
   (*k'an chang*)

7) White Clouds Chasing
   the Stars (*pai yun chui hsing*)

8) Sliding the Window Shutter to Look
   at the Moon (*tui ch'uang wang yue*)

Each of these palm exercises is designed to train specific striking mechanics. By diligently practicing each of these exercises thousands of times the student in Park's school learns how to use the palm in striking upward, downward, to the side, to the rear, forward and diagonally in an efficient and effective manner. By gaining a body knowledge through these repetitive exercises, the practitioner can easily understand how each movement of a form can be applied in a tactical situation and how each movement can be varied in order to be adopted to fit the changes which inevitably occur in the heat of combat.

Supplementary Palms

In addition to the "48 month" palms, the student in Park's school will learn and practice supplementary palm striking skills in order to

develop a full arsenal of defense and attack options in combat. Whereas the "48 month" palms are single palm techniques practiced repeatedly to develop power in applying the palm striking skills in all directions, the supplementary palms are primarily made up of striking combinations. These combinations are not developed from any of the "48 month" palms, however, many are derived from techniques which appear in the Pa Kua Chang combat forms. Park believes that after the student has practiced these palms in isolated, repetitive sets, he or she will be able to easily apply them in forms practice. As we have stated earlier in this book, the philosophy behind this method of practice is that the practitioner develops proficiency and skill with any movement while practicing that movement in an isolated, repetitive manner. In this manner the mechanics are trained, the body is developed, and a "muscle memory" is ingrained. After all of this development occurs, the student can then use the forms practice to refine these skills and link them with other skills.

The first few supplementary palms a student will learn are as follows:

1) Piercing Palm
   (*ch'uan chang*)

2) Three Basins Settling to the Ground
   (*san pan luo ti*)

3) Swallow Penetrates through the Forest
   (*yen tzu ch'uan lin*)

4) Scooping the Moon from the Sea Bottom
   (*hai ti lao yue*)

Fighting Skill: Adding Power and Speed

Adding Power to the "Hand + Step + Body" Equation

Looking back at the exercise described earlier in this book where the *fan chang* technique was combined with footwork, one may wonder how this slight turning of the palm can generate enough power to damage an opponent. Keep in mind that the application of an internal strike is much different than the familiar "external" punch, or external strike. As we have stated above, the application of a powerful internal strike does not require a "pull back and throw" type movement as is executed in an external strike. An internal strike can be "thrown" effectively from zero distance.

In Park's school, after the student has worked with a few of the palm exercises and begins to develop the basic striking mechanics, these mechanics are applied to the "hand + body movement + footwork" equation and the student begins to understand how the simple *fan chang* movement can produce a damaging attack. The stepping exercises start to look much different at this point. Until this stage in the training process the student has only practiced coordinating the *fan chang* movement with the stepping patterns as was discussed in the previous chapter. As we have mentioned in this chapter, training slowly and methodically not only helps the student learn how to execute the movements correctly in a fluid, smooth, and relaxed manner, but also helps the student develop the "heavy" or "long" energy application of the movement and condition the body for the next level of training.

The next stage in the training process is to add the quick snapping, or whipping, motion developed in the palm exercises to the *fan chang* maneuver executed in conjunction with the steps. The steps are now executed quickly and powerfully as are the changes. The student will practice these "hand + step + power" exercises just as the stepping exercises were first practiced. Simple straight line sets are practiced, then stepping patterns are

practiced, and then stepping combinations are practiced.

After the student has become familiar with these exercises, Park will teach a series of eight "straight-line" fighting sets. Each of these sets consist of two or three defense/attack combinations which are practiced while stepping forward along a straight line utilizing either the jump step, the full step, or the full step with a jump. The combinations expressed in these sets are designed to be utilized in opening up an opponent's body, or blocking an opponent's attack, and then moving in for an attack. After the student shows some proficiency in performing these sets in straight-line practice, the student will then pair up with a partner and research attack and defense strategies using these techniques. First the partner practice is performed with the partners facing each other squarely and later the partner's learn to employ these techniques while walking the circle.

Through the partner practice the student will gain experiential knowledge pertaining to the utilization of hand, body, and footwork in setting up an attack, opening up the an opponent for easy attack, evading an attack and counter-attacking, and obtaining superior body positioning. Once these skills are developed to a sufficient level of proficiency, the student will study combining skills which were developed in the "48 month" palm set, the supplementary palm set and the eight elbow set with the straight line attacking drills.

Adding Speed to the Equation

Park Bok Nam's equation for overall Pa Kua Chang fighting skill reads as follows:

Fighting Skill = Hand + Body + Step + Internal Power + Speed

171

The sub-components of this equation, as discussed thus far in this book, are as follows:

Hand Skill = Fan Chang + Circle Principle + "48 Month" Palms + Supplementary Palms

Body Skill = Flexibility + Stability + Coordination + Integration + Relaxation + Connection + Circle Principle

Stepping Skill = Pa Fang Ken Pu + Circle Walk + Pivot Step + K'ou Pu Pai Pu

Internal Power = Striking Mechanics + Ch'i Movement

Hopefully the reader now has a fundamental understanding of how Park teaches his students to develop these four sub-components of the fighting skill equation. We have yet to fully discuss the last element of this equation, which is "speed." Although, as one might imagine, this component does involve "swiftness of action," Park prefers to teach his students to develop this component while focused on "economy of motion."

In developing speed, one school of thought would employ training which will condition the practitioner to move faster through a given distance. While this is an appropriate approach, it is really a dead end street as the human body can only be trained to move so fast and as the body ages, that speed is naturally diminished. Instead of increasing the velocity at which the distance is traveled, Park's approach is to teach the student how to decrease the distance.

Decreasing the distance one has to travel in order to apply his or her fighting art is attained through a study of geometry and combinations. The blueprint for this study is found in the combinations and angles described by the eight trigrams and their corresponding geometrical arrangements.

One rule of thumb Park will have his students utilize in developing the economy of motion necessary to increase fighting speed is "attack the closest part of the opponent's body with whichever one of your weapons is closest." An example Park likes to give to demonstrate this rule is as follows:

If opponent "A" exposes his flank to opponent "B" as depicted in the illustration on the next page, and "B" executes a side kick to that open area, one option "A" might employ to block that kick is to block down with his hand as shown in illustration #2. The problem with this block is that it is very slow. The blocking hand has to travel through an 180° arc to reach the kicking foot. No matter how hard "A" practices that blocking technique, he or she will only get the hand to move so fast through that 180° arc.

A much better solution to the problem is shown in illustration #3. "A" simply lowers the elbow and strikes the incoming foot. In order to make this technique work best, "A" will pivot step while he or she is striking with the elbow. If the pivot step is employed, the kick will not land even if the elbow strike misses its mark.

Although this example is very simple, one can see how the employment of smart and efficient methods of attack and defense can increase the practitioner's overall speed in combat. All of the "speed combination" exercises that a student in Park's school learns to employ are based on well researched attack and defense combinations that allow the practitioner to be very fast and efficient when employing this fighting method.

Researching optimum angles of movement and striking combinations to develop speed is rooted in the Pa Kua Chang philosophy of the eight direction circle and the eight diagram combinations (hexagrams). While a complete discussion of how these angles and combinations are used to develop incredible speed is beyond the scope of this book, the underlying premise is that the less movement the practitioner has to make when blocking, evading, or striking, the faster he or she is going to be.

Once a practitioner has developed the ability to strike using internal power, little or no movement is required to issue an effective strike. Given this internal striking ability and knowledge of how to combine blocking and striking movements using the hands, wrists, elbows, shoulders, hips, knees, heels, and feet as weapons, one can begin to see how a practitioner can learn to dispense a lot of damage on an opponent in a very short amount of time.

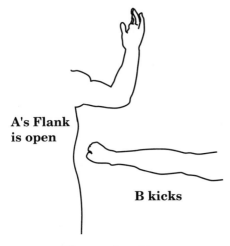

Illustration #1

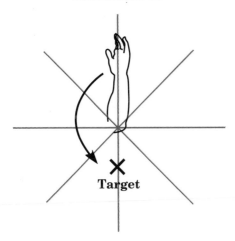

Illustration #2 - Inefficient

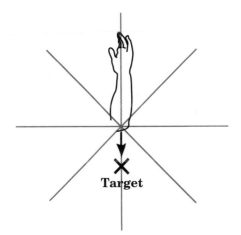

Illustration #3 - Efficient

Chapter 6
Pa Kua Chang Ch'i Kung

Chapter 6

Pa Kua Chang Ch'i Kung

In Park's Pa Kua Chang system, the development of *ch'i* through the practice of breathing exercises, meditation, and nonspecific body movements designed to increase distal circulation of *ch'i* and blood in the body are extremely important components in the overall Pa Kua Chang training program. Everyone has *ch'i* in their body, however, in some instances it is weak in areas and in other instances it does not flow smoothly or fully due to blockages. The goal of *ch'i kung* practice is to develop a full, balanced expression of the *ch'i* in the body. When the *ch'i* is full, balanced, and can flow without obstruction, the body's power can be optimally coordinated and unified for a specific purpose. Whether this purpose be healing or self-defense, the first priority of a *ch'i kung* system should be to balance the body's energy.

As we mentioned in the introduction to this book, every complete Chinese martial arts system will include elements of the following:

1) *Ch'i Kung* - breath control, visualization, and non-specific body movement techniques for various purposes - increased circulation to the distal points of the extremities, increased vital capacity, meditation, and *ch'i* development.

2) *Nei Kung* - training designed specifically for the development of muscle groups, ligaments, and tendons not usually under conscious control.

3) *Wai Kung* - external, i.e. visible, aspects of any martial art including firm balance, flexibility, good posture and stance work, proper structural and mechanical alignment, coordination, and stability.

Ideally, these elements will be developed in a progressive, balanced curriculum designed by an experienced teacher who will guide each student's individual development. Pa Kua Chang, being a complete martial art system, contains elements of all three of these disciplines.

In its final form, Pa Kua Chang movement will contain all of these elements integrated together. However, in Park Bok Nam's school the beginning students will train specific exercises designed to develop these three components separately. In this section of the book we will present the basic level of Park's Pa Kua Chang *ch'i kung* system.

What is *Ch'i*?

We will not try to strictly define *ch'i* in this book, but we are going to make the assumption that everyone has something in their body which the Chinese call "*ch'i*." We are going to further assume that this *ch'i* can be divided into the two general categories of internal *ch'i* (*nei ch'i*) and external *ch'i* (*wai ch'i*).

Park likes to give the following example to help define these two different types of "energy" in the body. Take two individuals and send them to work; one goes to a construction job and digs ditches, the other goes to an office job, sits at a desk, answers the phone and works on a computer. At the end of the day, both of these individuals feel tired even though their respective expenditure of energy is quite different. The construction worker has spent a lot of physical, external energy; the office worker has expended a lot of internal, mental energy. Even though the work performed and the energy expended is quite different, they both feel fatigue because they both have expended equal amounts of energy. This example of the difference between internal and external energy expenditure, although simple, will be enough to give the reader an idea of how Park defines internal and external *ch'i* on the most basic level.

While a practitioner of Traditional Chinese Medicine will define *ch'i* in much more complex terms, Park generally believes in keeping explanations very simple and letting the student reach deeper levels of understanding through direct experience. There is no need to strictly define *ch'i* or try and measure it, or even try to prove its existence through scientific methods. Any sort of definition or categorization would only serve to place bounds on one's potential experience. Those that experience it will know it and those that don't will never know.

Park's concern is that students gain an awareness of a feeling in the body which he calls the "*ch'i* feeling." Once the student gains an awareness of this feeling, he or she will learn to cultivate the feeling, deepen the awareness of the feeling, and utilize the results of the cultivation for both martial and healing purposes. What it is, where it comes from, and how it works is of little concern if the student can learn to use the results of the *ch'i* cultivation effectively.

When teaching, Park will give a student an exercise which produces specific results and allow the student to explain what he or she is feeling rather than give the student lectures on what he or she is supposed to be feeling. All the anatomy, physiology, and bioelectromagnetics lectures in the world will not take the place of actual practice. Park's philosophy is that if the student wants to know what *ch'i* is, they execute the exercises which are designed to cultivate *ch'i* and increase awareness of *ch'i*, not sit and talk about it.

Park emphasizes that there is a big difference between knowing something in the head and knowing something in the body. When it is "known" it in the body it becomes a reflex occurrence and it will not soon be "forgotten." Once when Lu Shui-T'ien was teaching, Park started to take notes on what his teacher was saying. His teacher asked, "What are you doing?" Park replied that he was taking notes so he would not forget what his teacher was telling him. Park's teacher

took away the notebook and said, "You go outside right now and practice this 1,000 times. This is the only way you will remember!"

Once the student has experienced a sensation as a result of an exercise, Park will ask the student to explain what he or she has felt and then guide the student to deeper experience by adding to the exercise or by teaching a higher level technique. In this manner, all of the student's knowledge of *ch'i*, or martial arts practice in general, is experiential.

The *Ch'i* Phenomenon

Park Bok Nam speaks of *ch'i* very matter of factly. There is no reason to become mystical, esoteric, or secretive about *ch'i* or its development. The awareness of *ch'i*, the movement of *ch'i*, the balancing of *ch'i*, the opening of *ch'i* blockages, the usage of *ch'i* in martial arts, the usage of *ch'i* in healing; these are not great achievements which one should hunger to attain. *Ch'i* is not something to be worshiped and *ch'i* related phenomenon is not something to be hungered for. Goals should not be set around achieving any particular *ch'i* sensation, ability, or technique.

Park believes that a student should simply practice in a natural, well balanced manner and let the *ch'i* be itself. If the training method is correct, positive results will occur. Once results do occur, the student should not become attached to them, as there is always something more. Students who hunger for phenomenal *ch'i* experience will usually run into problems.

When a student reaches a certain level of *ch'i* awareness or ability to utilize *ch'i*, Park simply takes these developments as guideposts in designing the student's training program. When the student reaches a new level, Park knows it is time to change the student's training. He does not allow the student to become hung-up on any particular *ch'i* sensation. Park changes each student's training program based on their individual experiences so that they can grasp the next level of experience.

Changing, or adding to, the basic training exercises is an integral part of continual development. Park's experience has told him that once a practitioner reaches a certain level of development with one exercise, he or she needs to change the exercise, or change the breathing technique, or the change the meditation in order to progress further. No matter what the individual's experience, there is always something more.

If the practice is not continually changed at key points in the developmental process, the student will stagnate. However, the only person who can tell the student how and when to change an exercise in order to reach higher levels is an experienced teacher. Everyone is different and thus there are no cookbook methods - all *ch'i kung* practice should be closely monitored by an experienced instructor. In the realm of *ch'i kung*, an exercise that could help one person could easily damage another.

Balancing Internal and External

In order to live a healthy life, an individual should exercise (in a balanced manner) both the internal *ch'i* and the external *ch'i*. External exercise (swimming, biking, running, weight lifting, martial arts forms and fighting, etc.) will strengthen the external, but will not efficiently or fully exercise the internal. Internal exercise (breath control, meditation, visualization, yoga, and other *ch'i kung* training methods) will not efficiently or fully train the external, but will develop the internal. To achieve optimum levels of health, martial arts development, or fighting skill, internal and external training should be balanced.

Modern health, fitness, and physical education disciplines tend to emphasis the external methods of physical development. However, in terms of health and longevity, internal development is equally, if not more, important. As a simple example Park likes to point out that a man who is physically very strong can easily be overcome by internal disorder or disease while an old person, who may be physically weak in terms of muscle strength, could be very robust and strong internally and thus live a long, healthy life.

While internal martial arts practice is designed to train the internal and the external together, bringing these elements together at the same time is very difficult for the beginning or intermediate level student. Until the student reaches an advanced stage of practice and can fully integrate the internal and the external in practice, Park feels that supplemental internal training, such as breathing exercises, meditation exercises, and specific *ch'i* circulation exercises should be practiced.

The Pa Kua Chang *Ch'i Kung* System

Park's system of *ch'i kung* has three component parts. These components are initially trained separately in a series of progressive exercises so that the practitioner can develop each component in isolation. Once a student has reached certain levels of development in each of the component areas, more advanced training is initiated which combines the component elements. The component parts in this system include breathing development and breath control exercises to help increase the body's vital capacity, meditation exercises to help increase awareness, focus and concentration, and body movement exercises to help increase circulation of blood and *ch'i*. Park's "equation" for *ch'i* development is as follows:

Ch'i Development = Breathing + Body Movement + Mind (Intention)

Park believes that each component of this equation should be trained in isolation starting with very simple exercises. If a beginning student were to try and train breath control, meditation/ visualization, and body movement in the same exercise he or she would not gain full benefit from the exercise - it is too much to digest all at once. There is also a higher risk of developing an internal disorder when something too difficult is attempted by a novice. One of Park's favorite phrases in this regard is, "You cannot feed a baby steak."

All systems of *ch'i kung* will contain elements similar to those listed above and the simple *ch'i kung* methods discussed in this book, although attributed to Pa Kua Chang, will not differ much from other system's methods. *Ch'i kung* development which is specific to Pa Kua Chang will not be attempted until the student has experience with the fundamental methods of *ch'i* development. The three component parts of Park's Pa Kua Chang *ch'i kung* training are discussed in this chapter with an explanation of some of the introductory exercises.

Breathing Exercises

When referring to internal development, the first aspect that Park likes to address is breathing. He points out that a person can live for a number of weeks without food, and days without water, but one cannot survive more than several minutes without air. Developing the ability to breathe efficiently and fully will greatly improve the quality of life and health of an individual.

Replenishment of expended energy in the body is accomplished through the intake of food and air. If one's breathing is inefficient, the body can easily expend more energy than is replenished. Park feels that one reason so many people become very tired by the end of the day is that their breathing process is inefficient. Through breathing development and breath control exercises one can learn to breathe fully and efficiently, help the body rid itself of toxins, and strengthen the body's vital capacity.

Breathing exercises and breath control are also key elements in developing skill in internal martial arts practice. To effectively apply "internal energy," whether it is in a martial application or healing application, a practitioner needs to not only develop proper alignments and mechanics, but they also need to develop the ability to concentrate *ch'i* in their body and move it with the mind. This is no small task. However, through breathing exercises, combined with meditation and other *ch'i kung* work, this ability can eventually be attained.

Breath control and development exercises are powerful techniques which can greatly improve health, longevity and martial arts development, however, if practiced incorrectly they can also be very dangerous. Moreover, a breathing exercise practiced perfectly by one whose body is not ready, or is not suited, for that specific exercise can also cause damage. Park teaches breathing exercises as an integral part of his program, however, his teaching is by prescription. Each student is given personal breathing exercises based on their unique needs and their level of development. Park explains that a doctor who is treating a number of patients will not prescribe the same thing to everyone. One person may need more of a certain vitamin, one may need to increase mineral intake, another may need to cut back on cholesterol, etc. Park uses the same approach when assigning breathing techniques to students. His teacher taught him over twenty breathing methods, each with a specific purpose and designed to provide a different result.

Park also states that the amount of time one practices *ch'i kung* is an important factor in proper development. When speaking of *ch'i* training, Park likes to use the analogy of cooking food. He says that when cooking, if the food is not cooked long enough it is not ready for eating. If the food is cooked too long, then it is overdone and not good to eat either. Park firmly believes that students who are practicing intermediate or advanced breathing techniques should be monitored closely by a competent instructor. The instructor will need to continuously fine-tune the student's practice so that the *ch'i* is "cooked" enough, but not too much.

Although Park's approach to teaching breathing exercises is by prescription, there are two basic breathing techniques that he will give to almost all of his students in order to build a foundation. (Students who should not practice these exercises are those with asthma, high blood pressure, and/or other heart or lung disorders. These students will be given separate exercises). When a student begins in Park's school he or she will be given three breathing exercises, the first two build a foundation and the third is the prescription breathing. Park will generally give the student a new breathing exercise every 3-4 months depending on his or her progress. When practicing breathing, the student will always practice the first two foundation breathing exercises prior to the third prescription exercise. When the student is ready for a higher level technique, the third exercise is discarded and replaced with a new breathing exercise, however, the first two remain the same.

The first two fundamental breathing exercises Park teaches are the "cleansing breath" and the "filling breath." Park's philosophy is that before the *ch'i* development breathing exercises are practiced, the air in the body needs to be clean and the lungs need to be working at full capacity. When we breathe, we inhale good air (what Park calls "life force energy"), however with that good air we also take in dirty air (what Park calls "bad chemicals"). Anyone who has read the ingredients label on most processed or packaged food also knows that we consume "bad chemicals" in our food as well. In order to operate efficiently, the body will naturally try to rid itself of these bad chemicals. One device the body employs is the digestive/elimination system and another is the respiratory system. With the exhale, the body will eliminate some of the "bad chemicals" it has consumed. The majority of this cleaning process is accomplished at night while the body rests. If the reader wants to test this theory, have someone smell your breath when you first wake up. What most people call halitosis, Park calls "getting rid of bad chemicals." The "cleansing breath" exercise is designed to help the practitioner eliminate the bad chemicals from the body before he or she practices the *ch'i* development breathing exercises.

The second breathing exercise which is practiced prior to the *ch'i* development breathing exercises is the "filling breath." Most breathing exercises from the East Indian or Chinese yogic traditions focus the breath down in the lower abdomen or *tan t'ien*. Park states that while the student should eventually learn this type of breathing, a preliminary step is to insure that all five lobes of the lungs are able to fill to capacity. Individuals who have never practiced breathing exercises will usually take shallow breaths. Shallow breathing only exercises the upper part of the lungs and thus breathing is inefficient. On the other hand, some individuals who have been practicing only lower abdomen breathing exercises for a number of years will tend to breathe only in their lower abdomen and the upper chest becomes tight and thus full breathing capacity is restricted. By practicing the "filling breath" everyday before the *ch'i* development breathing exercises, the practitioner will insure that all the lobes of the lungs are exercised and the chest can expand properly.

Park recommends that when practicing breathing exercises it is best to practice them in the morning before ten o'clock. The optimum time for practice is the period of time from one-half hour before sunrise to one-half hour after sunrise. During this period of time the air is best for breathing because when the sun is rising, the night air, which is *yin*, is changing to the day air, which is *yang*. In Chinese *yin-yang* theory, when *yin* is in the process of changing to *yang* (or vice-versa), the energy is strongest. It is best to practice breathing exercises outdoors and facing the sun. If practicing indoors, the practitioner may open a window to get fresh air and even if indoors, it is still best to face the sun.

Although Park recommends that his students practice the breathing exercises before ten o'clock in the morning, this is strictly a guideline. The underlying factor to consider when determining the best time of day to practice breathing exercises is the balance of *yin* and *yang* energy in the air. As a rule of thumb, cold, wet air is yin and warm, dry air is *yang*. Therefore, Park says that if a person lives in Texas and it is summer time, by ten o'clock in the morning it will be too hot (too much *yang* air) to practice breathing exercises efficiently. On the other hand, Park also recommends that if it is raining for three days in a row, the student skip the breathing exercises for a day because the air is too wet (*yin*).

A practitioner can gain benefit by practicing breathing exercises at anytime - in other words, practicing a correct breathing technique at the wrong time of the day will not generally damage the body. However, when the air is too *yin* or too *yang*, the benefit gained will not be worth the effort expended. If the student sticks with practicing sometime between one half hour before sunrise and one half hour after sunrise, he or she will gain the most benefit for the effort expended.

As for the correct body posture to use while practicing breathing exercises, Park states that as long as the body is relaxed and natural, the posture is correct. The practitioner can sit on the floor, in a chair, or stand. Sitting on the edge of a straight backed chair, with the spine straight and hands placed on the knees will probably be most comfortable. The tongue lightly touches the upper palate behind the front teeth. Placing the hands on the knees will help to complete an "energy circuit" in the body. If the lower abdomen area is weak, Park will recommend that the student place his or her hands there.

The two basic breathing exercises are described below:

The Cleansing Breath

As described above, the purpose for the cleansing breath is to "clean" the air we inhale, separating the "life force energy" from the "bad chemicals." To practice this breathing method the practitioner will sit in a comfortable position as described above and initiate the exercise by taking a long, deep inhale through the nose, filling the chest cavity with air. At the conclusion of the inhale, the practitioner begins to exhale through the mouth. The lips are mostly closed during the exhale. The practitioner will only allow a very small hole to open between the lips and exhales slowly through this hole. The length of the exhale should be two to three times the length of the inhale, however, the practitioner will want to remain comfortable. Park advises students not to try and force the inhale or exhale to be so long that the student is not comfortable.

The purpose of exhaling slowly through a very small opening in between the lips is to allow the "bad chemicals" to escape while retaining the "life force energy." Park explains through a simple analogy. Imagine you have a clear plastic bottle in your hand which is three-quarters full of water and has a nozzle at the top (like one of those plastic ketchup or mustard bottles you see in a diner). Imagine you are holding the bottle so that the nozzle is facing up. If you squeeze the bottle very slowly and then stop applying pressure just before the water comes out of the nozzle, the only thing that escapes is the air that was in the top quarter of the bottle. On the other hand, if you were to squeeze the bottle rapidly with force, the air would come out and you would also lose part of the water.

In this analogy, the air in the bottle corresponds to the bad chemicals in the air which was inhaled and the water corresponds to the life force energy. If the practitioner exhales very slowly through a small opening between the lips, only the bad chemicals will escape and the life force energy will be retained. If the exhale is rapid and in large quantity, life force energy will escape along with the bad chemicals.

The cleansing breath exercise should be practiced each morning 15 times.

The Filling Breath

After executing the cleansing breath exercise, the student in Park's school will then practice the "filling breath." The filling breath exercise is very straight forward. It is designed to help the chest cavity expand completely and thus allow all five lobes of the lungs to fill with air. In this exercise,

the practitioner will inhale slowly through the nose while trying to expand the chest cavity to full capacity. When no more air can be taken in, he or she will then exhale slowly through the nose. The exhale should be 2-3 times the length of the inhale. During any breathing exercise the practitioner should remain comfortable. If the inhale is too great, too forceful, or too slow, the practitioner may start to feel uncomfortable or get a slight headache when exhaling. If this is experienced Park advises the student to back off and be more gentle. He recommends that his students should always be gentle, comfortable and relaxed during the breathing exercises and advises them to never be forceful or attempt to rush progress.

The filling breath exercise is executed 10 times.

Prescription Breathing

After "warming up" with the cleansing breath and the filling breath exercises, the practitioner will then execute the prescription breathing exercise. This exercise is personally assigned by Park and progress is monitored closely. The exercise is based on individual needs and thus is different for each student. This third exercise is practiced for as many repetitions as the student desires, but the minimum number executed is 15. The student will typically practice this exercise for a minimum of three months at which time Park will check the individual's progress by feeling different areas of the their body while they inhale and exhale. If the student is ready to progress, he or she will discard the old prescription breathing and be given a new one to practice.

After the student has developed sufficient levels of breath control and improved their breathing capacity through the progressive stages of closely monitored prescription breathing, Park will begin to explain to the student how the breathing method is combined with the palm exercises. As mentioned in the previous chapter, Park believes that even if the student's palm striking mechanics are flawless, they will not reach the higher levels of striking ability without combining these mechanics with the correct breathing and *ch'i* movement method. The equation for internal power must be complete in order to achieve the highest levels of practice. The *ch'i* movement part of that equation is discussed in the next section.

Basic Ch'i Circulation Exercise

The second part of Park's Pa Kua Chang *ch'i kung* training system involves body movements which are designed to improve distal circulation of blood and *ch'i*. This series of exercises starts out with a very simple exercise which will aid the student in initially attaining the "*ch'i* feeling." Typically this feeling will first manifest itself in the hands as fullness, heat, and/or tingling. The practitioner will continue to practice this first exercise, which Park calls the "basic *ch'i* exercise" until the "*ch'i* feeling" is experienced throughout the body.

Park's "basic *ch'i* exercise" is performed as follows:
1) The practitioner stands in a relaxed posture with the feet parallel and slightly farther than shoulder width apart. The hands hang comfortably down by the sides as shown in photo 1. The eyes are closed, the tongue is on the soft palate behind the upper teeth and the shoulders are relaxed.
2) From the starting position, the practitioner will raise the hands, with the palms facing up, until they reach shoulder height. The shoulders remain relaxed and the elbows are slightly bent (see photos 2 and 3).
3) From this position the palms turn in towards each other as the arms move out to the sides. The hands continue to move out to the sides until they are almost extended out directly to the sides (see photos 4 and 5). The shoulders remain relaxed and the elbows are slightly bent.
4) Now the arms come back in towards each other traveling the same path as when they were out to the sides (see photo 6).

1   2   3   4   5   6

7   8   9   10   11   12

Basic Ch'i Circulation Exercise

5) From here the arms bend and the hands come in towards the shoulders with the palms facing out away from the body (see photo 7 and 8).

6) Now push the hands back out as if pushing something away from the body (see photo 9).

7) Finally, the arms come down and with the palms facing down as if pushing on a table (see photos 10 and 11).

8) When the hands get down to waist height, you totally relax the body and allow the arms to hang loosely by the sides (see photo 12).

9) Repeat steps 1 through 8 for at least 15 repetitions.

While performing the exercise the body, shoulders, and arms should be completely relaxed. The movements should be executed using only about ten percent muscle strength (children should use 20 percent). Concentration is focused on the hands and the awareness is tuned into trying to perceive the *ch'i* feeling. At this stage of training, the body movement is not chained to the breathing and the student does not try to use mental visualization to achieve movement of energy in the body or illicit a particular sensation. Remember that Park likes the student to train each component in isolation before the components are combined. The main purpose of this exercise is to become aware of the *ch'i* feeling in the body. Throughout this entire exercise set, the awareness is focused on maintaining a "*ch'i* feeling."

Upon completion of the entire set of repetitions of the basic *ch'i* circulation exercise, the student will then allow the hands to slowly fall down by the sides of the body and then he or she will stand quietly for a few moments to allow the *ch'i* to settle. After any exercise which is designed to bring *ch'i* to distal points in the body, the practitioner should allow the hands to hang loosely by the sides and concentrate on what Park calls the *"ch'i* feeling."

Typically this *ch'i* feeling will first manifest itself in the hands as fullness, heat, and/or tingling. When students have obtained this feeling during the execution of any *ch'i* circulation exercise, Park recommends that they relax for several minutes and concentrate on this feeling after the exercise has been completed. By concentrating on the feeling, the student begins to develop a mind/body/nervous system connection associated with this feeling. The more developed this connection becomes, the easier it will be to bring *ch'i* to the palms. With continued practice, the student will be able to produce this effect just by thinking about it. Later, increased amounts of *ch'i* will flow to the palms naturally, when it is needed, without conscious thought.

One goal in practicing Pa Kua as a self-defense art is to be able to move *ch'i* very rapidly to the palms (or any other part of the body) when striking. When the mind/body/nervous system connection has been fully developed, as soon as the body moves, the *ch'i* will be there. The movement of *ch'i* to the palm will be rapid and spontaneous. Forging the mind/body/nervous system connection during and after the basic *ch'i* circulation exercises will help the practitioner reach this goal.

While the main purpose of this exercise will be to give the student a feeling of *ch'i*, this is also a *ch'i* balancing exercise. Any *ch'i kung* exercise which contains non-specific symmetrical body movement and is practiced with a calm mind and relaxed muscles will help to balance the *ch'i* in the body. Areas in the body which are weak will naturally receive attention in terms of increased *ch'i* and blood flow. When the mind is calm and the circulation in the body is increased, the body, in its innate wisdom, will balance itself. The breathing exercises, which are practiced before the basic *ch'i* exercise, will "prime the pump" by collecting *ch'i* in the body. The movements of the basic *ch'i* exercise will help distribute that *ch'i* where it is most needed.

A third benefit of this exercise is achieved through the performance of the slow, focused movements. As we stated in the previous chapter, when the body moves slowly in a relaxed manner and the intention is focused, a more complete physical development occurs. Secondary muscles are conditioned and the body learns to act in an integrated, connected fashion. In this particular exercise all of the major motions which the hands and arms can perform are executed. They move up and down, in and out, and side to side. By repeating this exercise many times, the body is conditioned to move in a manner consistent with the internal martial arts principles.

An eventual goal of Pa Kua *ch'i kung* training is to maintain the full body *ch'i* feeling and whole body connection while executing the complex turning, twisting, and coiling movements associated with Pa Kua Chang. This is not an easy task, and thus the training should progress gradually. After the student can maintain the full body *ch'i* feeling in the basic *ch'i* exercise, a slightly more complex *ch'i kung* set is practiced which begins to incorporate some of Pa Kua Chang's characteristic body movements. Once this basic *ch'i kung* set is practiced for a sufficient amount of time, the student will then graduate to a more complex set of exercises and then to simple Pa Kua Chang *ch'i kung* circle walking form.

As in all aspects of training, Park starts the student practicing the *ch'i kung* form with very simple movements and then continues to add more complex maneuvers in progressive stages. The focus of the *ch'i kung* form will be to maintain the full body *ch'i* feeling, however, by this stage in the training process the student will begin experiencing this "feeling" at deeper levels in the body.

As we have discussed in the chapter of body movement, the straight *fan chang*, circle *fan chang*, and *t'ien fan chang* exercises can also be practiced together as one continuous *"ch'i* circulation" exercise to help bring *ch'i* to the palms and increase the overall *ch'i* feeling in the body.

Ch'i Awareness

As we have mentioned above, the feeling of *ch'i* in the body will usually first be experienced in the palms, however, with continued practice, it will be experienced throughout the entire body. The feeling is typically felt in the hands first, however, it will eventually be sensed in the arms, shoulders, torso, and legs. As the *ch'i* feeling is experienced moving up the arms and to the rest of the body, the practitioner will also gain an awareness of the *ch'i* moving deeper into the body.

In terms of *ch'i* circulation, Park speaks of three areas of concern: the skin, the nerves, and the bones. By "circulation of *ch'i* in the skin" Park is referring to circulation through the meridians and channels defined in traditional Chinese medicine. This would include circulation in the major meridians and channels as well as the smaller network of collaterals, or *lo*. The sensation of *ch'i* and blood circulation at the skin level will typically be the first *ch'i* awareness the student will experience. If anyone has practiced *ch'i kung* or internal martial arts for any length of time they will most likely be familiar with this sensation.

Circulation of *ch'i* in the nerves is slightly more advanced and will usually be experienced after the student has been practicing *ch'i kung* for a fairly long time, although it will vary from person to person. The student will typically experience a sensation in the hands, or other part of the body, like an electrical shock or current when *ch'i* begins to circulate at this level. This feeling can be somewhat uncomfortable at first.

Feeling the *ch'i* circulation in the bones is usually experienced at the more advanced stages of practice. This sensation is experienced within the bones. Again, the exact sensation will vary from person to person. When a student begins to feel *ch'i* circulation at the nerve or bone level, Park will modify their training program to help bring the student to still higher levels of experience.

When Park teaches *ch'i kung* seminars, he will ask students what experiences they have had with feeling *ch'i*. Most will indicate that after a number of months of training they experienced the heat, fullness, and/or tingling sensations in their hands and various other parts of their body. Since the first experience with this *ch'i* sensation, most students have gradually felt stronger degrees of these same sensations, but have not had any other drastically different experiences. In Park's view, these students have reached a plateau in their training and have not progressed because they have not had adequate breathing and meditation training in conjunction with their other practices. Park states that once a certain level is reached, the breathing practice or meditation practice changes in order to take the student to higher levels.

An eventual goal of training to maintain a full body *ch'i* feeling during the execution of relatively simple training drills, such as the basic *ch'i* circulation exercise and the three fan chang exercises, is to be able to maintain the full body *ch'i* feeling while executing the complex turning, twisting, and coiling movements associated with Pa Kua Chang. This is not an easy task. The training must progress gradually. The more flexibility, relaxation, and suppleness the practitioner can develop in his muscles, joints, and tendons, the easier it will be to generate strong, balanced *ch'i* flow and maintain a full body *ch'i* feeling.

Through a progressive methodology, starting with very simple exercises and working gradually to more complex exercises, the student's development will be complete.

Meditation Exercises

The term "meditation" means many different things to different people. Depending on the intent and focus of the meditative process a wide variety of results can be obtained. Some individuals meditate to reduce stress and tension, others meditate to increase levels of awareness or improve the ability to concentrate, while many others meditate for spiritual development. The type of meditative technique practiced will depend on the result one wants to obtain.

Like all techniques taught in Park's school, the first meditation exercise the student will learn is very direct and simple. This method is designed to help relax the body and mind and improve the ability to concentrate and maintain focus. Calming the mind and maintaining focused on one thing will help increase the ability to concentrate and will aid in the body's natural recovery and replenishment process. When the mind is calm and focused, the body, in its innate wisdom, will begin to naturally rejuvenate its energy and heal itself.

Practicing the stepping exercises, palm exercises, and body training exercises as described in this book is very physically demanding exercise. If the practitioner does not balance this external exercise with internal exercises such as the breathing exercises, *ch'i* circulation exercises, and meditation exercises as outlined in this chapter, the body will break down. Without a balanced training program, the student will have trouble continuing to practice a very hard external training routine. Exercises which are designed to replenish expended energy are equally as important as exercises designed to increase fighting skill.

The practitioner will start the basic meditation exercise sitting in a comfortable position with the eyes closed. The breathing is relaxed and follows a natural rhythm, the meditation at this level is not chained to a breathing technique. While maintaining a natural breathing rhythm, a relaxed body and mental calmness; the practitioner starts

slowly counting backwards from 300. Each number is visualized clearly in the mind's eye and spoken, either silently or aloud. Exactly what form the number appears when visualized will vary with each person. It is best to keep it plain and simple. While counting, the mind will inevitably wonder off to other thoughts and the practitioner will loose track of the numbers. Each time this happens, come back to the counting.

Park recommends that the student practice the meditation exercise in a quiet, comfortable location free from distraction. Any external distraction can easily take the mind off the focus of the meditation. A quiet and comfortable environment facilitates better focus, increased levels of relaxation, and deeper meditation. Park states that during the last several years of his life Lu Shui-T'ien spent much of his time in meditation. Park was forbidden to enter his teacher's room when his teacher was meditating. On one occasion Park forgot and opened the door to his teacher's room. As the door swung open Park was hit in the head with a book that Lu had flung across the room. Lu said, "I told you not to enter my room when I was meditating!"

Park will occasionally check the student's progress by having the student perform the meditation and count out loud. If the student has developed their ability to concentrate sufficiently, Park will allow them to move up to a higher number, maybe 500. Eventually the students will move on to other concentration and visualization techniques which will help their ability to maintain mental calmness and focus for longer periods of time. The above mentioned visualizations are not chained to the breathing and do not entail visualizing the circulation of *ch'i* in the body or attempting to move *ch'i* with the mind. Remember, every part of Park's *ch'i kung* training is practiced in isolation until the student has attained certain levels of development.

While there are many techniques which involve mental visualization to aid the flow of *ch'i* through specific meridians or to certain points of the anatomy, Park says that these exercises are dangerous for the beginning student to practice. While these exercises are valid at a certain stage of training, the beginner to meditation has not yet developed the ability to focus the attention, without distraction, long enough to practice visualization techniques effectively. Park states that the practitioner is not ready for visualization techniques which involve *ch'i* circulation until he or she can maintain meditative focus while counting from 500 down to 0 slowly. If the practitioner tries this exercise and looses count or

becomes distracted from the steady, deliberate counting, then he or she is not ready for *ch'i* movement visualization techniques.

If the practitioner is mentally moving *ch'i* through the body - through the "microcosmic orbit" or any of the other circuits used in popular *ch'i kung* training - and he or she cannot maintain complete focus and concentration on what they are doing, they are in danger of having an over abundance of *ch'i* get trapped in the head. Once a sufficient amount of *ch'i* is flowing in the body through mental visualization, if the mind becomes distracted, the *ch'i* will rise to the head. Park calls this *shang ch'i* (rising *ch'i*). *Shang ch'i* can result in severe headaches, intense pressure in the head, or migraines and is not much fun. Sometimes it takes weeks to go away.

Brand new students may not be in a lot of danger because they have not built up strong enough energy in the body. However, once the practitioner has practiced the powerful breathing exercises and *ch'i* circulation exercises for a few months, your *ch'i* is sufficiently strong enough to cause damage if the *ch'i kung* meditation is practiced incorrectly. This is one reason why meditative techniques are kept separate from *ch'i* circulation and breathing training in Park's school until the student has developed to certain levels in all three of these areas. Only an experienced teacher will know when you are ready to move on to advanced *ch'i* circulation visualization techniques.

Ch'i Kung Circle Walk Form

Park Bok Nam believes that the Pa Kua Chang practitioner should be able to maintain the "full body *ch'i* feeling" which has been developed through the meditation, breathing, and *ch'i* circulation exercises while performing any of the complex turning and twisting movements associated with this fighting art. To that end, the first form a student in Park's school will encounter is a basic *ch'i kung* circle walking form, the purpose of which is strictly *ch'i* development and training alignments.

Park feels that if the student begins with a form that is too complex, he or she will not be able to maintain the full body *ch'i* feeling and he or she will not fully understand the subtle mechanics of each movement. Once the student can maintain the full *ch'i* feeling during this simple form, executed with simple changes, more complex changes are added which serve to train the *ch'i* in various ways.

Park's simple Pa Kua *ch'i kung* circle walking form is described in this section. The form consists of walking the circle in both the clockwise and counter-clockwise directions while holding a series of static upper body postures. The practitioner holds one posture while walking the circle in one direction, executes a simple directional change, and then walks the circle in the other direction

holding that same posture on the other side. Once the practitioner has walked around the circle in both directions holding one posture, he or she executes a change and walks in the original direction holding the next posture in the series.

The first posture held in this form is a "warm-up" posture which proceeds the core form of eight "animal" postures. The number of times the practitioner walks around the circle holding each posture will vary from person to person - the longer the better. Park recommends that the practitioner continue to walk the circle holding the first posture until the full body *ch'i* feeling is obtained. Once the practitioner has cultivated this feeling, he or she changes direction. The change of direction is executed in such a manner that the practitioner does not loose the *ch'i* feeling that was developed during the previous walking. In order to insure the feeling is not lost during the change, the change must be executed in a smooth, continuous manner. The practitioner walks the circle the same number of times in each direction.

Once the student has practiced the basic *ch'i* kung circle walking form, which we present here, for a sufficient amount of time and can maintain the full body *ch'i* feeling throughout the entire set, Park will begin to add more complex transitions and changes to the set.

1 - Start standing with the feet together and body relaxed. Face the path of the circle.

2 - Slowly raise the arms straight out in front. The body and shoulders remain relaxed.

3 - Slowly turn the hands in preparation to move out to the sides.

4 - Slowly move the arms out to the sides. Relax the body and shoulders.

5 - Bring the arms back in towards the center. The left hand comes under the right elbow. Both hands are along the body's center line. The kness bend as the arms move toward the center.

6 - Toe-out with the left foot as the right foot steps forward. Both hands turn over so that the palms face up. The feet are in *pai pu*.

7 - Step into *k'ou pu*. The left arm comes under the right. The right palm is facing down, the left palm is facing up. The back is to the center of the circle.

8 - The body turns back to face the path of the circle as the left hand comes up and out in front of the face. The right hand is positioned behind the left elbow.

9 - The palms turn over. The practitioner has assumed the "dragon" posture.

10 - Step out and start walking the circle. The eyes look into the center of the circle.

11 - *K'ou pu* and bring the left arm over the right, both palms facing down. The body faces the center of the circle. This is the "white snake" changing posture.

12 - Twist the body to the left. The right arm comes out in front of the face and the left hand comes down under the right elbow. Walk the circle holding the "dragon" posture.

13 - *K'ou pu* facing the center of the circle. The left hand comes under the right, both palms facing up. The right hand remains at face level. The eyes look at the right (inside) palm. This is the "panther" changing posture.

14 - Turn the body to the right as the left arm is raised up to eye level, palm facing up. The right arm comes up over the head, palm facing down. This is the "lion" posture. Walk the circle holding this posture.

15 - When ready to execute a change of direction, slowly drop the right arm down and bring it under the left elbow as the palms turn over. Transition back to the "dragon" posture while walking.

16 - *K'ou pu* facing the center of the circle and assume the panther changing posture with the right arm underneath the left. Eyes look at the left (inside) hand.

17 - Twist the body to the left and transition to the "lion" posture on the other side. Begin walking the circle in this direction holding the lion posture.

18 - When ready to change directions, slowly transition back to the "dragon" posture while continuously walking.

19 - *K'ou pu* facing the center of the circle and assume the panther changing posture with the left arm underneath the right. Eyes look at the right (inside) hand.

20 - Twist the body to the right and transition into the "giraffe" (unicorn) posture. The left hand (palm up) is held at face level and the right hand is by the left elbow (palm down).

21 - *K'ou pu* facing the center of the circle and assume the panther changing posture with the right arm underneath the left. Eyes look at the left (inside) hand.

22 - Twist the body to the left and transition into the "giraffe" posture on the other side. Walk the circle holding this posture.

23 - *K'ou pu* facing the center of the circle and assume the panther changing posture with the left arm underneath the right. Eyes look at the right (inside) hand.

24 - Twist the body to the right as the left arm drops down by the right hip, palm facing down. Bring the right hand up over the head, palm facing up. This is the "snake" posture. Walk holding this posture.

25 - *K'ou pu* facing the center of the circle and twist the body to the left. As the body twists, the left arm begins to move up in front of the body and the right arm begins to move down with the palm down.

26 - The left arm continues to move up and the right arm moves down as the palm turns over to face up.

27 - The left palm begins to turn as it reaches face height.

28 - The left palm continues turning over and as the right palm reaches hip level it turns over to face down.

29 - Step off in the other direction and walk the circle holding the "snake" posture.

30 - When ready to change direction again, start to bring the left hand down and the right hand up while continuing to walk.

31 - Execute the fan chang maneuver while walking.

32 - Transition back to the "dragon" posture after the *fan chang*.

33 - *K'ou pu* facing the center of the circle and assume the panther changing posture with the left arm underneath the right. Eyes look at the right (inside) hand.

34 - Begin to twist the body to the right and commence the *fan chang* maneuver.

35 - As the left palm moves outward, the right palm moves upward.

36 - The left hand comes up in front of the face and points back toward the left (palm facing up) and the right hand comes up over the head and turns to face up and back to the left. Walk holding the "swallow" posture.

37 - When ready to change directions, slowly transition back to the "dragon" posture while continuously walking.

38 - *K'ou pu* facing the center of the circle and assume the panther changing posture with the right arm underneath the left. Eyes look at the left (inside) hand.

39 - Twist the body to the left and begin to transition to the "swallow" posture on the other side.

40 - Continuing the transition to "swallow."

41 - Walk the circle holding the "swallow" posture.

42 - When ready to change directions, slowly transition back to the "dragon" posture.

43 - *K'ou pu* facing the center of the circle and assume the panther changing posture with the left arm underneath the right. Eyes look at the right (inside) hand.

44 - Twist to the right and allow the left hand to slide up next to the right. The forearms touch and the palms face upward with the fingers pointing out.

45 - Separate the hands and allow them to move out to the sides.

46 - Extend the hands fully and begin to walk. The shoulders are relaxed and the elbows are slightly dropped. This is the "dragon flying" posture. Walk the circle.

47 - *K'ou pu* facing the center of the circle and assume the panther changing posture with the right arm underneath the leftt. Eyes look at the left (inside) hand.

48 - Twist to the left and allow the right hand to slide up next to the left. The forearms touch and the palms face upward with the fingers pointing out.

49 - Separate the hands and allow them to move out to the sides.

50 - Extend the hands fully and begin to walk. The shoulders are relaxed and the elbows are slightly dropped. Walk in the other direction in the "dragon flying" posture.

51 - *K'ou pu* facing the center of the circle and assume the panther changing posture with the left arm underneath the right. Eyes look at the right (inside) hand.

52 - Keep the arms crossed while the palms turn over.

53 - Twist to the right and allow the arms to separate and move down.

54 - Extend the hands fully, fingers pointing forward, and begin to walk. The shoulders are relaxed and the elbows are slightly dropped. Walk the circle in the "bear" posture.

55 - *K'ou pu* facing the center of the circle and assume the panther changing posture with the right arm underneath the leftt. Eyes look at the left (inside) hand.

56 - Keep the arms crossed while the palms turn over.

195

57 - Twist to the right and allow the arms to separate and move down. Walk in the other direction holding the "bear" posture.

58 - *K'ou pu* facing the center of the circle and assume the panther changing posture with the left arm underneath the right. Eyes look at the right (inside) hand.

59 - Keep the arms crossed while the palms turn over.

60 - Twist to the right and allow the arms to separate and move outward at shoulder level.

61 - Extend the hands fully, fingers pointing outward, hands at shoulder hieght and begin to walk. Walk the circle in the "phoenix" posture.

62 - *K'ou pu* facing the center of the circle and assume the panther changing posture with the right arm underneath the leftt. Eyes look at the left (inside) hand.

63 - Keep the arms crossed while the palms turn over.

64 - Twist to the left and allow the arms to separate and move outward at shoulder level.

65 - Extend the hands fully, fingers pointing outward, hands at shoulder height and begin to walk. Walk the circle in the "phoenix" posture.

66 - *K'ou pu* facing the center of the circle and assume the panther changing posture with the right arm underneath the leftt. Eyes look at the left (inside) hand.

67 - Begin to twist to the right and allow the left palm to slide up the right forearm as in the *fan chang* maneuver.

68 - Continue twisting to the right and bring the forearms together. The palms face up with the fingers pointing outward. Stretch the lower back. The palms are at eye level.

69 - Twist the body back toward the center of the circle and begin walking in the "monkey" posture.

70 - *K'ou pu* facing the center of the circle and assume the panther changing posture with the left arm underneath the right. Eyes look at the right (inside) hand.

71 - Twist to the left and bring the forearms together. The palms face up with the fingers pointing outward. Stretch the lower back. The palms are at eye level.

72 - Twist the body back toward the center of the circle and begin walking in the "monkey" posture.

73 - While continuing to walk, let the arms separate and move out to the sides.

74 - Once the arms get out to the sides, the arms start to move up.

75 - Once the arms are over the head, they start to come back down.

76 - Allow the hands to come down the center line of the body, palms facing down.

77 - The hands continue to fall while the practitioiner continues to walk.

78 - The hands continue to fall while the practitioiner continues to walk.

79 - Just before the hands fall all the way down by the sides, turn the body in towards the center of the circle, stop walking and relax the entire body.

Putting It All Together

Once the student has developed all of the component parts of the *ch'i kung* practice, the training will shift and the student will then begin to learn how to piece together all of the component parts and execute them simultaneously. Park is fond of saying that no matter how good the parts of an engine are, unless you know how to put them together to build the engine, you don't have anything but a pile of expensive parts. Although the elements of the Pa Kua Chang *ch'i kung* system are trained separately at first, the key to advanced development is in knowing how to fit the component parts together to form the complete equation.

Ch'i Development = *Mind + Breathing + Body movement*

However, the manner in which all of these pieces fit together and the specific training employed to accomplish this is beyond the scope of this book and should only be attempted under the guidance of an experienced teacher. As we have emphasized throughout this book, the beginner will practice the components separately. However, this is not accomplished in a random manner. There is a specific sequence utilized in daily training in order to achieve the best results.

When practicing the complete spectrum of a martial arts training system including the *ch'i kung*, *nei kung*, and *wai kung* components, the *ch'i kung* is always practiced as the last part of any practice session. The external is trained first and then you move towards the internal practice to end the workout. If practicing all three elements of this *ch'i kung* method, the first exercise to practice is the breathing component. The breathing exercises will help relax and calm the body while gathering the *ch'i* that will be utilized during the *ch'i* circulation practice.

After the breathing exercises, the next component that will be trained is the meditation exercise. The breathing exercises, which help to calm the mind, relax the body and cleanse the system prepares the practitioner to obtain the best results from meditative practice. After meditation, the *ch'i* circulation exercise is practiced. This exercise will help circulate and balance the energy in the body. After practicing the *ch'i* circulation exercise, the practitioner will want to remain relaxed and calm for ten to fifteen minutes and not practice any "external" exercise for appropriately one hour. This will give the newly circulated *ch'i* and blood time to help the body heal itself without disturbance.

Conclusion

This section has provided a brief introduction to the *ch'i kung* training system of Park Bok Nam. The exercises described above will typically be given to the beginner during his or her first few weeks of training and thus they are very basic. Park's complete system of *ch'i kung* training is designed to gradually lead the beginner from these basics through progressively advanced techniques in a balanced and individually prescribed curriculum. In order to gain the greatest benefit from *ch'i kung* practice it is wise to participate in a balanced, progressive program under the guidance of a qualified instructor. If the student starts out with very simple exercises and builds slowly without trying to rush results, development will be complete and the student will avoid complications.

199

Chapter 7

Conclusion

Some of the characteristics of Pa Kua Chang are as follows: high mobility attained through evasive footwork; quick directional changes; supple twisting, turning, and coiling body movements; smooth, continuous, flowing motion; varied rhythm and tempo; economy of movement; relaxed, stable, and connected body; close-in fighting techniques; and powerful palm strikes which seem to appear out of nowhere. The skilled Pa Kua Chang stylist is able to change, adapt, and vary his movement to ideally fit any given situation. He acts quickly, efficiently, and with purpose. His spontaneous response to his opponent's movement springs forth from an innate body knowledge of Pa Kua Chang principles which have been trained through hundreds of hours of repetitive drills.

As we have emphasized throughout this book, Park Bok Nam believes that the ability to adapt, change, and respond spontaneously to any given situation cannot be attained if the practitioner has only been taught a structured form set and some basic self-defense techniques based on the form movements. Training must be much deeper and be built up systematically from a strong foundation of Pa Kua Chang fundamentals.

The beginner in Park's school will be given fundamental training drills which specifically train each of the components we have emphasized in this book. These components are first trained in isolation so that the student can fully develop each piece before the components are fit together.

The beginner in Park's school will first practice exercises which train flexibility, balance, stability, coordination, and full body integration in order to develop what Park calls a "kung fu body." In conjunction with this "external" training, the student will also begin practicing basic breathing,

meditation, and *ch'i kung*, or "internal" exercises. Park strongly believes that there should be a balance between internal and external training.

Basic stance work and flexibility training are followed by specific exercises which isolate the footwork components of Pa Kua Chang practice and teach the student to develop a "body knowledge" of Pa Kua footwork principles, theory, and usage. Park says that if you want to use Pa Kua in fighting, knowing something in your head is no good, you have to "know it in your body" and it has to be a reflex action. Repetitive footwork drills are practiced for hours a day for months at a time before the practitioner can even begin to develop this "body knowledge."

Footwork drills are the most important part of Park's training program because he believes that unless the Pa Kua Chang practitioner knows how the Pa Kua Chang footwork is used, he or she will never know how to fight using Pa Kua Chang. Footwork drills are followed by similar repetitive exercises which isolate the components of blocking, seizing, trapping, palm striking, elbow striking, sweeping, kicking, throwing and overall coordinated body motion.

At the next level of training, exercises which combine footwork with hand techniques are practiced. Each stage of training is designed to teach the student how Pa Kua Chang is specifically applied in fighting. At each level the student learns to how the principle is applied, when it is applied, and why it is applied. Once a fundamental principle begins to become a reflex action, then the student works with a partner to learn how to vary the response based on the partner's movements.

Through partner practice the student researches how to obtain optimal body position at all times

201

through use of footwork and how to continuously attack using effective, lightning-fast striking combinations. The tools the student uses to help research the fighting method are found in the Chinese theories of *yin yang, wu hsing,* and *pa kua*.

In this book we have tried to present a very detailed description of Pa Kua Chang's fundamentals as taught by Park Bok Nam. The training presented in this book is very basic. The student in Park's school will be taught all of this material within the first year or two of practice.

This material lays the foundation. Without practicing the material contained in this book for many hundreds of hours, Park feels that the student in his program will not be able to get very far in developing real fighting skill utilizing the art of Pa Kua Chang.

We hope that the reader has been able to gain some valuable insights into the study of this magnificent art by reading this book and practicing the exercises.

Comments and questions are welcome.

List of References

1. Bell, E.T., *Men of Mathematics*, Simon & Schuster, New York, 1937.
2. Brennan, Herbie, *The Synchronistic Barometer*, Analog Science Fiction/ Science Fact, August 1973
3. Fung Yu-Lan, *A History of Chinese Philosophy*, Volume II, Commercial Press, Shanghai, China, 1934, republished Princeton University Press, 1973.
4. Govinda, Lama Anagarika, *The Inner Structure of the I-Ching*, Wheelwright Press, San Francisco, 1981
5. K'ang Ko-Wu, "Studying the Origins of Pa Kua Chang", 1984
6. Larre, Claude, *Survey of Traditional Chinese Medicine*, Institut Ricci, Paris, 1986.
7. Wong, K. Chimin and Wu Lien-Teh, *History of Chinese Medicine*, National Quarantine Service, Shanghai, China, 1936.

Appendix
Ch'iang Shan Pa Kua Chang
Association

In 1987 Park Bok Nam opened his school in Richmond , Virginia and began teaching his teacher's Pa Kua Chang method in the United States. For the first few years teaching here, Park kept a fairly low profile. He was happy teaching a handful of dedicated students in Richmond. One of Park's first students in Richmond, other than his long time student Glenn Wright, was Glen Moore. When Moore met Park he was a twenty year martial arts veteran who had studied Escrima, Arnis, Wing Chun, T'ai Chi Ch'uan and Pa Kua Chang among other arts and was already a skilled fighter. Glen has studied Pa Kua Chang with Park since 1987 and now helps Park run the school in Richmond.

By 1990 the word was out that Park was very skilled at Pa Kua Chang and students from Northern Virginia, Maryland, and North Carolina had begun traveling to Richmond to study with him. At the encouragement of some of these students, Park began teaching seminars in Maryland and New York. The seminars were very well received and so a student of Park's, Greg Hatza, who was traveling from Baltimore to Richmond every week to study with him arranged for Park to teach a weekly class in Towson, Maryland. This class started in November 1991 and currently students from Virginia, Maryland, Pennsylvania, Delaware, New Jersey, and New York travel to Towson to study with Park once a week. Greg Hatza is Park's senior student in this class.

In addition to the regularly scheduled seminars Park teaches in Maryland and New York, which started in 1991, he has also

taught seminars in Texas, Florida, Colorado, California, Massachusetts, and Washington State. All of these seminars have been well received and Park plans to continue teaching seminars throughout the county. Those readers who are interested in attending one of Park Bok Nam's Pa Kua Chang seminars can write to High View Publications for a current seminar schedule or contact Park directly.

Park's Assistant Instructors

As of April 1993, Park Bok Nam has designated four students in the United States who are authorized to teach the material which is printed in this book. These students are as follows:

1) Glenn Wright - Glenn is Park Bok Nam's senior student in the United States and has been studying with Park since 1978. Glen currently resides in Tacoma, Washington.

2) Glen Moore - Glen has been studying with Park since Park arrived in the United States in 1987. He currently helps Park run his school in Richmond, Virginia.

3) Greg Hatza - Greg, who has been studying with Park since 1990, is the senior student at Park's Saturday class in Towson, Maryland. Additionally, Greg continues to study with Park privately on a weekly basis at Park's school in Richmond.

4) Dan Miller - Dan is the co-author of this book and the director and producer of the companion video to this book. He currently resides in Pacific Grove, California. He has been studying with Park since 1991 and helps organize and facilitate Park Bok

Glenn Wright

Glen Moore

Greg Hatza

Dan Miller

Nam's West Coast seminars. He is also the publisher and editor of the *Pa Kua Chang Journal*, a bi-monthly publication covering all aspects and all styles of Pa Kua Chang.

Park Bok Nam has authorized each of these individuals to begin teaching students under his supervision. Anyone wishing to contact any of these individuals, please write to:

> High View Publications
> P.O. Box 51967
> Pacific Grove, CA 93950
> (408) 655-2990

Plans for the Future

In 1992 Park Bok Nam and his students formed the *Ch'iang Shan Pa Kua Chang Association*. This association was formed to help promote the art of Pa Kua Chang and the Pa Kua Chang of Lu Shui-T'ien in the United States. *Ch'iang Shan* is the Pa Kua Chang generation name given to Park Bok Nam by his teacher when Park was accepted as a

formal disciple in the lineage of Tung Hai-Ch'uan. Each of the generations in Tung's lineage has a generation name associated with it. Park is of the *Ch'iang* (6th) generation.

Every year (starting in 1992) Park holds a Pa Kua Chang training camp in the mountains of West Virginia. This camp is open to all of Park's students and provides an opportunity for everyone studying Park's Pa Kua Chang in the United States to train together and get to know each other. The camp also acts as the yearly Association meeting and Park uses the opportunity to promote students and accept formal disciples if he feels any students are ready for promotion. This camp is open to all interested Pa Kua Chang practitioners, however, Association members pay a discount price. Those readers who may be interested in the Pa Kua Chang Association can contact Glenn Moore by writing to the following address:

> Pa Kua Kung Fu School
> 11101 Midlothian Turnpike
> Richmond, VA 23236
> (804) 794-8384

In addition to this book and its companion video, Park plans to continue to present his material in video format so that he can share his method with interested students in the United States who may not have the opportunity to study with him directly on a regular basis. Additionally, he will be increasing and expanding his seminar program in the United States and Europe. In March, 1993 he conducted his first European seminar in Italy.

Park Bok Nam's goal is to share his Pa Kua Chang knowledge and experience with interested students so that the next generation of Pa Kua Chang practitioners can carry on the Pa Kua Chang lineage and the art of Pa Kua Chang will continue to be respected in martial arts circles.

About the Author

A native of Springfiled, Virginia, Dan Miller graduated from the United States Naval Academy in Annapolis, Maryland in 1982 with a Bachelor of Science in Mathematics and accepted a commission in the United States Marine Corps. He subsequently served for ten years as an officer of Marines. While in the military he was sent to study at the Naval Postgraduate School in Monterey, California (1987-1989) and earned a Masters Degree in Electrical Engineering.

Dan began his study of Chinese martial arts in 1983 with T'ai Chi Ch'uan. He has since spent time studying T'ai Chi Ch'uan, Hsing-I Ch'uan, and Pa Kua Chang. In 1990 he and his wife founded High View Publications and began publishing the *Pa Kua Chang Newsletter*. In 1992 the newsletter was upgraded to a Journal. In July 1992 Dan left the military service and now lives in Pacific Grove, California where he is writing and publishing full time.

Unique Publications Book List

Action Kubotan Keychain: An Aid in Self-defense • Kubota, Takayuki • 1100

Advanced Balisong Manual, The • Imada, Jeff • 5192

Advanced Iron Palm • Gray, Brian • 416

Aikido: Traditional and New Tomiki • Higashi, Nobuyoshi • 319

American Freestyle Karate • Anderson, Dan • 303

Art of Stretching and Kicking, The • Lew, James • 206

Balisong Manual, The • Imada, Jeff • 5191

Beyond Kicking • Frenette, Jean • 421

Bruce Lee's One and Three Inch Power Punch • Demile, James • 502

Bruce Lee: The Biography • Clouse, Robert • 144

Bruce Lee: The Untold Story • Editors of Inside Kung-Fu • 401

Chi Kung: Taoist Secrets of Fitness & Longevity • Yu, Wen-Mei • 240

Chinese Healing Arts • Berk, William • 222

Choy Li Fut • Wong, Doc-Fai • 217

Complete Black Belt Hyung W.T.F., The • Cho, Hee Il • 584

Complete Guide to Kung-Fu Fighting Styles, The • Hallander, Jane • 221

Complete Iron Palm • Gray, Brian • 415

Complete Martial Artist Vol. 1, The • Cho, Hee Il • 5101

Complete Martial Artist Vol. 2, The • Cho, Hee Il • 5102

Complete Master's Jumping Kick, The • Cho, Hee Il • 581

Complete Master's Kick, The • Cho, Hee Il • 580

Complete One and Three Step Sparring, The • Cho, Hee Il • 582

Complete Tae Geuk Hyung W.T.F., The • Cho, Hee Il • 583

Complete Tae Kwon Do Hyung Vol. 1, The • Cho, Hee Il • 530

Complete Tae Kwon Do Hyung Vol. 2, The • Cho, Hee Il • 531

Complete Tae Kwon Do Hyung Vol. 3, The • Cho, Hee Il • 532

Deadly Karate Blows • Adams, Brian • 312

Deceptive Hands of Wing Chun, The • Wong, Douglas • 201

Dynamic Strength • Wong, Harry • 209

Dynamic Stretching and Kicking • Wallace, Bill • 405

Effective Techniques of Unarmed Combat • Hui, Mizhou • 130

Effortless Combat Throws • Cartmell, Tim • 261

Enter The Dragon Deluxe Collector's Set (25% max. discount) • Little, John • EDSP2

Essence of Aikido, The • Sosa, Bill • 320

Fatal Flute and Stick Form • Chan, Poi • 215

Fighting Weapons of Korean Martial Arts, The • Suh, In Hyuk • 355

Fundamentals of Pa Kua Chang, Vol. 1 • Nam, Park Bok • 245

Unique Publications Book List

Fundamentals of Pa Kua Chang, Vol. 2 • Nam, Park Bok • 246
Gene LeBell's Grappling World • LeBell, Gene • 593
Hapkido: The Integrated Fighting Art • Spear, Robert • 360
Hsing-I • McNeil, James • 225
Internal Secrets of Tai Chi Chuan • Wong, Doc-Fai • 250
Jackie Chan: The Best of Inside Kung-Fu • Little, John R. and Wong, Curtis F. • 599
Jean Frenette's Complete Guide to Stretching • Frenette, Jean • 420
Jeet Kune Do: Entering to Trapping to Grappling • Hartsell, Larry • 403
Jeet Kune Do: Its Concepts and Philosophies • Vunak, Paul • 410
Jeet Kune Do Kickboxing • Kent, Chris • 526
Jeet Kune Do Vol. 2: Counterattack, Grappling & Reversals • Hartsell, Larry • 404
Jeet Kune Do Unlimited • Richardson, Burton • 440
Jo: The Japanese Short Staff • Zier, Don • 310
Jun Fan Jeet Kune Do: The Textbook • Kent, Chris • 528
Kata and Kumite for Karate • Thompson, Chris • 558
Kendo: The Way and Sport of the Sword • Finn, Michael • 562
Kenjustu: The Art of Japanese Swordsmanship • Daniel, Charles • 323
Kokushi-ryu Jujutsu • Higashi, Nobuyoshi • 322
Koryu Aikido • Higashi, Nobuyoshi • 321
Kung-Fu: History, Philosophy, and Techniques • Chow, David • 103
Kung-Fu: The Endless Journey • Wong, Douglas • 230
Kung-Fu: The Way of Life • Wong, Douglas • 202
Making of Enter the Dragon, The • Clouse, Robert • 145
Man of Contrasts • Cho, Hee II • 508
Martial Arts Around the World • Soet, John • 140
Ninjutsu History and Tradition • Hatsumi, Masaaki • 105
Northern Sil Lum #7, Moi Fah • Lam, Kwong Wing • 213
Nunchaku: The Complete Guide • Shiroma, Jiro • $12.95
Pangu Mystical Qigong • Wei, Ou Wen • 242
Practical Chin Na • Yuan, Zhao Da • 260
Science of Martial Arts Training, The • Staley, Charles I. • 445
Searching for the Way • Sutton, Nigel • 180
Secret History of the Sword, The • Amberger, J. Christoph • 150
Shaolin Chin Na • Yang, Jwing-Ming • 207
Shaolin Fighting Theories and Concepts • Wong, Douglas • 205
Shaolin Five Animals Kung-Fu • Wong, Doc-Fai • 218
Shaolin Long Fist Kung-Fu • Yang, Jwing-Ming • 208

Unique Publications Book List

UNIQUE PUBLICATIONS

4201 W. Vanowen Place, Burbank, Calif. 91505

Please write or call for our latest catalog

(800) 332-3330

www.cfwenterprises.com

Notes

Notes

Notes